NATIONALISM,
ETHNOCENTRISM,
and
PERSONALITY

NATIONALISM, ETHNOCENTRISM, and PERSONALITY

Social Science and Critical Theory

H.D. Forbes

The University of Chicago Press
Chicago & London

H. D. Forbes is associate professor of political science at the University of Toronto.

The University of Chicago Press, Chicago 60637
The University of Chicago Press, Ltd., London
© 1985 by The University of Chicago
All rights reserved. Published 1985
Printed in the United States of America

94   93   92   91   90   89   88   87   86   85   54321

Library of Congress Cataloging in Publication Data

Forbes, H. D. (Hugh Donald)
  Nationalism, ethnocentrism & personality.

  Bibliography: p.
  Includes index.
  1. Authoritarianism.   2. The Authoritarian personality.
3. Nationalism.   4. Ethnocentrism.   I. Title.
II. Title: Nationalism, ethnocentrism, and personality.
HM271.F65   1985   303.3′6   85-1202
ISBN 0-226-25703-7

To Allan Bloom

Contents

Preface

Nationalism is often said to be an attitude or state of mind, but the psychological literature about nationalism is surprisingly thin—except for *The Authoritarian Personality*, which contends that nationalism has the same causes as ethnic prejudice. The present book, which began as a doctoral dissertation in the field of political socialization, is one result of an effort to think clearly about that contention. Writing it has taught me something about what Pascal must have had in mind when he contrasted *l'esprit de géométrie* and *l'esprit de finesse*, but most of all it has taught me about *l'esprit de l'escalier*.

It has taken me more than a dozen years to get the problems I here confront into clear enough focus to make it worthwhile to publish anything about them. Along the way I have contracted many debts.

First of all, to my wife and children. Studies like this one may make a man a better husband and father, but if so, it is only after a delay.

Secondly, to my thesis supervisor, Robert Dahl, who was an ideal supervisor—confidence that inspired his students, loose reins, quick reactions to drafts, sound advice when asked, solid emotional and even financial support when necessary, and a careful reading at the end. It was all a student could ask, and I am grateful to him for his help and for his easy acceptance of a thesis that differed greatly, in the end, from the one I had set out to write.

I owe thanks to the organizations that provided money for the project and the educational officials who helped me to collect the data I have used. Doctoral fellowships and travel grants from the Canada Council covered most of my expenses for two years while I worked on the research full-time. A grant from the H. P. Kendall Fund paid for the printing of questionnaires, the hiring of a research assistant, and the preparation of the data for analysis by computer. A grant from the Izaak Walton Killam Fund of the Canada Council, administered by the Institute for the Quantitative Analysis of Social and Economic Policy, University of Toronto, made possible a reduced teaching load during the year the main ideas of the study were first worked out. For permission to conduct my research in the public schools of Quebec, Ontario, and Manitoba, and for help in selecting participating schools, I am grateful to George Brown, G. P. Hillmer, Henri Lesage, Donell J. McDonald, G. T. MacDonell, Lucien Perras, John Rolley, R. K. Self, H. L. Softley, Denis Tanguay, and Jean-Guy Tremblay. I also owe a debt of gratitude, of course, to the students who completed the questionnaires, to their teachers, and especially to the school principals, too numerous to mention, who bore the main brunt of the disruption caused by my study.

For advice and assistance when the surveys were being planned and the questionnaires tested I wish to thank Léon Dion, A. B. Hodgetts, and the Reverend St. Clair A. Monaghan, S.J. The French part of the study would have been impossible without the generous help of Nicole Rolland, Guy Dumas, and André Mercier, who translated the questionnaires and took much of the responsibility for their distribution.

Over the years I have benefited from comments on rough drafts and conference papers from more people than I can properly acknowledge. I especially remember shrewd advice and suggestions from Richard Bird, Michael Denny, Fred Greenstein, Jerry Hough, Richard Simeon, and Paul Sniderman. For a decade the good-humoured skepticism of John Davis was more of an influence than I realized at the time, and I am grateful to him for his interest and encouragement. More recently I have benefited from the detailed and sympathetic criticism of earlier versions of the final chapter by Tom Pangle and Jone Schoeffel.

Finally, a decade ago, when I was starting to become aware of the hidden complexities of *The Authoritarian Personality*, I also started to become friends with the remarkable man to whom this book is dedicated. My debt to him is difficult to express and will perhaps be understood only by those who have had the good fortune to know a great teacher who gave freely of his knowledge to his students.

Introduction

Thirty-five years ago a book appeared that answered all the main questions about the psychology of nationalism. It said what kind of an attitude nationalism is, analyzed its relations to other attitudes, particularly patriotism and ethnic prejudice, and explained how it develops. Is nationalism simply learned, like most other attitudes, or does it derive from personality processes? Both, according to this book, but the important thing to remember is that personality processes are involved. Is it a sign of internal conflict or does it indicate a healthy relation between the different parts of the psyche? Internal conflict, we learn, due to an unbalanced psyche. Are nationalists generally strong and secure or weak and emotionally unstable? Weak and unstable. Are they modest folk who are easily led, or are they proud and domineering? Both, for they have bicyclist's personality, bowing above and kicking below. To which motives or emotions does nationalism appeal? Are they primitive and aggressive or generous and cooperative? Primitive and aggressive. Are they rational or irrational? Irrational. Are questions like these simply foolish? No. Are they so broad and vague, and are we so far from being able to answer them rigorously, that they should be put beyond the pale of science? Certainly not—indeed, we are on the threshold of being able to produce, at will, nonethnocentric personalities.

The book was, of course, *The Authoritarian Personality*, written in the late 1940s by a group of German and American sociologists and social and clinical psychologists usually called "the Berkeley group."[1] It dealt with the psychology of fascism, anti-Semitism, and the antidemocratic personality. It analyzed data from more than two thousand questionnaires and more than eighty lengthy clinical interviews. Drawing on Marx and Freud, it argued that nationalism is a species of ethnocentrism; that ethnocentrism is a characteristic expression of authoritarianism; and that authoritarianism is a defect of personality rooted, not in any unalterable features of human nature or the human situation, but in the strains of modern capitalist society. To understand nationalism and ethnocentrism fully, it suggested, we have to understand the type of person for whom such attitudes have a special appeal, the weak, inhibited, and resentful "antidemocratic personality." And to understand contemporary capitalism, it implied, we have to see how it depends upon nationalism, ethnocentrism, and psychopathology.

The present book takes a new look, from a critical perspective, at *The Authoritarian Personality*. It raises once again some old questions in the area of politics and psychology. What are the relations between nationalism, ethnocentrism, and authoritarianism? Is authoritarianism the essential psychological basis for ethnocentrism? Does ethnocentrism have an identifiable "psychology"? Does it even exist? These are the main questions, apparently settled, that may be seen in a new light if we scrutinize the Berkeley group's theory about nationalism.

Part I of this study explains the Berkeley group's novel concepts and hypotheses. The right interpretation of *The Authoritarian Personality* is not disputed among social scientists, but a careful reading of the secondary literature reveals some vagueness and uncertainty. The three chapters of Part I provide a more accurate and detailed restatement of the theory we wish to test than is available elsewhere.

We shall see that the California studies were designed to throw light on the psychology of the bigoted or ethnically prejudiced personality type. The first step in the research was to construct a scale to measure anti-Semitism, one that could be included in a questionnaire and filled out by a large number of people. The next step was to correlate different degrees of anti-Semitism with other attitude variables and to compare extreme groups by means of interviews and other clinical techniques. These clinical studies gave access to the deeper personality factors behind prejudiced opinions and suggested ways of investigating them on a mass scale. Then the problem was to find questions that could be included in a questionnaire to detect the relevant underlying trends. This whole cycle was repeated at least twice. Progress lay in finding more and more reliable indications of the central personality forces and in demonstrating more and more clearly the relation of these forces to antidemocratic ideological expression. In the end, not only had the dependent variable broadened from anti-Semitism to ethnocentrism, as will be explained more fully below, but the personality traits of the "authoritarian" personality type had been identified and a method for measuring their presence, the famous F scale, had been developed.

We shall see how the Berkeley group slowly and methodically, detail by detail, built up their main concepts of ethnocentrism and authoritarianism. Ethnocentrism, it will become clear, has little to do with ethnicity, but is rather the propensity to divide humanity into groups, identifying with some and rejecting others as alien and threatening. Its twin, authoritarianism, has little to do with power and authority, but rather, as the Berkeley group used the term, with the character structure resulting from weakness in the rational component of the psyche, the ego, because of excessive external pressure to repress basic impulses.

Finally, we shall see that the Berkeley group, when they developed their theory, employed an important distinction often neglected when their work is summarized. Very briefly, they distinguished between genuine patriotism and pseudopatriotism, and they derived this distinction from their fundamental distinction between authoritarian and democratic (or equalitarian) structures of personality. The way in which these two distinctions are interrelated, however, makes it very difficult to determine the operational meaning of their main concepts and to say what would constitute a fair test of their main hypotheses. The basic problem will be clear as soon as we try to apply their theory of nationalism to Canada, in Chapter 3, but its full significance may be apparent only after we have considered the so-called "functional approach" to attitudes, in Chapter 7.

Part II examines nationalism in Canada using the concepts and methods developed by the Berkeley group. Five of its six chapters deal with a single basic question: Do the hypotheses about nationalism found in *The Authoritarian Personality* apply to Canada? Our approach throughout this part will be *indirect* and *empirical*. Rather than directly contrasting the Berkeley group's conception of ethnocentrism with detailed descriptions of the main types of nationalism in Canada, these chapters will analyze the correlates of various nationalist attitudes among two samples of Canadian students. Rather than directly challenging the main assumptions of the Berkeley group's theory, they will try to test empirical hypotheses derived from the theory.

Two main hypotheses will be tested. First, that extreme nationalists are recruited disproportionately from those with the authoritarian structure of personality. And second, that different nationalist attitudes are structured, or interrelated, in such a way as to justify using the term "ethnocentrism" to describe the attitudes of extreme nationalists.

The data to be analyzed come from self-administered questionnaires given to students in twenty-eight schools in three provinces in the spring of 1968. The questionnaires, which were anonymous, were filled out in the classroom or in a larger hall during regular school hours. The respondents were high school students in their eleventh or twelfth years of schooling; their average age was slightly under eighteen. The sample of schools and classrooms was drawn unsystematically from five cities and two towns in Manitoba, Ontario, and Quebec. A total of 1,825 students completed questionnaires, 1,081 in the English language and 744 in the French language. The students came from a wide range of backgrounds, though disproportionately from the upper social strata. (Appendix A gives more details on the sources of the data.)

Obviously we must expect some difficulties in using these data from two "unrepresentative" samples to make broad generalizations about the psychology of nationalism. At this point I can deal with only the most elementary aspects of a large and complex question. An important axiom worth recalling immediately, however, is the following: the value of a sample must be judged in light of the generalizations to be made or tested. That all swans are white can be disproved by finding one black swan. This study aims to test some relatively simple hypotheses of essentially universal scope, that is to say, which are supposed to apply to all normal human beings in modern societies. On the face of it, therefore, to test these hypotheses we need only have respondents who show substantial variation on the relevant variables, nationalism and authoritarianism. Since our respondents are a large and heterogeneous sample of Canadians who were in their late teens in 1968, a time when nationalist policies were being widely debated in Canada, they seem to qualify. A variety of more specific questions about possible sampling biases will of course have to be dealt with in connection with particular interpretations of particular findings, and some broader questions about the role of precise factual studies in the development of social theory will also have to be faced eventually. But it will be best to defer discussion of these questions until they can be examined in detail and some relevant evidence considered.

Many readers may wonder, at this point, whether the material just described merits book-length presentation. What can possibly be revealed that is not already well known? Surely everything there is to say about *The Authoritarian Personality* has already been said.

The publication of *The Authoritarian Personality* stimulated a vast, in some respects unprecedented, outpouring of research by psychologists, sociologists, and political scientists.[2] Most of this research was modestly constructive in aim, designed to refine and extend the Berkeley group's concepts and hypotheses. Some of it was adversely critical, however, and sought to reveal fundamental defects in the theory and methods of the California studies. Methodologists faulted the Berkeley group's empirical research for shortcomings in questionnaire design, sampling, measurement, and statistical analysis. Sociological theorists scrutinized the Berkeley group's integration of psychology and sociology and concluded that they had no understanding of the importance of conformity to social norms. Most readers noticed that the Berkeley group feared the Right and favored the Left, and some suspected that their entire analysis was vitiated by pervasive bias. Few if any recent studies in the social sciences have received the attention from professional as well as lay audiences that *The Authoritarian Personality* did, and few have been exposed to the searching criticism and damaging attacks it suffered.

During the 1950s and 1960s the book's critics gradually prevailed over its defenders. A consensus slowly developed among social scientists that the Berkeley group had been guilty of one main error and that they were vulnerable to one serious objection.

"Too psychological" is now the standard criticism of the Berkeley group's theory about anti-Semitism, ethnocentrism, fascism, and the authoritarian personality. The California studies neglected, it is said, the social, political, and economic causes of both ethnocentrism and anti-democratic opinions. They exaggerated the importance of psychological factors and unconscious motives. They reflected preoccupation with the impulsive, irrational behavior of the mentally disturbed and failed to appreciate the balance, resourcefulness, and lucidity of the normal mind. As a result, they failed to understand the relation between individual psychology and the functioning of social institutions. In particular, they grossly underestimated the importance of conformity to social norms or social roles as an explanation for social behavior. As Edward Shils wrote, in a classic criticism of *The Authoritarian Personality*, "the Berkeley group has no realization of the extent and importance for the proper functioning of any kind of society of . . . adaptiveness to institutional roles." They discuss conformity, he admitted, but they distort its nature and significance. "For them conformity is only compulsive conformity, adherence to conventions is rigid conventionalism, both of which are obviously more closely related to the substantive content of the dispositional system than the ordinary run of conformity and respect for conventions which enables any society to run peacefully and with some satisfaction to its members."[3] The merit of this criticism is generally conceded today: it is said that "personality factors" certainly play some role in the determination of most people's beliefs and their social and political behavior, but that the Berkeley group exaggerated how large that role is.

"Biased" is the popular but still controversial objection to *The Authoritarian Personality*. The Berkeley group were sensitive to the pathologies of the extreme Right, the critics charge, but blind to the same pathologies on the Left. Consequently their book leaves the impression that left-wing views are healthier and more rational than right-wing views, when in fact both political extremes tend to be neurotic and authoritarian by comparison with moderate liberals and conservatives. This objection is controversial, not because anyone denies that the Berkeley group equated authoritarianism with right-wing authoritarianism, but because some think that they were right to do so. Did they unfairly denigrate conservative movements by calling them authoritarian and whitewash left-wing movements by calling them democratic? Again Edward Shils provides the classic statement of the case against the Berkeley group. He cited the theory and practice of Russian communism as evidence of a Left authoritarianism alongside that of the

Right. Bolshevism and fascism, he insisted, are fundamentally similar. "Their common hostility towards civil liberties, political democracy, their common antipathy for parliamentary institutions, individualism, private enterprise, their image of the political world as a struggle between morally irreconcilable forces, their belief that all their opponents are secretly leagued against them and their own predilection for secrecy, their conviction that all forms of power are in a hostile world concentrated in a few hands and their own aspirations for concentrated and total power—all of these [show] that the two extremes [have] much in common." Any objective scientific analysis of authoritarianism, according to Shils, would have to take these similarities into account. The Berkeley group's did not, and he concluded that the California studies were tendentious, designed to blur "the distinction between Leftists authoritarians and reasonable persons of humanitarian, equalitarian dispositions."[4] The defenders of the Berkeley group, on the other hand, argue that there is no such thing as "left-wing authoritarianism," or that there are fundamental differences, as well as striking similarities, between the extreme Left and the extreme Right.[5]

The criticisms just outlined will be familiar to anyone acquainted with the literature on psychology and politics of the past thirty years. In a fuller discussion of the professional reaction to *The Authoritarian Personality* these criticisms would have to be related to a number of specific issues, for example, response set, the ideological content of the F scale, and the effects of education on authoritarianism. We should also have to tackle the formidable problem of objectivity in social science. Is objectivity within our reach? Can it be achieved by attaining objectivity in value judgments, or only by eschewing value judgments altogether and avoiding topics that would require such judgments? Can the language used to describe differences in personality be purged of evaluative connotations? Must science, to be nonpartisan, discover equally flattering things about the partisans of all different political options and, in particular, about the supporters of progressive and reactionary political movements? Fortunately we need not confront these difficult questions immediately, nor need we consider even the narrower methodological questions at this point, since there will be ample opportunity later to review the classic arguments and current thinking on the most important specific issues. It suffices, for the present, to note the main shortcomings critics have detected in the Berkeley group's work.

The two standard criticisms can be summed up as follows: *The Authoritarian Personality* offers a biased account of a system of statistical relations with little explanatory power. It is not to the California studies that we should turn, it seems, for a comprehensive explanation of the rise of racism, nationalism, and totalitarianism in Germany and Italy in the 1920s and 1930s. But what if the book is seen (as I shall argue it should be seen) as an attempt to delineate the prejudiced personality? Can a theory about the *psychology* of anti-Semitism and ethnocentrism really be criticized for being "too psychological"? Can an analysis of the differences between bigoted and tolerant Americans be dismissed as "biased" because it neglects similarities between the Soviet Union and Nazi Germany?

These questions remind us that even the Berkeley group's harshest critics have found some things to praise in the California studies. During the past thirty years, there has been virtual unanimity that the Berkeley group, whatever their shortcomings as methodologists and psychometricians, and whatever their political biases, were saying something novel, plausible, and important about nationalism, ethnocentrism, and personality. Innumerable expressions of this opinion can be found in the literature on authoritarianism. The sheer bulk of that literature is impressive testimony to the prevailing opinion about the importance of the Berkeley group's work. And not surprisingly, the most eloquent tributes have come from the Berkeley group's most eloquent critics.

No critique of *The Authoritarian Personality* has been more widely read or more influential than that of Edward Shils. He argued that the California studies were deeply flawed in conception as well as execution. The Berkeley group exaggerated what could be learned from public opinion polls, he claimed, and they labored in the grip of a narrow and deforming intellectual tradition. Their treatment of interview data showed obvious bias, and their famous F scale measured only Right authoritarianism. They had absolutely no understanding of the importance of conformity for the smooth operation of any society. Yet Shils also said that the Berkeley group had "demonstrated in a more plausible manner than any previous investigators that there is a determinate relationship between particular attitudes towards public objects and symbols and 'deeper' cognitive and emotional attitudes or dispositions." He described their conjectures about repression and reaction formation as "plausible," and he concluded that the data they presented "provide grounds for accepting their claim that general disposition[s] and particular concrete attitudes are intimately related."[6]

Herbert Hyman and Paul Sheatsley provided a thorough and justly famous methodological critique of *The Authoritarian Personality*. But after showing in great detail the inadequacy of the Berkeley group's sampling, the weaknesses of their scales, and the likelihood of serious biases in their coding procedures—after showing, in short, the self-deluding character of most of the Berkeley group's "empirical" research, Hyman and Sheatsley concluded with the following wistful observation: "One feels intuitively that they have wisdom in their views and soundness in their conclusions, and it is sad that the acumen which inspired the project, the energy in executing a research task unparalleled in scope, and the intuitive power devoted to the appraisal of the results, were not matched by equal methodological skill."[7]

Brewster Smith has done more than any other psychologist to develop and popularize the "functional approach" as an alternative to that of the Berkeley group. Yet his opinion of their achievement has always been highly favorable. Writing in the mid-1960s he said that *The Authoritarian Personality*, despite its methodological weaknesses, "remained rich in conception and fertile in implication. . . . [It has] proved bigger than the swarm of critical studies that one would have thought would destroy it. And evidence kept coming in that lent support to aspects of its underlying conceptions. It has rightly joined the elect of classics in paperback." He encouraged social scientists to "carry forward the unfinished task of reformulating and transforming the insights of *The Authoritarian Personality* into well-grounded understanding."[8]

Two authors who came very close to adopting a simply debunking account of *The Authoritarian Personality*, Gertrude Selznick and Stephen Steinberg, nevertheless credited the Berkeley group with discovering that "anti-Semitism is but one element in a syndrome of unenlightened beliefs and values." They were careful to affirm that "the 'true' authoritarian is a pathological personality in the sense that he has an emotional investment in rigid, punitive, and 'paranoid' beliefs." They themselves had no doubts that "some people seek out such beliefs and score high on F (and similar measures) for reasons of personal psychopathology." Where the Berkeley group went astray, they suggested, was only in believing that the F scale was a pure measure of true authoritarianism (since "the evidence suggests that most people score high on F for lack of intellectual sophistication") and in failing to appreciate the role of formal education in strengthening the ego and inhibiting "the more primitive psychic mechanisms."[9]

Glenn Wilson has developed a concept of "conservatism" to replace, among other things, the Berkeley group's concept of authoritarianism. He has some harsh things to say about the methodological shortcomings of the Berkeley group's F scale, but a glance at his definition of conservatism shows that he accepts many of their most important ideas. His "ideal" conservative is ethnocentric and intolerant of minority groups; fearful of foreign corruption; a fervent nationalist; a militarist and warmonger; a punitive authoritarian who defers to persons higher in the "pecking order" and who insists on strict obedience from those below; a religious fundamentalist; a partisan of all that is traditional and conventional; an opponent of pleasure and scientific progress; and a dupe of occult nonsense. Wilson presents fresh evidence to support his assumption that all of these things do in fact go together.[10]

Among contemporary critics of *The Authoritarian Personality*, Michael Billig and John Ray stand out. Billig's discussions of the book embrace a far broader range of sources and themes than is usual; he has sharp eyes for things that others miss; he hints at a devastating criticism when he says that the Berkeley group "showed an intolerance for ambiguity by concentrating their analysis on the minority of highly and lowly prejudiced subjects."[11]

But he sets the California studies in the context provided by the Frankfurt School of "critical theory" ("one of the aims of the enterprise was to produce a 'critical theory' by which contemporary society could be opposed at least on an intellectual level")[12] and his criticism of their blind spots and errors is always qualified by his approval of their general aim. His summary judgment of the book is favorable: "*The Authoritarian Personality* constitutes a major landmark in the history of psychology, as well as being the single most important contribution to the psychology of fascism."[13] John Ray, on the other hand, is the least accommodating of all the critics, and his various objections constitute a comprehensive indictment of the Berkeley group's work. His key idea that their F scale measures only conservatism and response set has great merit and will be considered at length below. But he emphasizes the distinction between authoritarian attitudes and authoritarian behavior and concedes, so far as attitudes are concerned, that the Berkeley group "did describe the characteristics of a real class of people," namely, "tough-minded conservatives."[14]

The authors of textbooks and specialized monographs in neighboring areas have naturally echoed the judgments of these eminent critics. Thus John Madge, the author of an instructive history of social science based upon detailed analyses of twelve landmark studies, devoted a chapter to *The Authoritarian Personality*. He began by calling it "undoubtedly one of the key modern works in the empirical social sciences"; went on to characterize it as "enormously ambitious"; reviewed its methodology, carefully noting the objections of the critics; and then concluded that "no one has dented the outstanding quality, or indeed the essential truth, of this work."[15] Martin Jay, in his standard history of the Frankfurt School, said that "to dwell on [the difficulties in the methodology and conclusions of *The Authoritarian Personality*] unduly would be to miss the tremendous achievement of the work as a whole."[16] David Held, in his recent comprehensive introduction to critical theory, sides with critics of the Berkeley group who find them guilty of hasty generalizations about personality and prejudice, but he adopts the California account of the authoritarian character structure, praising "the revelation of the syndrome itself," and echoes the Berkeley group's conclusion, that "*eros* belongs mainly to democracy."[17]

The ideas of the Berkeley group are now encountered in unexpected places. Stanley Rothman and Robert Lichter have recently published a bold, careful, and not very flattering psychological analysis of the New Left, *Roots of Radicalism*. The two authors argue that the New Left was in large measure an expression of the resentment of a marginal but influential minority, American Jews, against mainstream America. They describe the typical New Leftist as an "inverted authoritarian" or "authoritarian rebel":

> The classic authoritarian adopts conservative ideas to defend himself against his underlying conflicts and insecurity. But this

process, we believe, can be turned inside out. The same set of
personal conflicts can give rise to either a fervent espousal or
rejection of the Establishment. The traditional authoritarian
deflects his hidden hostilities onto outsiders and outgroups. The
inverse authoritarian unleashes his anger directly against the
powers that be while taking the side of the world's "victims"
and "outcasts." The anarchist thus may have much in common
with the conventionalist, just as embarrassing similarities have
been observed between the motivation and behavior of Stalin-
ists and fascists.[18]

 Rothman and Lichter discriminate two main styles of inverse authoritarianism and they concede that most protesters during the 1960s and early 1970s
did not conform to any clear type. They bluntly reject, however, the
conventional portrait of the New Leftist as democratic, humanitarian,
psychologically liberated, and morally advanced. Rather they conclude that
the typical New Leftist was a victim of the same internal conflicts, and
manifested the same motivational patterns, as those conventionally called
authoritarian. "The evidence suggests that [the young radicals who dominated the early stages of the movement] were attempting to deal with
narcissistic injuries by further undermining an already weakened cultural
superego and ego. They fantasized that, by so doing, they could bring an
end to western scientific rationality and hence to time itself. Thus they
would achieve a feeling of immortality in a world in which they could safely
swim in a sea of experience."[19] Sex, drugs, and rock and roll, it seems, are
part of the authoritarian syndrome.

A clear explanation of the Berkeley group's achievement must await a
detailed presentation of their theory. Very briefly, its hypotheses about the
characteristic motives for ethnocentrism transformed the study of prejudice
against domestic minorities and popularized a new psychology of politics.
Today it is widely accepted that the Berkeley group were the first to
demonstrate a lawful relation between politically important opinions, on
the one hand, and a structure, or syndrome of traits, of personality, on the
other, and that in doing so, they provided an essentially accurate portrait of
the genuinely prejudiced or ethnocentric personality. The critical assault on
The Authoritarian Personality has left these important ideas virtually un-
touched.

    The findings reported in Part II of this book challenge the contemporary
consensus about ethnocentrism and authoritarianism. They suggest that
there is not the connection between these two things that even the critics of
The Authoritarian Personality have assumed.

    Any satisfactory interpretation of the results of an empirical study must
of course reckon with the results of other studies in the same area. The

surprising and anomalous statistical results of the present study will not lead us simply to reject the Berkeley group's theory, on the ground that it has now been falsified, rather they will force us to consider in some detail the differences between nationalism in Canada and nationalism and ethnocentrism in the United States and the other countries where strong correlations between nationalism and authoritarianism have been found. How should we distinguish between different types of nationalism or ethnocentrism? Are the distinctions we should make the same as the distinctions implicit in the Berkeley group's theory? Do different nationalisms call for different psychologies of nationalism? These are the theoretical or conceptual questions that we shall have to consider. They require that we reflect on the language we use to describe, and in a sense to create, the phenomena we study. To what extent is that language permeated by ideology? Must we see in it deviations from the ideals of freedom and reason that science upholds—deviations that we must attribute, upon reflection, to the manipulative activities, conscious or unconscious, of interested parties? Does our language distort the phenomena?

Part III of this study consists of a long train of reflections about types of nationalism, the meaning of authoritarianism, the psychology of democracy, and the methodology of the social sciences. I have tried to achieve two objectives in the two chapters of this part. One, as just suggested, is to supply the need for a new and more satisfactory account of the empirical relations between nationalism, ethnocentrism, and personality. The other is to clarify what *The Authoritarian Personality* has to teach us about the theory and practice of social science.

The first objective presents relatively few problems. In Chapter 10 I shall argue that we can make sense of the huge literature on ethnocentrism and authoritarianism only by assuming that the F scale measures conformism as well as conservatism. I shall not be able to offer much hard evidence for this hypothesis, but I shall try to show that is is sensible and that it is consistent with the results of a great many careful empirical studies.

My second objective is far more problematic. Why should *The Authoritarian Personality* have anything in particular to teach us about the philosophy of social science? Why use it rather than any other large study as the occasion for philosophical reflections? My answer to these questions will emerge only slowly, as this study progresses. But it may be helpful at the outset to note some simple points. *The Authoritarian Personality* has been an oddly influential book; it is in some important ways typical of the best social science (a powerful theory tested by the most advanced empirical methods); its theory derives from "critical theory," one of the most influential schools of German philosophy; [20] critical theorists are experts at overcoming bias and exposing false consciousness; false consciousness is a central problem of social science.

The opposite of false consciousness, true consciousness or "objectivity," is plainly a basic goal of social science and psychology. We strive for an objectively valid understanding of ourselves and others. The ultimate test of our ideas may be the future development of humanity (present-day experiments and observations may throw only a flickering light on our most important hypotheses) but, even so, we can hardly rest content with obviously partisan or tendentious descriptions and explanations. Of what could social science boast if it could provide nothing more than obscure elaborations of the political prejudices of its practitioners? We wish to rise above the conventional wisdoms; we wish to escape the confusions and misconceptions others have propagated in the course of pleading their special interests. We wish to see ourselves from a distance, as it were, undistorted by contemporary passions and prejudices, so that our way of life appears in its true colors, neither darkened by unreasonable gloom (due perhaps to the frustration of unreasonable hopes) nor brightened by unreasonable enthusiasm (due perhaps to ignorance of better ways of living than our own). We strive, in short, for *knowledge* or *science;* we wish to be rid of *opinion* or *ideology* or *false consciousness.* But we live in the medium of opinion. Parents, teachers, friends, and employers, not to mention lawmakers, are constantly supplying us with more or less plausible psychological, sociological, and historical opinions. To get on in the world and to enjoy easy relations with others, even to carry out our social scientific studies and to communicate their results, we are compelled to pay at least lip service to conventional opinion. At the same time we are trying to escape this mesh of opinion. We are trying to purge ourselves of our prejudices, not with the idea of killing all commitments, or all strong feelings, but only in order to get our emotions under the control of our reason, so that our reason can function unfettered by habitual or defensive beliefs that keep us from seeing things as they are.

Now false consciousness, as just noted, is a central theme of critical theory. Modern society, according to critical theorists, is tending to absolute ideological closure. Modern man is held more and more tightly in the grip of a single dominant ideology. His thinking is "one-dimensional." His philosophy is unphilosophical. His social sciences are conformist, technical, and atheoretical: they no longer challenge, but simply help to legitimize, unjust domination; they repress the old philosophical ideas of freedom and reason in the interest of an increasingly irrational "rationalization" of society and domination of nature. "Critical theory conceives of itself as a protest, . . . impotent in practice, against an apocalyptically self-obdurating system of alienation and reification, and as the spark whose preservation in a self-darkening world will keep alive the memory of something quite different."[21] Critical theorists can write like this because they are able to stand outside the ideological fog in which others are lost. Critical theory offers its adepts a cure for bias, and it is a novel cure, more psychological and historical than the "positive science" usually recommended in the textbooks of methodology. Chapter 9, which briefly canvasses some of the issues in this area, is meant to serve as a bridge from the rigorously empirical to the more loosely theoretical chapters of this book.

Only one point need be stressed immediately to explain the direction the following discussion will take. Critical theorists emphasize the importance of recollection as an antidote to one-dimensional thinking. Thus Russell Jacoby, drawing on the ideas of Max Horkheimer and Theodor Adorno, has recently provided a brilliantly clear attack on the neglect of the past that seems to be characteristic of contemporary psychology and even contemporary social and political philosophy.

> The history of philosophy is the history of forgetting: so T. W. Adorno has remarked. Problems and ideas once examined fall out of sight and out of mind only to resurface later as novel and new. If anything the process seems to be intensifying: society remembers less and less faster and faster. The sign of the times is thought that has succumbed to fashion; it scorns the past as antiquated while touting the present as best. Psychology is hardly exempt. What was known to Freud, half-remembered by the neo-Freudians, is unknown to their successors. The forgetfulness itself is driven by an unshakeable belief in progress: what comes later is necessarily better than what came before.[22]

The danger, as Jacoby points out, is that society, in losing its memory, may lose its mind. Thought, trapped in the commonplaces of the day, may be unable to examine the grounds for their validity, unless it is able to reexamine the arguments of earlier thinkers. "The inability or refusal to think back takes its toll in the inability to think."[23]

No one would deny, of course, that many important questions are best tackled in ignorance—ignoring all but the most recent research. Contemporary questions about the tradeoff between unemployment and inflation, for example, or the hereditability of intelligence, or the neurophysiology of aggression, can be answered only on the basis of recent experience and precise quantitative analysis. It would be foolish to expect any great enlightenment on such questions from authors who wrote before the present century. Recent research has simply eclipsed earlier speculation. But when the questions are the age-old ones about human nature, it is not so clear that we have more to teach Freud than Freud has to teach us, or even that our century has more to teach earlier centuries than we have to learn from them. There may be nothing new under the sun, psychologically, and there is a danger, therefore, that the progress made on some important questions in recent times, together with the prevailing philosophies of social science, will blind us to the need to take into account the rival, and perhaps superior, insights of earlier writers. *The Authoritarian Personality* is an interesting test case for this hypothesis.

Ethnocentrism, authoritarianism, pseudopatriotism, conventionalism, ego weakness, the antidemocratic personality—the Berkeley group's terms are contemporary, but the underlying questions are very old, and the discussion of them is not confined to recent social psychology. They were being discussed in classical times and even earlier. They are being discussed today in many different branches of social science and philosophy. Over the centuries they have been treated from many radically different points of view. How much attention should today's political psychologist pay to these earlier discussions? Should he, like the natural scientist, ignore all but the most recent literature in his field? Or should he make the reading of that earlier literature the most important part of his research?

The Berkeley group paid little attention to the older literature about the psychology of politics. Their hypotheses about ethnocentrism and authoritarianism were derived directly from the writings of Freud. Certainly they were not, like the neo-Freudians criticized by Jacoby, insensitive to Freud's great insights. But the most interesting question raised by their influential work may still be Jacoby's question about forgetfulness. Horkheimer and Adorno drew attention to the shortsightedness of contemporary social science and philosophy; they charged it with forgetting the great ideas of freedom and reason that had animated earlier philosophy. But were they themselves forgetful, and did they encourage forgetfulness in others?

There is no way to answer these questions except by making explicit comparisons with earlier treatments of their main themes. There is no way to do this briefly except by selecting a single writer to represent, as it were, the forgotten past.

The writer chosen must, of course, merit serious consideration. His hypotheses must have as much claim on our attention as those of the Berkeley group. No purpose would be served by rummaging through the histories of philosophy and psychology for obscure adumbrations of the California studies. Theophrastus, a little-known Aristotelian, once wrote a brief sketch of a personality type called (in a recent translation) "the authoritarian."[24] But it would be foolish to compare Theophrastus's 400-word sketch to the Berkeley group's 990-page treatise. The one is an exercise in subjective psychological portraiture, while the other is a systematic empirical analysis, deriving from sophisticated psychological theory and based upon masses of questionnaires and interview data. Only a pedant would blame the Berkeley group for failing to include Theophrastus in their bibliography.

The situation is somewhat different, however, with writers like Plato, Shakespeare, or Rousseau. Whatever their particular strengths or weaknesses, eminent authorities have testified that they merit our attention. And as Burke once said: "Great critics have taught us one essential rule. . . .It is this: that, if ever we should find ourselves disposed not to admire those writers or artists (Livy or Virgil, for instance, Raphael or Michael Angelo) whom all the learned had admired, not to follow our own fancies, but to study them, until we know how and what we ought to admire; and if we cannot arrive at this combination of admiration with knowledge, rather to believe that we are dull than that the rest of the world has been imposed on."[25] To compare and contrast the ideas of any of the great psychologists with the ideas of the Berkeley group might be to throw a very powerful light on the real novelty and enduring contribution of the California studies. Perhaps the most helpful of these writers, from our present perspective, would be the one furthest removed from us in time, whose theories may be the most alien and therefore the most challenging, namely, Plato.

In Chapter 12 I shall summarize the Berkeley group's politico-psychological typology, compare it with the classification of regimes and types of character in Books VIII and IX of Plato's *Republic*, comment on the methods the Berkeley group used in developing their typology, and conclude with some remarks on the bias in their work.

Only recently has it become relatively easy to discuss the Berkeley group's work with these broad questions in mind. During the 1950s and early 1960s, when the controversy about authoritarianism filled some social science journals, the situation was quite different. The philosophical stature of Max Horkheimer and Theodor Adorno was hardly ever properly appreciated. Only a tiny minority of English-speaking social scientists knew anything about "critical theory" or "the Frankfurt School." During the past twenty years the situation has changed dramatically because of the new respectability of national liberation movements and the influence of Herbert Marcuse on social scientists who were young in the 1960s. Critical theory is today one of the most influential forms of Marxism, and it provides a serious challenge to contemporary social science positivism. The time is ripe, it would seem, for a broad reexamination of the main concepts and underlying theory of *The Authoritarian Personality*. The result may be to throw some new light on the difficult questions of scope and method that trouble contemporary social science.

Part One

Hypothetical

1

Ethnocentrism

The research reported in *The Authoritarian Personality* began early in 1943 as an investigation of the psychology of anti-Semitism among Americans.[1] The investigators were a group of social psychologists at Berkeley who called themselves the Berkeley Public Opinion Study Group. This group, which seems to have centered around Nevitt Sanford, and which included Else Frenkel-Brunswik and Daniel Levinson, probably began their study without any very definite hypotheses about the causes of anti-Semitism. Their working hypothesis was perhaps only that the objective methods of psychology, and a focus on the individual, might turn up something of interest. The research acquired a more definite direction and some broader objectives as a result of three developments—the discovery of strong correlations between hostile attitudes towards many different ethnic outgroups, the discovery of some interesting psychological correlates of attitudes towards the war, and finally and most important, the decision to collaborate with Max Horkheimer and Theodor Adorno, who had moved from New York to Los Angeles in 1941.

The result of these influences and discoveries was a mammoth volume that made a monumental contribution to the discussion of racial and religious prejudice, nationalism, political ideology, and the causes of fascism. Today it belongs to the literature of empirical social science, of history, and of philosophy. It evoked, as already noted, an enormous amount of criticism.

This criticism was essentially methodological, however, and the Berkeley group's theory has never received the attention it deserves. This is partly due to the form of *The Authoritarian Personality*, which is a collection of research reports by seven different authors, without a clear theoretical framework. The great majority of both critics and defenders used small empirical studies to pick at isolated points. Many of these studies were as controversial, conceptually and methodologically, as the original work of

19

the Berkeley group. A large and complicated empirical literature on authoritarianism gradually took shape and itself became the object of concern. A
number of specific controversies of an essentially methodological character
raged for about ten years and then died away. A simplified account of the
main findings of the research became part of the lore of social science,
entombed in its textbooks. The broad theoretical issues raised by the
California studies gradually faded from view without there ever having been
a clear confrontation between the Berkeley group's ideas and alternative
treatments of the same phenomena.

   To see that this is so, we must first clarify the question the California
studies were designed to answer. Once this question is clear, it will also be
clear that much of the criticism of *The Authoritarian Personality* over the past
thirty years has missed the point.

Towards a Psychology of Prejudice

The Berkeley group began their research by developing a scale to measure
anti-Semitism.[2] The scale consisted of short statements of unfavorable
opinions about Jews. Respondents agreed or disagreed with these statements, and depending upon the number and intensity of their agreements
and disagreements, they were assigned a position along the dimension of
interest, from intense anti-Semitism at one end to consistent *anti*-anti-
Semitism[3] at the other. The scale was "intended to measure the individual's
readiness to support or oppose anti-Semitic ideology as a whole" (AP, 71),
and the fifty-two statements of the original scale contained practically all the
important stereotypes, fears, demands, and generalizations that constituted
the "everyday American" form of that ideology (AP, 94).

   Statistical tests supported the basic assumption that anti-Semitism was
an *ideology*, that is to say, "a relatively organized, relatively stable system of
opinions, values, and attitudes concerning Jews and Jewish-Gentile relations" (AP, 58). The various parts of the scale "hung together" statistically;
they all seemed to be getting at essentially the same thing.

   The consistency of responses to the diverse statements of the scale—"the
inclusiveness of anti-Semitic ideology" (AP, 93)—pointed to the inadequacy
of any theory of anti-Semitism that highlighted only a single ground for
anti-Semitism, presenting it as an instance of *racial* prejudice, for example,
or *religious* fanaticism, or *economic* competition. "None of these conceptions
of anti-Semitism has adequately grasped its generality, its psychological
complexity, and its function in the emotional life of the individual" (AP,
93). The problem was not to investigate the subjects' possible reasons for
accepting or rejecting particular, arguable opinions about Jews. Rather
what was required was "a psychological approach which seeks to grasp both

anti-Semitic ideology and *anti*-anti-Semitic ideology in their full complexity and scope, and which then attempts to discover the various sources of each viewpoint in the psychological development and social background of the individuals holding it" (AP, 93-94). The main question would be "why [it was] so important for anti-Semites to reject Jews on any and all grounds" (AP, 95).

The generality of anti-Semitism was in line with earlier quantitative research on ethnic attitudes in the United States, which had made a single basic discovery, that hostile attitudes towards any particular ethnic minority tend to be associated with similar attitudes towards other ethnic outgroups and with vociferous national loyalty.[4] Ethnic prejudice seemed to be general rather than specific, and it seemed to be closely related to nationalism.

[handwritten margin note: NATIONAL LOYALTY ⇓ CONNECTION WITH NATIONALISM]

The Berkeley group constructed three new scales, a 12-item scale of attitudes towards Negroes, a 12-item scale of attitudes towards various other minorities (foreigners, Japanese, "the Oklahomans who have recently flooded California," criminals, Filipinos, zootsuiters, etc.), and a 10-item scale of "patriotic" sentiments. The idea was to combine the scores from these different scales in order to get an overall measure of the tendency to accept ethnocentric ideology and to support ethnocentric political movements. This approach would be justified if the intercorrelations among the scales showed that they were all tapping a single, underlying dimension of variation. In fact, the intercorrelations ranged from + .69 to + .83, very high values for psychological measures of this sort (AP, 113 and 122). The Berkeley group concluded that an ethnocentric ideology, or an "ethnocentric approach to group relations," did indeed exist, and that it should be the focus of their study. "Anti-Semitism is best regarded, it would seem, as one aspect of this broader frame of mind; and it is the total ethnocentric ideology, rather than prejudice against any single group, which requires explanation" (AP, 122).

The strong intercorrelations among different prejudices naturally encouraged the Berkeley group to relate differences in prejudice to differences in personality. The intercorrelations effectively discredited what might be called the "personal experience" or "overgeneralization" theory of prejudice.[5] Evidently most people were forming their opinions about minorities on some basis other than personal experience. These opinions might, therefore, indicate more about the prejudiced subjects than about the objects of their prejudice. The Berkeley group concluded that prejudice has little to do with individuals' experiences with members of minority groups or with the characteristics of any of these groups as wholes. Ethnocentrism, Levinson wrote, "must . . . have to do primarily with psychological trends within the ethnocentrist rather than with the actual characteristics of the outgroups" (AP, 149). Adorno emphasized the difference between the subject and the object of prejudice: "prejudice, according to its intrinsic content, is but superficially, if at all, related to the specific nature of its object" (AP, 612).

The Meaning of Ethnocentrism

It is one thing to combine different measures into an overall index, using the correlations between the different measures to show that their sum (or average) corresponds to some real communality of content. It is often quite another matter to say precisely what this communality is and what the composite index measures. In the case at hand, there is a considerable jump from the subscales that make up the E scale—the meanings of which are fairly clear—to the theoretical definition of ethnocentrism.

William Graham Sumner had coined the term "ethnocentrism" at the turn of the present century.[6] For him it connoted two key ideas, first, that groups are naturally at war with one another, so that peace within a nation, tribe, or state can be explained only by the demands of war with outsiders, and second, that this situation of open or latent warfare necessarily produces appropriate sentiments, namely, loyalty towards ingroups and approval of their distinctive customs and beliefs, combined with hatred and contempt for outsiders.[7] By 1950 the term had come to stand for the ordinary person's unsophisticated reaction to cultural differences—unthinking defense of familiar ways as absolutely right, and unqualified rejection of alien ways as simply wrong. The ethnocentrist was someone who judged foreign groups by domestic standards. Ethnocentrism was contrasted with cosmopolitanism and cultural relativism. The term no longer referred to a supposedly universal process but to the manifestations of a widespread, but curable, pathology. Thus Levinson explained that "the term had the general meaning of provincialism or cultural narrowness; it meant a tendency in the individual to be 'ethnically centered,' to be rigid in his acceptance of the culturally 'alike' and in his rejection of the 'unlike'" (AP, 102). This is essentially the meaning the term still has today.[8]

The term had important advantages as a label for the opinions that the Berkeley group were interested in studying. By comparison with *prejudice*, for example, it drew attention away from specific complaints against specific groups. "Prejudice is commonly regarded as a feeling of dislike against a specific group; ethnocentrism, on the other hand, refers to a relatively consistent frame of mind concerning 'aliens' generally" (AP, 102). By comparison with several terms referring primarily either to ingroups (e.g., *patriotism*) or to outgroups (e.g., *xenophobia*), *ethnocentrism* highlighted the mutual interdependence of attitudes towards ingroups and outgroups. "Ethnocentrism refers to group relations generally; it has to do not only with numerous groups towards which the individual has hostile opinions and attitudes but, equally important, with groups toward which he is positively disposed" (AP, 102). Finally, the related term *ethnic group* provided a good description of the two most important groups for the California research, Negroes and Jews. By comparison with the main alternatives, *race* and *nation, ethnic group* highlighted cultural traditions and individual socialization, rather than biological inheritance, but without restricting attention to territorially based nation-states. In short, it did not have the seriously misleading connotations of *race,* and it was more comprehensive than *nation.* "From the point of view of sociology, cultural anthropology, and social psychology, the important concepts are not race and heredity but social organization (national, regional, subcultural, communal) and the interaction of social forms and individual personalities" (AP, 103).

The Berkeley group liked the breadth of the term *ethnocentrism,* and they broadened its meaning even further. It would be wrong, they argued, to think of ethnocentrism only in connection with *ethnic* groups, that is to say, peoples or nationalities with a distinctive character or way of life—an ethos and mores—that set them apart from others. Ethnocentrism should rather be conceived as "an ideological system pertaining to groups and group relations." The relevant groups might include labor unions, college sororities, and one's own and other families (AP, 104). "The term 'group' is used in the widest sense to mean any set of people who constitute a psychological entity for any individual" (AP, 146). A psychological entity is a "differentiated region" in the individual's conception of the social world, and each such region can be considered a group.

> This sociopsychological definition includes sociological groups such as nations, classes, ethnic groups, political parties, and so on. But it also includes numbers-of-people who have one or more common characteristics but who are not formal groups in the sense of showing organization and regulation of ways. Thus, it is legitimate in a sociopsychological sense to consider as groups such sets of people as criminals, intellectuals, artists, politicians, eccentrics, and so on. Psychologically, they are groups in so far as they are social categories or regions in an individual's social outlook—objects of opinions, attitudes, affect, and striving. (AP, 146)

The defining characteristic of the ethnocentric person, according to the Berkeley group, is his propensity to divide humanity into groups with which he either identifies or "contraidentifies." The ethnocentrist either accepts a particular group without reservation or else he rejects it as alien and threatening. The groups he accepts are his ingroups; those he rejects are his outgroups. For the ethnocentric person there are only the two extreme possibilities; there is no such thing as qualified support or moderate criticism. The ethnocentrist cannot be neutral or indifferent; he must reject all outgroups—all groups with which he is not able to identify. "It is as if the ethnocentric individual feels threatened by most of the groups to which he does not have a sense of belonging; if he cannot identify, he must oppose; if a group is not 'acceptable,' it is 'alien'" (AP, 147). And for the ethnocentrist, contraidentification, or the rejection of outgroups, is fundamental, while identification with ingroups is only derivative. He cannot identify with a group unless there is some complementary group which he is simultaneously rejecting. Consequently the ethnocentrist cannot identify with humanity as a whole, and he necessarily approaches political life as the partisan of some more limited cause. "The inability to identify with humanity takes the political form of nationalism and cynicism about world government and permanent peace" (AP, 148). Particular ethnocentric people will have particular pet aversions, but all will have ethnocentric opinions and attitudes regarding a great many groups, including humanity as a whole.

    A related characteristic of the ethnocentric person is his propensity to shift his ingroup–outgroup distinctions, depending upon the issue being discussed. The social world as seen by the ethnocentric person is comparable to a series of overlapping circles of varying sizes around some central region.⁹ "Each circle represents an ingroup–outgroup distinction; each line serves as a barrier to exclude all outside groups from the center, and each group is in turn excluded by a slightly narrower one" (AP, 148). No single loyalty has sovereignty, one might say. The ethnocentrist shifts his identifications so as always to have an outgroup. "Once the social context for discussion has been set, ethnocentrists are likely to find an outgroup-ingroup distinction. Thus, in a context of international relations ethnocentrism takes the form of pseudopatriotism; 'we' are the best people and the best country in the world, and we should either keep out of world affairs altogether (isolationism) or we should participate—but without losing our full sovereignty, power, and economic advantage (imperialism)" (AP, 147). But the national "we" breaks down as soon as attention turns to domestic affairs. Then the ethnocentric person identifies himself with particular groups within the nation—regional, religious, racial, class, or ethnic groups, depending upon circumstances—and rejects all other citizens as aliens. "It seems, then, that the individual who has a pseudopatriotic conception of America in relation to other nations actually regards most of America as an outgroup: various religions, non-whites, 'the masses,' too-educated people and too-uneducated people, criminals, radicals, and so on, tend largely to fall in the outgroup category" (AP, 148).

    The nonethnocentric person, by contrast, is not rigidly compelled to make distinctions between ingroups and outgroups. For him most groups are neither "ingroups" nor "outgroups." His behavior demonstrates that one can sympathize with a group without actually identifying with it, and conversely that one can criticize a group without regarding its members as alien and categorically different from oneself. "One may be opposed to many groups in the sense of feeling a difference in interest or values, or merely of feeling that their aims and existence are irrelevant to him; but these are not outgroups if there is not the sense of contraidentification, of basic conflict, of mutual exclusiveness, of violation of primary values" (AP, 147). The opinions of the nonethnocentric person reflect this general outlook. "The democratic alternative—humanitarianism—is not a vague and abstract 'love for everybody' but the ability to like and dislike, value and oppose, *individuals* on the basis of *concrete specific experience;* it necessarily involves the elimination of the stereotypical ingroup-outgroup distinction and all that goes with it" (AP, 148).

How people talk about groups will reveal their ethnocentric or humanitarian "frame of mind." The ethnocentric person regards outgroups—all groups with which he is not at the moment identifying—as threatening and inferior. They are criticized in moralistic terms. Ingroup virtues are contrasted with corresponding outgroup vices. Traits that are virtues in the ingroup become vices in the outgroup: "moral righteousness, self-defence, and loyalty" are praised in the ingroup but condemned as "power-seeking and clannishness" in the outgroup. Ingroups are regarded as "superior in morality, ability, and general development," and it is felt that they should also be "superior in power and status." Conflict between groups is accepted as inevitable. "The only alternatives are dominance and submission; justice requires dominance by the superior ingroup, and the subordinate group will always remain resentful and rebellious." Ingroup solidarity is essential, therefore. "Obedience and loyalty are the first requirements of the ingroup member." In short, "the ingroup is idealized and blindly submitted to" (AP, 149).

It is harder to describe the humanitarian's views about groups; the point is that he does not have a rigid, stereotyped ideology about groups. He can criticize the groups to which he belongs as well as support them enthusiastically. His criticism of opposing groups is moderate and discriminating. He is able to sympathize with and support some groups to which he does not belong. He recognizes social and economic causes of group differences; he can appreciate, for example, how a history of slavery or discrimination may have developed some undesirable traits in the groups discriminated against. He does not place all the blame for group conflict upon outgroups. His approach to a new or strange person or culture is one of curiosity, interest, and receptivity, not one of fear and hostility. He approaches individuals *as* individuals, not as sample specimens of reified groups. The nonethnocentric person identifies with humanity as a whole. He sympathizes with the efforts of subordinate groups to attain equality and mutual interaction, and he looks forward to a world in which power considerations are largely eliminated and in which no group controls the lives of other groups (AP, 148–49).

The difference between ethnocentrism and humanitarianism is not, strictly speaking, the difference between identification with the groups to which one belongs and alienation from them. The intended contrast is not simply between those who are loyal and those who are not so loyal. Nor is it a contrast between different objects of loyalty—different nations, classes, or religions. The difference concerns rather the style, exclusiveness, and emotional intensity of group loyalties. The difference is manifested in contrasting ethnocentric and humanitarian ideologies of group relations.

Levinson summarized the ethnocentric ideology of group relations as follows: "Ethnocentrism is based on a pervasive and rigid ingroup-outgroup distinction; it involves stereotyped, negative imagery and hostile attitudes regarding outgroups, stereotyped positive imagery and submissive attitudes regarding ingroups, and a hierarchical, authoritarian view of group interaction in which ingroups are rightly dominant, outgroups subordinate" (AP, 150, also 104).

Measuring Ethnocentrism

This definition of ethnocentrism suggests that there must be four basic ways of separating the humanitarian sheep from the ethnocentric goats.

1. By asking questions about people's feelings of belonging to or distance from various groups. The ethnocentric person will make relatively sharp and explicit distinctions between the groups with which he identifies and those with which he "contraidentifies"; he will identify with relatively few groups; and where a choice is possible, he will give priority to his narrower or more exclusive identifications. He is more concerned with what he is *against* than what he is *for*. He maximizes the number of his outgroups by defining his ingroups as narrowly as possible, given the context of discussion. The nonethnocentric person, by contrast, will tend to identify with the widest possible group, ultimately with humanity as a whole, and to resist regarding any group as an outgroup.

2. By asking questions about the respondents' most salient ingroups. The ethnocentric person will describe his ingroups not just extremely favorably, but in such a way as to suggest that the group rightly exercises authority over its members and over foreigners in its midst.

3. By asking questions about the characteristics and intentions of important or salient outgroups. The ethnocentric person will disparage outgroups, yet regard them as threatening, and he will reveal a desire to avoid or humiliate their members.

4. By asking questions about conflicts between groups and the policies that should be followed by ingroups when dealing with outgroups. The ethnocentric person should be distinguished by his strong support for policies that increase the power and status of his ingroups and that segregate or demean outgroups. He should resist any effort by subordinate groups to

improve their status so as to deal with other groups on a footing of equality. He should oppose any institutions or policies that would increase the influence of powerful outgroups in the affairs of his ingroups. If his ingroups cannot, in their relations with outgroups, maintain their full power and independence, then they should, according to the ethnocentric person, withdraw altogether from relations with such groups.

According to the Berkeley group's conception of ethnocentrism, it is of no importance whatever whether the context of discussion for these questions is provided by controversies in domestic or international politics or by any other problem that involves groups. No matter what the issues being discussed, and no matter what the relevant groups are, whether they be nations, classes, religions, races, political parties, occupational categories, private associations, or even psychological types—"any set of people who constitute a psychological entity for any individual"—ethnocentrism should reveal itself as a distinctive way of thinking about groups and group relations generally.

The Berkeley group's measure of ethnocentrism, the E scale, consisted almost entirely of statements about ethnic minorities, and almost all of these statements expressed opinions that would fall in classes 3 and 4 above. The "patriotism" subscale, too, consisted mainly of opinion statements belonging to classes 3 and 4, rather than, as one might expect, class 2. None of the statements in the scale were openly about national or ethnic identity (the first class).

Conclusions

Since 1950 critics of *The Authoritarian Personality* have given far more attention to the concept of authoritarianism, and to its operational definition, the famous F scale, than to the concept of ethnocentrism and its scale, the E scale. Yet the latter concept is perhaps the more important of the two, for it implicitly defines the problem to which the whole theory of authoritarianism is a response. And the right formulation of a problem often provides the key to its solution.

The concept of ethnocentrism transformed the problem of understanding particular ethnic prejudices into the problem of understanding a way of thinking about groups and group relations generally. The attitude studies summarized above suggested that prejudices should not be studied in isolation. Any satisfactory explanation for an individual's hostility towards Jews, for example, would have to be an explanation for the whole syndrome of hostile attitudes—against Negroes, Mexicans, Oklahomans, etc.—of which this particular hostility was only one aspect. No satisfactory explanation could be framed on the assumption that attitudes towards Jews are somehow a reaction to the distinctive characteristics of the Jewish group, whatever these characteristics may be. The explanation would have to be framed in terms of the common characteristics of Jews, Negroes, Mexicans, Filipinos, zootsuiters, and Oklahomans. And these common characteristics are perhaps exhausted by saying that the objects of prejudice are human and that they can be distinguished, no matter how "formal" or artificial the distinctions, from the prejudiced subjects. What had to be explained, then, was not particular animosities but rather ethnocentrism.

The attitude studies also suggested that ethnic prejudice might be associated with a single personality type, a single dominant motive, or a single complex structure of motives. There was no need to consider many different kinds of prejudice and therefore many different relations between prejudice and personality. There was simply ethnocentrism and—potentially—the ethnocentric personality type. The problem was to understand *the* relationship between ethnic attitudes and personality. Having thus defined the problem, the Berkeley group had opened the way for the marriage of Freudian psychology, European "critical" sociology, and American statistical method that *The Authoritarian Personality* as a whole represents and that the contemporary concept of authoritarianism, in particular, epitomizes.

2

Authoritarianism

Any discussion of human affairs requires distinctions between different types of men—the good and the bad, the just and the unjust, the cruel and the compassionate, the rational, the proud, the stingy, the indulgent, the tyrannical, and so on. The authoritarian is one of these types. He and his opposite, the equalitarian, have become important types only quite recently, as a result of important discoveries in psychology and sociology. About fifty years ago the pioneering work of Erich Fromm, Max Horkheimer, and Wilhelm Reich gave the term *authoritarian* its current meaning. Behind these great contemporaries stood Marx and Freud. Marx provided a theory of the irrationality of modern capitalist society; Freud provided an analysis of irrationality, because of sexual repression, in the human soul; Fromm, Horkheimer, and Reich combined Marx and Freud to produce a theory about "the human basis of fascism."

To create this theory they had to envision a political type (representing definite governmental policies and principles) that was also a psychological type (constituted by a particular relation between the major components of the psyche), and they had to relate the development of this type to the circumstances of contemporary society. The authoritarian, as this type is now called, is the natural opponent of democracy. He has a deep-rooted antipathy to democratic values. He is driven to uphold reactionary, autocratic, and inegalitarian policies and forms of government. In Germany, in the early 1930s, where the concept was developed, he was the ideal Nazi, the kind of person who supported Hitler, not from economic motives or to please a friend, but simply because he thought that Hitler should rule Germany. More generally, he is the type of mass man who makes possible the destructive and irrational dictatorships needed to defend private property in the era of late capitalism. His reactionary politics have a psychological basis and a social cause: ego weakness, rooted in sexual repression, which is fostered by the organization of family life in bourgeois society, is the essence of authoritarianism.

The first detailed analysis of authoritarianism was developed in a study of American anti-Semitism. The connection is not just accidental. The authoritarian has a natural affinity for all kinds of irrational ideology, but particularly for national, racial, and religious prejudice. Himself the victim of an irrational society, maimed by domination, the ordinary fascist needs an outlet for his irrational anger, and he finds this above all in the persecution of the Jews. Fascist society creates a need for anti-Semitism which fascist leaders coldly and systematically supply, but anti-Semitic ideology also emerges in part as the spontaneous result—along with nationalism and racism—of the psychic disorders of dominated man. The study of fascism and authoritarianism must be joined, therefore, to the study of anti-Semitism and general ethnocentrism.[1]

To understand these complex conceptual linkages, we must retrace the main steps in the research of the Berkeley group. Step one, as noted above, was some research on American attitudes towards World War II by Nevitt Sanford and Herbert Conrad.

Militancy and Strength of Character

Sanford and Conrad had two objectives, to develop a technique for estimating the general level of wartime morale, and to ferret out unconscious psychological determinants of low morale. Their first two studies were based upon a scale to measure civilian morale that equated high morale with realistic fear of the Axis powers and a strong commitment to democratic ideals, and low morale with fascist sympathies and cynicism about democracy.[2] The data for these two studies were collected on December 4, 1941, three days before the Japanese attack on Pearl Harbor, so respondents with high morale must generally have been interventionists, while those with low morale must have been isolationists. Their third study used a less political measure of optimism-pessimism regarding the consequences of the war, and the data for this study were collected in September 1942.[3]

The extreme groups on these scales differed in ways that suggested the concept of authoritarianism already developed by Fromm, Horkheimer, and Reich.[4] The interventionists, among the men, tended to identify with their mothers rather than their fathers. The researchers contrasted their "manly disposition to defend the weak against the strong" with the doubts of the isolationists about their own strength which they denied by asserting that they resembled their fathers. The isolationists, it seemed, admired "maleness" and tended "to identify social values with softness." The researchers concluded that the isolationists tended to be those "who

[attached] high value to the purely conventional or the 'here and now'—
those . . . whose attitudes [were], in general, superficial, selfish, materialistic, and lacking in inner conviction or spiritual depth."[5]

The most interesting of the studies compared two students, Vito and
Marco, who had extreme scores on the morale scale. Although similar in
many respects, the two students differed greatly in their strength of character. "Vito [the isolationist] is a man whose manifest self-assertion, hostility,
and drive for power are overcompensations for underlying weakness, submissiveness, and possibly passive homosexuality, while Marco [the inter-
ventionist] appears as a man whose vigorous self-assertion is based on
security and confidence, whose aggression is sublimated, whose social
values and humanitarian ideals express genuine warmth of feeling, and
whose strong social conscience is integrated with his ego."[6]

The third of the personality studies, which was based on a separate
sample and a different measure of optimism-pessimism, came to similar
conclusions regarding the psychological determinants of a militant commitment to democracy. "The most important basis for optimism concerning
the consequences of the war is personality integration, that is to say, an Ego
that is sufficiently well developed so that it can honestly integrate with itself
both conscience and the basic emotional impulses."[7]

Portrait of the Anti-Semite

The Berkeley group employed the same approach when they turned their
attention from wartime morale to anti-Semitism. Their first step was to
construct an attitude scale to measure different degrees of anti-Semitism.
Then they correlated this scale with other scales and compared extreme
groups by using interviews and a variety of projective tests.

In the first major report of their research, Frenkel-Brunswik and Sanford identified a number of differences, some superficial, others having to
do with deeper trends in personality, between anti-Semitic college women
and those who rejected anti-Semitism.[8] On the surface, the anti-Semitic
girls were well-groomed, "their appearance being in the best middle class
social tradition"; they were composed and untroubled, "satisfied with
themselves and with their situation generally"; they had narrow interests,
mainly focused on marriage and social standing; they were unwilling to talk
about themselves, having "little familiarity with their inner lives, but rather
a generally externalized orientation"; and finally, they "declared without
exception that they liked their parents." The anti-anti-Semites, by contrast,
"were predominantly nondescript in appearance, less at ease socially, pos-
sessed of varied interests, quite willing to talk about themselves and their
situations, and able to make critical appraisals of their parents."[9]

Regarding deeper trends in personality, the report drew attention to eight distinguishing traits of the anti-Semitic women. These traits, which were mainly inferred from responses to TAT-type pictures,[10] might be summarized as follows:

1. *Destructiveness.* Prominence of aggressive themes; preoccupation with cruel and unusual crimes and punishments.
2. *External focus.* Emphasis on externalized and physical causation of events rather than personal responsibility; dependence on fate.
3. *Social anxiety.* A conventional type of conscience that has not been fully internalized; strict conformity to a superficial morality; moralistic use of conventional standards of propriety.
4. *Utilitarianism.* Religion and nationalism used as sources of support in place of genuine effort and achievement; a worldly understanding of religion rather than a deeper experience of it imbued with the character of ethics and philosophy.
5. *Denial and projectivity.* Repressed sexual and aggressive impulses which are rendered ego-alien and projected onto alien groups; suppression of conscious guilt and anxiety.
6. *Parents.* Ambivalent attitude towards parents; conscious admiration and devotion, but unconscious hatred, jealousy, and suspicion; ability to love crippled by ambivalence.
7. *Paranoid trends.* Suspiciousness, fear of prying, confusion about sex roles.
8. *Power complex.* Human relationships seen as a matter of dominance or submission and the struggle between the two.

In addition the researchers noted a ninth broad feature of the personalities of the anti-Semitic subjects, a general falseness arising from discrepancies between the overt and covert layers of the personality. The best example of this was the ambivalence towards parents just noted, but ambivalence was pervasive among the prejudiced subjects—kindness and charity on the surface, but destructiveness just beneath it; optimism, on the one hand, and fear of catastrophes, on the other; overt conservatism but covert anarchism; belief in the supernatural combined with materialistic striving for social success; and so on.

Summarizing the results of all their comparisons, Frenkel-Brunswik and Sanford wrote that the outstanding feature of the anti-Semitic college women seemed to be "a restricted, narrow personality with a strict, conventional superego, to which there is complete surrender. It is the conventional superego which takes over the function of the underdeveloped ego, producing a lack of individuation and a tendency to stereotyped thinking. In order to achieve harmony with the parents, with parental images, and with society as a whole, basic impulses . . . have to be kept repressed and can find only devious expressions, as for instance, in projections and 'moral indignation'."[11]

Portrait of the Ethnocentrist

Very similar results, derived from much more extensive testing, are reported in *The Authoritarian Personality*. Here the touchstone of bigotry is general ethnocentrism rather than just anti-Semitism. As noted above, the Berkeley group found strong correlations between anti-Semitism, hostile attitudes towards other minorities, and a narrow, aggressive loyalty to the national ingroup ("patriotism"). They called the combination of all these things "ethnocentrism," and their most important studies of personality investigated the differences between those high and low on ethnocentrism, as measured by the E scale.[12]

Chapter 7 of the book summarizes the main differences between the ethnocentric and nonethnocentric subjects. On page 228 we find essentially the same list of traits as above, but classified under different headings.

a. *Conventionalism.* Rigid adherence to conventional, middle-class values.

b. *Authoritarian submission.* Submissive, uncritical attitude toward moral authorities of the ingroup.

c. *Authoritarian aggression.* Tendency to be on the lookout for, and to condemn, reject, and punish people who violate conventional values.

d. *Anti-intraception.* Opposition to the subjective, the imaginative, the tender-minded.

e. *Superstition and stereotypy.* The belief in mystical determinants of the individual's fate; the disposition to think in rigid categories.

f. *Power and "toughness."* Preoccupation with the dominance-submission, strong-weak, leader-follower dimension; identification with power figures; overemphasis upon the conventionalized attributes of the ego; exaggerated assertion of strength and toughness.

g. *Destructiveness and cynicism.* Generalized hostility, vilification of the human.

h. *Projectivity.* The disposition to believe that wild and dangerous things go on in the world; the projection outwards of unconscious emotional impulses.

i. *Sex.* Exaggerated concern with sexual "goings-on."

These were the underlying trends that, as hypothetical constructs, seemed best to explain the responses of the highly ethnocentric subjects. Each trend was thought of as a variable within the person, and "the variables were thought of as going together to form a single syndrome, a more or less

enduring structure in the person that renders him receptive to antidemocratic propaganda" (AP, 228).

The Problem of Susceptibility

On the first page of *The Authoritarian Personality*, the Berkeley group stated
that their research was concerned with "the *potentially fascistic* individual,
one whose structure is such as to render him particularly susceptible to
antidemocratic propaganda" (AP, 1). The following ten pages, which explained this statement, unfortunately put the emphasis squarely on *fascistic*
and *antidemocratic*, but to understand the book these terms must be understood as synonyms for *ethnocentric* and *anti-Semitic*. The California studies
were designed, as we have seen, to reveal the psychological underpinnings
of ethnocentrism, and not directly of fascism. What the Berkeley group
were able to do, on the basis of their research, was to delineate the ideal
bigot, one whose structure is such as to render him particularly receptive or
susceptible to ethnocentric propaganda.

The Berkeley group's method was ideally suited to the end they had in
view. They wanted to generalize about the psychology of bigotry, so they
systematically compared their most tolerant and least tolerant subjects. The
dominant motives and psychodynamic structures typical of each group
were inferred from their typical concerns, interests, values, fantasies,
preoccupations, worries, opinions, imagery, and so on. The motives and
structures that might be generally important among the proponents of
ethnocentric ideology, but that were equally important among its opponents, receded from view. As a way of investigating all the causes of
ethnocentrism (or anti-Semitism or fascism) the procedure just outlined has
obvious limitations, for it can take into account only the factors that vary
from individual to individual in a given society at a particular point in its
history. It ignores all those factors that are common to all the individuals
whose ideas are being studied, including the "climate of opinion" in which
they live. But as a way of investigating the narrower question of the
personality traits that predispose some people to accept ethnocentric ideology and others to reject it, the method is simple, straightforward, and
without inherent limitations.[13]

The Berkeley group did not find a perfect correlation between ideology
and personality, nor did they expect to. "The same ideological trends may
in different individuals have different sources, and the same personality
needs may express themselves in different ideological trends" (AP, 2). They
believed that crude economic interests and group norms were as important
as personality forces in determining ideological choices. They recognized
that "people in general tend to accept political and social programs which
they believe will serve their economic interests," and that these interests

depend upon "the individual's position in society as defined in economic and social terms" (AP, 8). They conceded, as well, that "individuals, out of their needs to conform and to belong and to believe and through such devices as imitation and conditioning, often take over more or less ready-made the opinions, attitudes, and values that are characteristic of the groups in which they have membership" (AP, 9). Differences in ideology should be correlated, therefore, with socioeconomic status and group memberships as well as personality.

But there is a fundamental difference, they suggested, between these external determinants of ideological differences and the internal determinants that have to do with natural affinities between particular ideologies and particular types of personality. We learn practically nothing about the real meaning and ultimate causes of an ideology from a purely external study of its determinants. We do not understand anti-Semitism any better when we observe people using it to make money or to make friends. For practically any ideology—given appropriate circumstances—can be adopted from economic interest or to conform to (or rebel against) family and friends. We may, however, understand an ideology better when we investigate its "psychology" and discover what kinds of people find it intrinsically appealing. Many thinkers during the past century have thought so, and the Berkeley group were among them.

Stated most broadly, the Berkeley group's problem was to relate differences in political thinking to different ways of coping with the primitive emotional needs, impulses, or instincts that are the driving forces behind all behavior. They assumed that people differ in the affinities they have for particular ideologies. Even when all the external or "climatic" factors are the same, some show a greater "readiness" than do others to exhibit particular ideological tendencies (AP, 4). By studying an irrational ideology at this "readiness level," they believed, we can gain some real insight into its causes and possible cures.[14] We may also, they hoped, acquire a solid basis for estimating the latent potential for its exploitation by "crude economic interests." Ultimately they hoped to use the results of their research on anti-Semitism and ethnocentrism as a basis for estimating the potential mass support for a fascist movement in the United States.[15]

The problem they tackled might be further clarified by contrasting two apparently similar, but really very different, questions about motivation. One might ask: What motives lead men to accept anti-Semitic ideas and to support segregation and discrimination in practice? This question demands, in effect, a list of possible motives. Any answer that pointed to only a single motive, particularly an uncommon one, would be open to the reasonable objection that ethnic prejudice and discrimination are obviously complex and serve many different purposes. (Some get rich from bigotry, others gain votes, many no doubt simply keep peace in the family or ingratiate themselves with bigoted friends, and so on.) But one might also ask: Are there any motives that are distinctly or characteristically motives for ethnocentrism? This question does admit an answer in terms of a single motive or identifiable complex of motives, and the Berkeley group are among those who have advanced hypotheses about what the characteristic motive or motives for ethnocentrism might be.[16]

The Berkeley group were, in effect, trying to delineate the genuine or authentic bigot. They were not concerned with his more numerous cousins, the simple conformists who echo his ideas or the political or economic entrepreneurs who flatter him and pretend to support his cause in order to gain his money or his vote. They turned away from these shadows on the wall of the cave, one might say, in order to see more clearly the ideal form of the bigot.[17]

The Cause of Susceptibility

When presenting their overall picture of the ethnocentric type, the Berkeley group emphasized the potential fascist's lack of individuality and his dependence upon external direction because of his failure to internalize genuine moral values.

> The most essential feature of this [personality type] is a lack of integration between the moral agencies by which the subject lives and the rest of his personality. One might say that the conscience or superego is incompletely integrated with the self or ego, the ego here being conceived of as embracing the various self-controlling and self-expressing functions of the individual. It is the ego that governs the relations between self and outer world, and between self and deeper layers of the personality; the ego undertakes to regulate impulses in a way that will permit gratification without inviting too much punishment by the superego, and it seeks in general to carry out the activities of the individual in accordance with the demands of reality. (AP, 234)

When the superego is incompletely integrated with the ego, the result is an "authoritarian" relation between conscience and the self; the superego is like "a foreign body within the personality," and its rule is "rigid, automatic, and unstable" (AP, 234).

The failure to internalize the prohibitions of conscience is due to the weakness of the ego. "Weakness in the ego is expressed in the inability to build up a consistent and enduring set of moral values within the personality; and it is this state of affairs, apparently, that makes it necessary for the individual to seek some organizing and coordinating agency outside of himself" (AP, 234). When such outside agencies are depended upon for moral direction, we can say that conscience has been *externalized*.

Several of the traits of the ethnocentric personality are easily understood as direct consequences of ego weakness. Anti-intraception, or opposition to introspection, is probably the best example. Ego weakness means that the person must rely on crude defenses like repression rather than on conscious control of his impulses; a weak ego is one that is too weak to deal with the person's emotional needs—all his energy is bound up in internal conflict, rather than being deployed in constructive impulse fulfillment. The person with a weak ego can thus ill afford the luxury of introspection.

> The extremely anti-intraceptive individual is afraid of thinking about human phenomena because he might, as it were, think the wrong thoughts; he is afraid of genuine feeling because his emotions might get out of control. Out of touch with large areas of his own inner life, he is afraid of what might be revealed if he, or others, should look closely at himself. (AP, 235)

Superstition and stereotypy, which are forms of obtuseness in psychological and social matters, are also understandable as defenses adopted by a weak ego against disturbing thoughts.

> It might be hypothesized that one reason why people in modern society—even those who are otherwise "intelligent" or "informed"—resort to primitive, oversimplified explanations of human events is that so many of the ideas and observations needed for an adequate account are not allowed to enter into the calculations: because they are affect-laden and potentially anxiety-producing, the weak ego cannot include them in its scheme of things. More than this, those deeper forces within the personality which the ego cannot integrate with itself are likely to be projected onto the outer world; this is a source of bizarre ideas concerning other peoples' behavior and concerning the causation of events in nature. (AP, 236)

Finally, "power and toughness," the variable which has to do with "overemphasis on the conventionalized attributes of the ego," is easily understood as an unconsciously motivated compensation for ego weakness (AP, 237). The person with a weak ego is driven to exaggerate his own strength and rationality by his unconscious awareness of his own weakness and blind submissiveness.

Several of the most important traits of the susceptible type—conventionalism, authoritarian submission, authoritarian aggression, projectivity, and destructiveness and cynicism—could perhaps be understood without reference to ego weakness, but to see exactly what the Berkeley group understood by these variables, we must examine their definitions in the light of this unifying concept.[18] What they meant by conventionalism, for example, was not simply support for conventional values, but rather rigid adherence to convention based upon an underlying, pervasive fear of being different. Their research clearly showed that conventional people could be either prejudiced or tolerant, that is to say, potential fascists or conservative democrats, depending upon their reasons for being conventional.

> What might make the difference was the deeper source of the conventionality, or rather the type of broader personality structure within which it had a functional role. If the adherence to conventional values was an expression of a fully established individual conscience, then we should expect no necessary connection between these values and antidemocratic potential. . . . If, on the other hand, adherence to conventional values is determined by contemporary external social pressure, if it is based upon the individual's adherence to the standards of the collective powers with which he, for the time being, is identified, then we should expect a close association with antidemocratic receptivity. (AP, 230)

They wished to distinguish this "conventionalism" from mere acceptance of conventional values, and it was "conventionalism" that they identified as a cause of fascism and a consequence of ego weakness.[19]

The distinction will be clearer if we pause for a moment to consider what the Berkeley group meant by ego weakness. They assumed that the ego exists to find ways to satisfy the individual's id impulses, his "primitive emotional needs," while avoiding punishment and keeping the goodwill of the social group. A weak ego is one that cannot properly serve this function. It fails to secure the gratifications that the individual needs and that others are enjoying. A person with a weak ego is disabled by internal conflict between his id and his superego. What the Berkeley group say about his attitude towards power applies generally, namely, that "he wants to get [it], to have it and not to lose it, and at the same time he is afraid to seize and wield it" (AP, 237). He naturally envies those freer and bolder individuals who deliberately seek and successfully acquire more from life than a scrupulous respect for convention would allow. Such a weak person will preach conventional values—hard work, loyalty to family, respect for authority, "the homely virtues of living"—but he cannot help secretly desiring leisure and its delights, freedom from family obligations, the power to disregard the restraints of authority and convention, and, generally, an exciting rather than a homey and conventional existence. The individual with a weak ego is really not an *individual* at all, but rather an outwardly submissive, inwardly rebellious, and generally envious and dissatisfied reflection of the demands imposed upon him by others, which he lacks the strength to resist. Such a person's "values" and "style of life" will be conventional and styleless, not because he really values conventional ways, or because he gets any great rewards from society as a result of his outward respect for its conventions, but only because he is too timid to challenge those conventions. Impotence transforms his envy into resentment. Rather than struggling openly for the rewards he covets, the person with a weak ego nourishes a malignant resentment against those more fortunate natures that demand more and get more. He resents the whole society that denies him what he secretly craves. He unconsciously fears his own enormous desire for revenge, however, and he avoids any open condemnation of those "authorities" who benefit from his submissiveness and timidity. His lust for revenge can find expression only in insincere glorification of his own condition, attacks on lower status groups and individuals, and a general denigration of human nature.

Conventionalism rooted in ego weakness is thus closely related to authoritarian submission, authoritarian aggression, and projectivity. The antidemocrat's attitude towards authority is not "a realistic, balanced respect for valid authority," but rather "an exaggerated, all-out, emotional need to submit" (AP, 231). It is a way of handling ambivalent feelings towards authority figures: "underlying hostile and rebellious impulses, held in check by fear, lead the subject to overdo in the direction of respect, obedience, gratitude and the like" (AP, 232). Overdoing submissiveness in one direction, he compensates with extreme aggressiveness in another. It is hardly surprising that "the conventionalist who cannot bring himself to utter any real criticism of accepted authority will have a desire to condemn, reject, and punish those who violate these values" (AP, 232). But the antidemocrat's attacks on unconventional groups and individuals go far beyond ordinary moralism. Repressed and unsatisfied desires for revenge make this sort of person unusually vindictive, constantly on the lookout for moral laxness, even driven to see immorality where none exists.

> As the emotional life which this person regards as proper and a part of himself is likely to be very limited, so the impulses, especially sexual and aggressive ones, which remain unconscious and ego-alien are likely to be strong and turbulent. Since in this circumstance a wide variety of stimuli can tempt the individual and so arouse his anxiety (fear of punishment), the list of traits, behavior patterns, individuals, and groups that he must condemn grows very long indeed. . . . [And] once the individual has convinced himself that there are people who ought to be punished, he is provided with a channel through which his deepest aggressive impulses may be expressed, even while he thinks of himself as thoroughly moral. If his external authorities, or the crowd, lend their approval to this form of aggression, then it may take the most violent forms, and it may persist after the conventional values, in the name of which it was undertaken, have been lost from sight.(AP, 232-33)

These are only the reactions naturally to be expected of people who have been "forced to give up basic pleasures and to live under a system of rigid restraints, and who therefore [feel] put upon" (AP, 232). Only by condemning others can they counter (while secretly gratifying) their own inhibited tendencies. Such people are disposed to believe that "wild and dangerous things go on in the world," and they readily agree that deviants and nonconformists need to be punished severely. They project their own unacceptable impulses onto others and then try to fight their temptations by attacking and rejecting those others. "Projectivity is thus a device for keeping id drives ego-alien, and it may be taken as a sign of the ego's inadequacy in carrying out its function" (AP, 240).

Finally, the true ethnocentrist's pervasive resentment finds expression in a more diffuse ill will than the moral indignation just noted. This ill will the Berkeley group called "destructiveness and cynicism," and they described it as "generalized hostility, vilification of the human" and as "rationalized, ego-accepted, nonmoralized aggression" (AP, 239). What they meant is that the antidemocratic type, because "he has had to accept numerous externally imposed restrictions upon the satisfaction of his needs, harbors strong underlying aggressive impulses," and therefore stands ready, at the slightest excuse, even without the usual moralizing rationalizations, for "all-out aggression" (AP, 239).

The discussion so far has been based on the analysis of authoritarianism in Chapter 7 of *The Authoritarian Personality,* which was written jointly by the four main members of the Berkeley group. But essentially the same account of the "high" (ethnocentric, antidemocratic, or protofascist) type is found in a number of other places in the book. The concluding section of Chapter 15, which was written by Daniel Levinson, provides a brief and clear statement of these basic ideas.

> The primary difference [between those high and low on ethno-centrism] seems to lie in the ego functioning, and particularly in the relation of the ego to the deeper levels of personality. In the lows . . . the underlying trends are more *ego-assimilated,* in the highs more *ego-alien.* . . . The ego defences of the lows are relatively more impulse-releasing: at best we find considerable sublimation, to perhaps a greater degree we find that impulses have been assimilated into the ego without being fully integrated. . . . In the highs, on the other hand. . . the ego defences are characteristically more countercathectic; there is less sublimation and more use of defences such as projection, denial, and reaction-formation, defences which aid the individual in maintaining a moral facade at the expense of self-expression and emotional release. . . . The highs have comparatively narrow, circumscribed egos. (AP, 595–96)

Then Levinson describes the "authoritarian" superego:

> The highs . . . have a punitive but poorly internalized superego. The ego, submitting out of fear, must constantly forego conscious, constructive impulse gratification; instead, it finds morally acceptable ways of gaining indirect satisfaction (e.g., aggression by means of ethnocentrism and moral indignation, dependency through submission to powerful authority), and it "cheats" the superego when fear of detection is minimized (e.g., at conventions). Again we have a contradiction in levels: the highs, so moral on the surface, are essentially most concerned with underlying anxiety and with the gratification of impulses which, being ego-alien, have developed but little beyond their primitive, infantile form; whereas the lows, often so rebellious and so opposed to traditional morality on the surface, have more fully internalized moral *principles* and in their emotional functioning are more troubled with moral conflict. (AP, 598–99)

Else Frenkel-Brunswik provides essentially the same synthesis of the differences between those high and low on ethnocentrism (AP, 452-59 and 474-86), as does Maria Levinson (AP 965-70).

The Measurement of Susceptibility

It is one thing to suspect that genuine ethnocentrics are distinguished, generally speaking, by a particular structure of personality; it is another to demonstrate that this is so. A demonstration requires, in addition to a valid measure of ethnocentrism, some way of measuring (or manipulating) the relevant variable (or variables) of personality. In the present case, we would like to be able to measure the strength of an ego in the same straightforward way we measure the strength of a man or a horse, or to manipulate its strength as easily as we manipulate a person's hunger or thirst. Unfortunately we cannot, so hypotheses about the causes and effects of ego weakness are hard to test.[20]

The Berkeley group's working hypothesis was that personality determines ideological receptivity, and consequently that the presence or absence of a particular character structure can be inferred from the acceptance or rejection of relevant "ideological" statements (cf. AP, 11). They considered ethnocentric opinions to be one of the expressions, or "give-aways," of the antidemocratic personality type, and their A-S and E scales had been designed specifically to evoke the relevant "emotionally determined antidemocratic trends in the person" (AP, 224). But on the surface the A-S and

E scales were measures of ethnic prejudice. They had been developed before the relevant personality trends had been investigated in detail, and the whole purpose of the California studies was, in a sense, to establish objectively that prejudice depends upon personality. To do so, an independent measure of personality was needed. The early results of the clinical interviews made it possible, as we have seen, to define the relevant personality trends more clearly. The Berkeley group then conceived the idea of developing a more precise and better disguised measure of these trends, suitable for use in mass surveys. The approach would still be through "ideology": personality would be inferred from the acceptance or rejection of particular controversial opinions. But they would no longer try to find statements that expressed different aspects of a preexisting, more or less standardized ideology, such as anti-Semitism, race prejudice, or politico-economic conservatism. Rather they would try to find statements that expressed, with as little distortion as possible, the relevant underlying trends in personality.

The researchers kept two goals in mind while developing their new F (for fascism) scale. One was "[to] measure prejudice without appearing to have this aim and without mentioning the name of any minority group" (AP, 222). Armed with such an instrument, psychologists would be able to circumvent some of the defenses usually aroused when "race issues" are broached, and they might even be able to study prejudice among its victims. The second and more important aim of the scale was "[to] estimate antidemocratic tendencies at the personality level," thus achieving "a better estimate of antidemocratic *potential* than could be obtained from scales that were more openly ideological" (AP, 223).

The researchers assembled a pool of ordinary-looking opinion statements designed to tap one or more of the nine personality variables listed above. The opinion statements were taken from a variety of sources, including the clinical interviews of their prejudiced subjects, responses to certain "projective questions" (AP, 547), and earlier attempts to measure fascist attitudes.[21] The scale went through three revisions. Items were selected for the final F scale partly on the basis of their correlations with the A-S or E scales and partly on the basis of theoretical considerations (including the correlation of each item with the scale as a whole). None of the items mentioned minorities. In the end they had a 30-item scale, disguised as a public opinion questionnaire, that in theory measured the weak ego of the antidemocratic personality type.

Critics of *The Authoritarian Personality* have covered the F scale under a pall of doubt and controversy. Some of the arguments about its validity will be considered at length in Chapter 5. For the present it must suffice to note that the Berkeley group made clear that the scale was primarily a measure of ideology and only indirectly a measure of personality. Chapter 7 of *The Authoritarian Personality*, which describes the development of the F scale, ends with a discussion of the relation between F-scale scores and personality. The authors note that the validity of the scale as a measure of "fascist receptivity at the personality level" has still to be demonstrated. "It remains to be shown conclusively," they write, "that the variables with which the F scale has been concerned are, in reality, variables of personality" (AP, 279).

Whatever the shortcomings of the original F scale, there is no denying the central place it has held in research on authoritarianism, ethnocentrism, and the democratic character. For more than a generation the F scale, or some relatively slight modification of it, has *defined* authoritarianism for most social scientists, and it is still widely used in empirical research.

The scale has been widely used because it provides a clear and plausible operational definition of an important but obscure concept. To this day the theory behind the Berkeley group's F scale is little known. Definitions can be quoted, and arguments summarized, as they have been here, but the fundamental ideas are hard to grasp. Fortunately, however, we do not always have to know exactly *what* we are measuring before we begin empirical research, provided we know *how* to measure it.[22] We can discover what we are measuring as research proceeds, and since 1950 a great deal of valuable research has proceeded on the simple assumption that the authoritarian is the person who scores high on the F scale.

The F scale secured this privileged status, as the definition and not just the measure of authoritarianism, because of its usefulness in demonstrating the great quantitative importance of ego weakness as a cause of ethnocentrism. The method of comparing extreme groups, which was the basis for the fundamental psychological discoveries of the Berkeley group, could show that personality variables had some effect on prejudice, and could help to identify the most important such variables, but the method had two serious limitations. It could not yield an estimate of the amount of variation in prejudice due to variation in personality, and it could not determine whether the categories used in coding the interview material were all getting at a single underlying difference in personality (rather than diverse personality differences). The F scale made it feasible to study large, more or less representative samples of the general population, and therefore to estimate the overall correlation between personality and prejudice. It also, of course, defined a single dimension of variation. It turned out that this dimension correlated strongly (about $r = .75$) with ethnocentrism, as measured by the E scale. This was one of the most remarkable discoveries of the research: more than half of the variation in ethnocentrism, it seemed, could be associated with variation along a single, well-defined personality dimension.

After the publication of *The Authoritarian Personality*, research on ethnic relations could no longer ignore "the psychological dimension." The book seemed to demonstrate the great importance of psychological variables as causes of prejudice, and it lent credence to a new and complex, indeed rather strange and unorthodox, theory about what the relevant variables were. Psychoanalytic theory was needed, it seemed, in order to understand the *why* of ethnocentrism, the motives it typically served, and the personality type of which it was a characteristic expression.[23]

The Freudian Roots

The Berkeley group's elaborate theory derived directly from Freud,[24] who developed the general formula under which their analysis of ethnocentrism can be fitted (the formula for "obsessional neurosis");[25] who provided their theory's basic concepts (id, ego, and superego); and who even delineated, in a few quick strokes, the personality type the Berkeley group called "authoritarian."

A brief essay which Freud published in 1931, "Libidinal Types," provides the most concise, and perhaps the clearest, analysis of the main features of the authoritarian type as conceived by the Berkeley group. In this essay Freud distinguishes three pure personality types on the basis of where in the mental apparatus the subject's libido is mainly allocated. There is an erotic type, in which the sexual impulses of the id are dominant; an obsessional type, in which the superego is supreme; and a narcissistic type, in which there is no conflict between ego and superego and the ego is dominant. The description of these types is exceedingly sketchy and vague, and Freud remarks dryly that they "will hardly escape the suspicion of being deduced from the theory of the libido."[26] He then distinguishes three mixed types, the erotic-obsessional, the erotic-narcissistic, and the narcissistic-obsessional. The first of these three, the erotic-obsessional type, is defined by the relative weakness of the ego. "In the *erotic-obsessional* type the preponderance of the instincts is restricted by the influence of the super-ego: dependence on persons who are *contemporary* objects and, at the same time, on the residues of *former* objects—parents, educators, and ideal figures—is carried by this type to the furthest point."[27] In short, this is the type of the anxiety-ridden, repressed, conventional conformist or authoritarian.

Freud's purpose in developing his typology is not clear. He says nothing about the causes of the different types. He briefly considers the relation of the six types to pathology and concludes that the classification throws no new light on the incidence or aetiology of mental disorders. "Experience testifies that persons of all these types can live free from neurosis."[28] The essay seems almost a playful attempt to see what might come of using some of the main concepts of psychoanalysis to define fundamental human types.

The Berkeley group provide a much more detailed description of the erotic-obsessional type, as we have seen, and they also offer some hypotheses about the social and political causes of this type, as we shall see in a moment. On one point, however, their treatment of the type compares unfavorably with that of Freud: they are not nearly so clear about the alternative, or alternatives, to the authoritarian type.

One might expect a type defined by ego weakness to be contrasted with a type defined by ego strength (the narcissistic type). The Berkeley group's scaling procedures almost forced them to make this contrast, but in fact they never did so. Instead they generally emphasized the diversity of types among the low E subjects (humanitarians or equalitarians), implying that all of Freud's types except the erotic-obsessional are to be found among the partisans of democratic ideology, and on at least one occasion they contrasted the authoritarian type with Freud's "erotic-narcissistic-obsessional type," which is defined by the equal strength of the id, ego, and superego. The occasion was Adorno's description of the "genuine liberal":

> This syndrome is very outspoken in reaction and opinion. The subject in whom it is pronounced has a strong sense of personal autonomy and independence. He cannot stand any outside interference with his personal convictions and beliefs, and he does not want to interfere with those of others either. His ego is quite developed but not libidinized—he is rarely "narcissistic." At the same time, he is willing to admit id tendencies, and to take the consequences—as is the case with Freud's "erotic type." One of his conspicuous features is moral courage, often far beyond his rational evaluation of a situation. He cannot "keep silent" if something wrong is being done, even if he seriously endangers himself. Just as he is strongly "individualized" himself, he sees the others, above all, as individuals, not as specimens of a general concept. . . . [H]e is little repressed and even has certain difficulties in keeping himself under "control." However, his emotionality is not blind, but directed towards the other person as a *subject*. His love is not only desire but also compassion—as a matter of fact, one might thing of defining this syndrome as the "compassionate" low scorer. (AP, 781)

If we were to consider general concepts, we could, as Adorno recognizes, talk here about the balanced development of the three different components of the psyche, the id, the ego, and the superego. Freud had written that an "erotic-obsessional-narcissistic" person in whom there was a perfect balance of mental forces "would no longer be a type at all, but the absolute norm, the ideal harmony."[29] Adorno echoed Freud when he wrote that "the *Genuine Liberal* may be conceived in terms of that balance between superego, ego, and id which Freud deemed ideal" (AP, 771).

In short, when defining a positive ideal, even in theory, it seems that we must not think of the fullest possible development of the rational faculty, the strongest possible ego, but rather of an ego of the *right* strength, just strong enough to introduce the voice of reason into the conflict between the id and society's surrogate, the superego, but not so strong as to kill all pleasure in life or to render a person dangerous to his fellows. The genuine liberal, according to Adorno, combines the reasonableness that results from ego strength, with the autonomy and devotion to principle that results from a strong superego, and finally the emotionality, or desire and compassion, that results from a strong id combined with relatively little repression of id impulses.

The Political Economy of Authoritarianism

The Berkeley group's greatest novelty was to link pathological ego weakness with contemporary capitalism. By joining psychoanalysis to Marxism, they gave Freud's psychodynamic typology a solid socioeconomic foundation and Marxism an appealing psychodynamic superstructure.

Why, we must ask, does the ethnocentrist have a weak ego? Wilhelm Reich provides the clearest statement of the answer implicit in *The Authoritarian Personality*. A weak ego, or the authoritarian character structure, is basically produced by early sexual inhibition; it is the result of the way childish sexual activity is "normally" blocked by terrifying threats and then extinguished from memory; it is a particular—and in bourgeois civilization, very common—resolution of the Oedipus complex. As Reich puts it, "the conflict that originally takes place between the child's desires and the parent's supression of these desires later becomes the conflict between instinct and morality *within* the person. In adults the moral code, which itself is unconscious, operates against the comprehension of the laws of sexuality and of the unconscious psychic life; it supports sexual repression ('sexual resistance') and accounts for the widespread resistance to the 'uncovering' of childhood sexuality."[30] This suppression of sexuality is rationalized in many ways, all of which Reich rejects. It does not exist, he says, for the sake of salvation beyond the grave, as the church contends; nor is it a direct result of man's eternal ethical and moral nature, as mystical moral philosophy claims; nor does it take place in the interest of "culture," as Freud himself argued. Sexual inhibition exists because it serves the interests of the minority of the rich and the powerful—because it changes the structure of economically supressed man in such a way that he acts, feels, and thinks contrary to his own material interests. He becomes incapable of rebellion—generally timid, conservative, afraid of freedom, and in a word, reactionary. "The moral inhibition of the child's natural sexuality . . . makes the child afraid, shy, fearful of authority, obedient, 'good,' and 'docile' in the authoritarian sense of the words. It has a crippling effect on man's rebellious forces because every vital life impulse is now burdened with severe fear; and since sex is a forbidden subject, thought in general and man's critical faculty also become inhibited."[31] Sexual repression is, in short, the psychological basis for human exploitation. The bourgeois family is the factory in which the capitalist state's structure and ideology are molded. Forced to adapt himself to such a family, the child is prepared for the general social adjustment required of him later.

The Berkeley group offer essentially the same explanation for ego weakness, even though their research procedures forced them to give some attention to variations in child-rearing practices within a single bourgeois society. According to Adorno, the authoritarian personality follows the "classic" pattern of Oedipal fear and repression, and the existence of this type is to be explained ultimately by the irrationality of modern society.

> External social repression is concomitant with the internal repression of impulses. In order to achieve "internalization" of social control which never gives as much to the individual as it takes, the latter's attitude towards authority and its psychological agency, the superego, assumes an irrational aspect. (AP, 759)

In other words, when the demands of society are irrational, as they are at present, adjustment to society requires that the rational component of the psyche, the ego, remain undeveloped. The subject must be made incapable of seeing and acting on his own interests; he must learn to take pleasure in obedience and subordination. Such traits can be instilled by a specific resolution of the Oedipus complex.

> Love for the mother, in its primary form, comes under a severe taboo. The resulting hatred against the father is transformed by reaction-formation into love. This transformation leads to a particular kind of superego. The transformation of hatred into love, the most difficult task an individual has to perform in his early development, never succeeds completely. In the psychodynamics of the "authoritarian character," part of the preceding aggressiveness is absorbed and turned into masochism, while another part is left over as sadism, which seeks an outlet in those with whom the subject does not identify himself: ultimately the outgroup. (AP, 759)

This kind of upbringing has great value, from the standpoint of contemporary society, because of the "blindness" it creates to the working of society and the subject's own role within it. "People who have the greatest difficulty facing themselves are the least able to see the way the world is made. Resistance to self-insight and resistance to social fact are contrived, most essentially, of the same stuff" (AP, 976).

In principle, therefore, authoritarianism, with all its concomitants, including ethnocentrism, has a simple remedy—better child-rearing. No archaic instincts, no immutable human nature, nor anything in the nature of society stands in the way of a fully democratic and enlightened politics. There is a particular structure of the basic drives and functions in the human psyche that finds its natural expression, politically, in ethnocentric and authoritarian ideology. There are other possible structures, equally natural, given appropriate education, that have no affinity for such ideology. As the Berkeley group say in their concluding chapter, "it would not be difficult, on the basis of the clinical and genetic studies reported in this volume, to propose a program which, even in the present cultural pattern, could produce non-ethnocentric personalities. All that is really essential is that children be genuinely loved and treated as individual humans" (AP, 975).[32]

The difficulty is, of course, that parents, even those with the best will and the best feelings, are thwarted by the need to mold their children to fit into present-day society. "Few parents can be expected to persist long in educating their children for a society that does not exist, or even in orienting themselves toward goals which they share only with a minority" (AP, 975). What is needed, then, is a general reform of society; the strengthening of the ego, on a mass scale, cannot be achieved by psychological means alone.

> The task is comparable to that of eliminating neurosis, or delinquency, or nationalism from the world. These are products of the total organization of society and are to be changed only as that society is changed. It is not for the psychologist to say how such changes are to be brought about. The problem is one which requires the efforts of all social scientists. All that we would insist upon is that in the councils or round tables where the problem is considered and action planned the psychologist should have a voice. (AP, 975)[33]

Parents should not be deterred, however, from doing what they can to produce rational children, and young people should not fear an increase in their capacity "to see themselves and be themselves." Self-aware individuals may suffer from being out of step with American society, and they may enjoy fewer material rewards from life, but "we need not suppose that the tolerant have to wait and receive their rewards in heaven, as it were" (AP, 967). The rational and tolerant, who accept neither the legitimizing ideology of their society's ruling class nor repress their basic impulses, lead happier lives than the prejudiced, because they get more gratification of basic needs. As the last sentence of the book proclaims, "*Eros* belongs mainly to democracy" (AP, 976).

3

Nationalism

Patriotism having become one of our topics, Johnson suddenly uttered, in a strong determined tone, an apophthegm, at which many will start: "Patriotism is the last refuge of a scoundrel." But let it be considered, that he did not mean a real and generous love of our country, but that pretended patriotism which so many, in all ages and countries, have made a cloak for self interest.

Boswell, *Life of Johnson*

Can the California studies of the antidemocratic personality be used to clarify the psychology of nationalism? The Berkeley group certainly thought so. They presented their generalizations about racial and religious bigots as a comprehensive theory of ethnocentrism and they treated nationalism as a species of ethnocentrism. A good deal of hard evidence supports their approach and assumptions. Since 1950 some three dozen studies have found positive correlations between nationalist attitudes and variables like ethnocentrism and authoritarianism. Yet only the most perfunctory attempts have been made to analyze and explain nationalism using the Berkeley group's concepts and hypotheses. The empirical studies just mentioned were all small in scale, usually resulting in the publication of a single journal article, and they all steered clear of fundamental theoretical questions. The more ambitious psychological studies of nationalism have based their analyses on concepts from learning theory[1] or have employed a general "functional approach,"[2] and thus they too have avoided any sustained discussion of the Berkeley group's theory. Generally speaking, the political scientists, sociologists, and historians who study nationalism have shown little interest in *The Authoritarian Personality*. Since 1950 research on ethnic prejudice has been deeply affected by the California studies, but research on nationalism has gone on much as before.

49

This is puzzling, for if the theory is true, it must surely help us to understand at least some types of nationalism. Conversely, if an attempt to apply the theory in the study of nationalism should fail, and if the results should thus be disappointing as a contribution to our knowledge of nationalism, such results should nonetheless help to reveal more clearly the real strengths and weaknesses of the theory as an explanation of ethnocentrism. For few would deny that the problems posed by the coexistence of different nations in the world community are similar in many respects to the problems posed by the contact between different ethnic groups within a single sovereign state, and further, that the reaction to these problems of the bigot on the domestic stage is matched by that of the chauvinist internationally.

Nationalism as Ethnocentrism

The publication of *The Authoritarian Personality* stimulated a wave of studies of the relation between nationalism and personality closely modeled on the original Berkeley research. Three of these stand out because they illustrate three different ways that nationalism can be linked to ethnocentrism and authoritarianism.

The first noteworthy study was designed to investigate the personality correlates of "worldmindedness," which was considered the opposite of "national-mindedness."[3] The operational definition of worldmindedness was a 32-item scale which dealt with eight topics—religion, immigration, government, economics, patriotism, race, education, and war. Just as in the California research, groups of extreme high-scoring, or worldminded, and extreme low-scoring, or nationally-minded, subjects were selected for intensive study. (The subjects were students enrolled in the summer programs of several metropolitan New York universities.) The personality variables investigated included self-expansiveness, love-orientation, equalitarianism, stereotypy, internalization-externalization, independence-compliance, optimism-pessimism, security-insecurity, and ego ideals. Measurements of personality were derived from the subjects' responses to a variety of open-ended questions during one- to two-hour interviews and also from their responses to a series of projective tests. The results of the research were in line with the findings of *The Authoritarian Personality*. Those who scored low on the W scale tended to resemble those who scored high on the E scale in the California studies: they tended to put other values ahead of personal growth, to endorse conventional values without qualification, to favor compliance over independence, to harbor pessimism regarding the possibility of solving social problems, and to prefer conventional (political-military) to unconventional (artistic-intellectual-humanitarian) heroes. The "lows" also differed from the "highs" in the expected ways regarding their relations with parents and the kinds of discipline they had experienced as children. The authors noted that such results did not "necessitate the use of psychiatric or psychoanalytic terminology to explain them," but they nonetheless showed "that the worldmindedness dimension is closely (and inversely) related to the dimension of authoritarianism" and that it was "parsimonious to consider them as slightly different aspects of the same basic personality structure." Just as the Berkeley group thought that their E and F scales were both tests of latent fascism, the authors of this study felt that the F and W scales could be used interchangeably. "It is more parsimonious to conceptualize the dimension of nationalism-internationalism as a variant of the authoritarian-nonauthoritarian syndrome rather than as a variable having independent psychodynamic validity."[4]

The second exemplary study, contributed by Daniel Levinson, provided direct and objective evidence of intimate connections between nationalism, ethnocentrism, and authoritarianism among Americans.[5] Levinson, of course, began with the assumption that nationalism can be identified with ethnocentrism.

> Nationalism may be seen as a facet of a broader ethnocentric orientation. It is, so to speak, ethnocentric thinking in the sphere of international relations. Like other forms of ethnocentrism, it is based on a rigid and pervasive distinction between in-groups and out-groups. The primary in-group in this case is the American nation; all other nations are potential out-groups, the focal out-groups at any time being those nations whose aims are seen, rightly or wrongly, as different from ours. The American nation as a symbol is glorified and idealized; it is regarded as superior to other nations in all important respects. Great emphasis is placed on such concepts as national honor and national sovereignty. Other nations are seen as inferior, envious, and threatening.[6]

The purpose of Levinson's study was to demonstrate that nationalism is, in fact, related to ethnocentrism, and that it has essentially the same relation to authoritarianism that ethnocentrism has. To support these hypotheses, Levinson conducted a survey of 84 students attending classes at Harvard University in the summer of 1951. He devised an Internationalism-Nationalism scale consisting of 12 items having to do with American foreign, defense, and immigration policies and used this scale, along with conventional measures of ethnocentrism and authoritarianism (16-item and 12-item versions, respectively, of the E and F scales developed in the original Berkeley research) to measure the attitudes of the students. Nationalism, as defined operationally by Levinson's scale, correlated strongly with both ethnocentrism ($r = +.77$) and authoritarianism ($r = +.60$). Having regard not only to these findings, but also to other studies of nationalism, ethnocentrism, and fascism, Levinson concluded that "personal authoritarianism constitutes an important inner source (though by no means the only source) of the disposition toward nationalism and related ideologies."[7]

The third study strengthened the evidence for the association between nationalism and ethnic prejudice that was one of the foundations of the Berkeley group's reasoning about ethnocentrism. An unusually thorough study, it related anti-Semitism to a great many antecedent variables, including *national involvement*.[8] Two different measures of national involvement—a National Involvement scale and a Differential Loyalty to Americans scale—correlated significantly, and in some cases rather strongly, with at least three different measures of anti-Semitism. "Those who felt that the nation was very important to them were on the whole more anti-Semitic than those who were less nationally involved."[9] In short, strong nationalists tended to be domestic bigots.

The last two studies exemplify the methods of more than a score of studies in this area, almost all of which have focused on the relation between nationalism and authoritarianism. Thirteen studies during the fifties and sixties reported the expected correlations between F-scale scores and attitudes having to do with nationalism—isolationism, provincialism, jingoism, militarism, and so on.[10] During the seventies, four studies reported correlations between authoritarianism and support for the war in Vietnam.[11]

At least five studies of nationalist attitudes have employed Milton Rokeach's D (for dogmatism) scale, a close relative of the F scale. (Dogmatism is defined as general authoritarianism, and the D scale is designed so that left-wing as well as right-wing authoritarians can get high scores on it.) The most ambitious of these found significant correlations between nationalism and dogmatism for a sample of American university students and also for a sample of foreign students resident in the United States.[12] Two studies found dogmatism related to patriotism and superpatriotism.[13] Three studies report positive correlations between dogmatism and support for the war in Vietnam.[14] One study reports a negative relation between dogmatism and enjoyment of the antiwar movie "Dr. Strangelove."[15]

A far-reaching study by McClosky yielded a variety of strong correlations supporting the general hypothesis that nationalists differ from internationalists in their psychological characteristics.[16] McClosky's study focussed on isolationism which was measured by means of a 9-item attitude scale. The statements in the scale expressed distaste for the increasing involvement of the United States in world affairs and a desire for greater independence of foreign countries. The study reports strong correlations between isolationism, so defined, and more than twenty personality variables, including authoritarianism, hostility, misanthropy, obsessiveness, rigidity, dominance (an inverse correlation), and anomie. The study also reports correlations between isolationism and a variety of other ideological dimensions including chauvinism, ethnocentrism, political cynicism, classical conservatism, populism and both left-wing and right-wing extreme belief. Isolationism, McClosky concluded, is "part of a network of attitudes that are related to common underlying personality dispositions."[17]

Using McClosky's data, Sniderman and Citrin found a strong correlation between isolationism and low self-esteem.[18] Still other studies show nationalist attitudes correlated with low faith in people,[19] respect for people with status and influence,[20] a tendency to emphasize differences in power where there are differences in status,[21] and a tendency to behave competitively in experimental Prisoner's Dilemma games.[22] One researcher, intrigued by the possibility that there is a connection between aggressive anticommunist sentiments and constipation (or better, "uptightness"), developed a short measure of anal personality characteristics and then found that such characteristics were indeed related to hostility to communism ($r = +.37$) in a sample of 130 college students.[23]

All of the studies mentioned so far concern the attitudes of Americans, but there are several studies that clearly show similar correlations in other populations. For example, there are two relevant studies of the opinions of white South Africans. One showed a strong positive correlation between authoritarianism and support for "white civilization," while the other showed a strong negative correlation between dogmatism and "world-mindedness."[24] Two studies report positive correlations between nationalist attitudes and authoritarianism among Australians.[25] An important study reports significant correlations between authoritarianism, as measured by a modified F scale, and various indicators of nationalism among samples of secondary-school student from Belgium, France, Germany, Italy, and the Netherlands.[26] There are hints in the literature that the standard correlation could be found in England, Wales, Sweden, Lebanon, Tahiti, the Cook Islands, and Samoa.[27] Three studies suggest, without clearly demonstrating, that it should be possible to find the same correlations between nationalist attitudes and authoritarian personality traits among Canadians as have repeatedly been found among Americans.[28]

Some relevant studies have probably been missed in this review of the literature, but enough have been cited, I trust, to establish the reality of a link between nationalism and authoritarianism. The studies cited also suffice to suggest a portrait of the nationalist.

The nationalist, as he appears in this literature, is the ethnocentrist and the authoritarian. He is of course critical of foreigners, suspicious of their motives, apprehensive about their designs, contemptuous of their customs and beliefs, unwilling to endure close contact with them, convinced of the need to keep them in check with superior military force, and thus zealous in his defense of his nation's power and independence. This much follows, so to speak, from the definition of nationalism. But the nationalist is also inclined to find fault with his own countrymen, particularly racial and religious minorities. He is the all-round bigot. His image of mankind is coloured by mistrust, envy, and resentment. Tightly controlled himself, he demands that deviants who offend conventional values be severely punished. He believes that only strong authority can restrain man's anarchic impulses. He admires autocratic leaders, and he seems to have a compulsive need to submit to powerful authority figures. More generally, he complies obsessively with the contradictory and irrational demands of external authority. He is rigid, closed-minded, and dogmatic. He exudes fear and hostility. He is more concerned with what he hates than what he loves, more concerned with protecting himself than expressing himself. He avoids introspection and is uninterested in "psychological" explanations of human action. All his opinions seem to be stereotyped manifestations of a pervasive underlying alienation, pessimism, and insecurity. This insecurity must derive from his difficulty conforming to society's demands, which he has never properly internalized, and in repressing his own aggressive and erotic impulses. In short, the nationalist has a weak ego.

Do all nationalists fit this mold? Let us call the belief that they do "the personality hypothesis." This hypothesis, which equates nationalism with ethnocentrism and authoritarianism, implicitly condemns nationalism. Could anyone accept the hypothesis and also be a nationalist?

Nationalism as Humanitarianism

Blanket condemnations of nationalism are hard to defend. Surely there is a nationalism that consists essentially of a real and generous love of a nation without any important admixture of antipathy towards outsiders, and surely we have to take this kind of nationalism into account before we generalize about nationalist movements and their supporters. What about national liberation movements? Admittedly their partisans hold negative attitudes towards certain outgroups, but these outgroups are imperialists, and the hostility against them may be the perfectly reasonable response of dominated and oppressed people to their oppressors. Did the Berkeley group really intend to denigrate all the patriots throughout history who have fought for the liberation of their countries from foreign domination? In analyzing the psychology of nationalism, did they mean to denounce a force that historians say created Germany and Italy in the nineteenth century and that in our own lifetimes has brought freedom to China and India, not to mention smaller countries like Algeria and Cuba?

Clearly a distinction is needed, and the Berkeley group were careful to provide one. They had no desire (to choose an example still closer to home) to impugn the motives of those Americans who had fought fascism in World War II. They recognized some perversions of loyalty by some Americans in the struggle against the Axis powers, and they certainly had these in mind when they developed their "patriotism" scale mentioned earlier. But revulsion against Hitler combined with unshakeable loyalty to American democracy and optimism regarding America's ability to crush Nazi Germany, while it might be regarded as a kind of patriotism or nationalism, was far from their notion of authoritarianism. Indeed, they considered such attitudes good signs of a harmonious balance between id, ego, and superego (see above, pp. 30–31).[29]

The Berkeley group distinguished genuine patriotism, based on love of country and attachment to national values, from pseudopatriotism, based on mere conformity. Explaining the labeling of the Patriotism (P) subscale within the Ethnocentrism (E) scale, Levinson wrote:

> The term "patriotism" as used here does not mean "love of country." Rather, the present concept involves blind attachment to certain national cultural values, uncritical conformity with the prevailing group ways, and rejection of other nations as outgroups. It might better be termed *pseudopatriotism* and distinguished from *genuine* patriotism, in which love of country and attachment to national values is based on critical understanding. The genuine patriot, it would appear, can appreciate the values and ways of other nations, and can be permissive toward much that he cannot personally accept for himself. He is free of rigid conformism, outgroup rejection, and imperialistic striving for power. (AP, 107–8)

It was pseudopatriotism, and not genuine patriotism, that the Berkeley group regarded as a form of ethnocentrism and a consequence of authoritarianism.

Since 1950 about a dozen different studies of the attitudes of American Jews and blacks have sustained the Berkeley group's earliest hypotheses and have illustrated their important distinction between genuine patriotism and pseudopatriotism. The results of these studies are at first glance puzzling, for they seem to show that authoritarianism, as measured by the F scale, tends to be associated, not with extreme declarations of loyalty to narrowly defined ingroups and denigration of outgroups, but rather with criticism of these ingroups and a tendency to favor wider groups. On the surface, in other words, authoritarianism is associated, not with ethnocentrism, but with humanitarianism. These results could be regarded as evidence against the Berkeley group's theory, but they are better understood as evidence of the importance of the distinction between genuine patriotism and pseudopatriotism. The authoritarian members of oppressed minorities, rather than defending the legitimate rights and interests of their own groups (genuine patriotism), tend to "identify with the aggressor" and to take over, in a purely conformist fashion, the prevailing bigoted stereotypes held by dominant groups (pseudopatriotism). In the context of racism and oppression, then, authoritarianism is associated with the narrow nationalism manifested in pseudoloyalties to wider groups—the political nation dominated by a different group.

Thus the classic study of "minority group authoritarianism" found that Jewish students with high scores on the F scale tended to blame Jews for the anti-Semitism of the Christian majority; they attributed anti-Semitism to the unconventional behavior of the Jewish group. It was the equalitarians, and not the authoritarians, who were more likely to identify with their own group and to defend its rights vigorously. In this sense, the equalitarians were more "nationalist" than their authoritarian compatriots, but only in the sense that they more vigorously rejected nationalist stereotypes. As the author explained, "the non-authoritarian Jew rejects [society's stereotype of the Jew], fights its existence within himself, and is sometimes ridden by guilt when he is unable to do so completely."[30] A study of the attitudes of black Americans found that those with high F-scale scores were *less* likely than those with low scores to support the civil rights movement and to adopt an overtly militant stance vis-à-vis white society. They were more likely to criticize blacks, less likely to support or participate in demonstrations, and more likely to acquiesce in segregation and discrimination.[31] A study of nationalism in the West Indies even more clearly illustrates this pattern. Charles Moskos reports that the leaders of the West Indian independence movement, as compared with elite opponents of the movement (i.e., supporters of colonialism), typically held equalitarian and democratic attitudes, not authoritarian attitudes. The ideological setting of nationalist demands was not the traditionalism and obscurantism commonly associated with nationalism in European and American politics, but rather the beliefs and values of the European Enlightenment—"belief in the possibility of progress, the use of reason, skepticism of the old order, the equality of man, the removal of inherited social barriers, and a faith in men collectively to govern themselves under democratic procedures."[32] It was the opponents of nationalism, not the nationalists, who were the authoritarians.

All this is not to suggest, of course, that minority-group nationalism is entirely without blemish, nor that loyalty to a dominant group must necessarily be authoritarian. Studies of the attitudes of minority groups in the United States suggest that "ingroup loyalty" would correlate *positively* with authoritarianism, even in the context of oppression, were "loyalty" to be defined operationally as exclusive attachment to a narrow ingroup and rejection of all other groups as outgroups. For example, the authoritarians in Gary Marx's sample of American blacks were more likely than the equalitarians to be hostile towards whites—high scores on the F scale were associated with high scores on a measure of antiwhite sentiment. The authoritarians were also more likely to endorse separatist proposals such as those of the Black Muslims.[33] These findings support the simpler generalization usually associated with the literature on ethnocentrism, namely, that authoritarianism predisposes an individual to be hostile towards out-groups and to avoid contact with them.

The relations between nationalist attitudes and personality are evidently complex. The usual "personality hypothesis," linking nationalism with ethnocentrism and authoritarianism, has to be complemented, it seems, by a second hypothesis relating democratic militancy to humanitarianism, equalitarianism, and strength of character. I shall call this the "mirror-image hypothesis," since the personality traits remain the same, but their apparent relation to politics is reversed.

Politics and Psychology

The genuine patriot (the antinationalist in the dominant group, the nationalist in the dominated group) is evidently the humanitarian and the equalitarian. He loves his own country, but not to the exclusion of other countries. He loves humanity, one might say, and loves his own country-men because they too are human. He is firmly attached to his country's culture and traditions, but not so firmly attached that he is blinded to the equal legitimacy of other cultures and traditions. He recognizes the relativity of all national values, and he has no inclination to claim absolute validity for the particular culture and tradition he happens to prefer. He has a strong (but not an "automatic") superego, and a strong (but not too strong) ego. He has internalized and rationally criticized genuine moral values. His values are firmly internalized, even though he is fully aware that they are really matters of choice and have no absolute validity. He demands only that his own personal convictions be respected, and he is willing to respect those of others, provided they are not intolerant or expressed dogmatically. He welcomes diversity and refrains from generalizations, except those based on an adequate theory of personality, for he is able "to like and dislike, to value and oppose, individuals on the basis of concrete specific experience" (AP, 148). He identifies with humanity as a whole, not just with his own nation, and he has no desire that his nation should dominate the world. The ideal that naturally appeals to him is the ideal of a world in which power considerations are largely eliminated and in which no group can control the lives of any other group.

The pseudopatriot (the nationalist in the one group, the comprador or *vendu* in the other) is the ethnocentrist and the authoritarian. His thinking about groups and intergroup relations is determined by the need to have an outgroup. The pseudopatriot is a hypocrite. He makes a show of loyalty, but without any real commitment or critical understanding, in order to have a pretext for behavior that has other motives. He pretends to value his own nation's culture and traditions—so that he can censure and deride those of others. His attachment to national values is at best mere conformity to the strongest powers within his own society; at worst, it is a thin disguise for unruly aggressive impulses.[34] Pseudopatriotism is the manifestation, in nationalist ideology, of an underlying authoritarian personality structure. The authoritarian lives by standards that, for him, are alien standards, even though they are the standards of the group with which, for the moment, he is identified. His conformity to these standards is essentially "conformism" or "conventionalism": it is really nothing more than fear of punishment, submissiveness to external authority, gullibility, and lack of individuality. His morality is false, rigid, and resentful. It finds its purest expression in bizarre beliefs about the moral defects of outgroups and in attacks upon such outgroups and other low-status scapegoats (zootsuiters, homosexuals, people with bad manners, Oklahomans, etc.). "If his external authorities, or the crowd, lend their approval to this form of aggression, then it may take the most violent form, and it may persist after the conventional values, in the name of which it was undertaken, have been lost from sight" (AP, 233).

The Berkeley group did not, of course, distinguish good and bad types of nationalism—no more than they distinguished good and bad types of anti-Semitism. For them, nationalism was something inherently bad. But implicit in their distinction between genuine and pseudopatriotism is a distinction between at least two types of nationalist movements. On one side of their dichotomy is an ethnocentric type that is aggressive, irrational, and ultimately authoritarian, a type represented by the Fascist movement in Italy and the Nazi movement in Germany. These movements were concerned above all with enhancing national power so as to be able to oppress weaker nationalities. They were imperialistic. On the other side is an opposite type—humanitarian, equalitarian, and reasonable—that might be represented by almost any of the anti-imperialist movements of the past generation that have opposed Western, particularly American, domination of smaller countries, for example, the Front de Libération Nationale in Algeria. Such movements have been concerned with attaining freedom and independence so as to be able to advance the legitimate rights and interests of their own peoples and to preserve and develop their distinctive cultures and traditions. They have not been expansionist or imperialistic.

Thus in a changed climate in which nationalism enjoys a better press, the Berkeley group's distinction between genuine and psueudopatriotism can be seen as implicitly a distinction between two types of nationalism—an imperialistic and reactionary *nationalisme de domination*, on the one hand, and a progressive and humanitarian *nationalisme de libération*, on the other hand. The Berkeley group did not present it as such, but such it is. The distinction is not one given must attention in the standard literature on nationalism, except perhaps as the distinction between nationalism and patriotism, but it is interesting and important, and it deserves careful scrutiny.[35]

The distinction is not the same as the popular and familiar distinction between political and ethnic loyalties.[36] No doubt the Berkeley group would have felt more sympathy, generally speaking, with a person who gave his greatest loyalty to a pluralistic, multinational democratic state, rather than to an ethnically homogeneous nation. But this is not the essence of the distinction they made between genuine and pseudopatriotism. In their view, not just any political loyalty that transcends ethnic particularisms can claim to be genuinely patriotic, and not all ethnic loyalties need be condemned as pseudopatriotic. In principle, as we saw earlier, ethnocentric people can use political differences (e.g., American capitalism vs. Russian communism) just as easily as "ethnic" ones (e.g., blacks vs. whites or Christians vs. Jews) to define outgroups. And just because a group claims to represent political principles of universal validity, and indeed even if it actually embodies such principles in its constitution and way of life, we should not conclude that all those who identify with the group are genuine patriots motivated by a genuine concern for the values of the group—some may be merely conformists. In addition, genuine patriotism is not incompatible with loyalty to a mere ethnic group, even though its distinctive customs do not embody any principles of universal validity, provided that loyalty to the group is based on commitment to the principle of the democratic equality of all groups. The Berkeley group upheld the basic principle that all such groups deserve to be treated fairly.[37]

Nor is the Berkeley group's distinction between genuine and pseudopatriotism simply the commonplace distinction between loyalty to one's own nation and hatred of foreign nations. Nationalists everywhere probably claim that they oppose foreign nations because they are *for* their own nation, not *against* the foreign nations. The problem is whether we can take them at their word. From the standpoint of the Berkeley group, the question concerns the psychological basis of the nationalist attitudes, and it is answered by careful psychological investigation. They recognized quite rightly that the simple presence or absence of hostility towards outsiders is of no real significance, since genuine loyalty to one group sometimes involves active hostility against other groups. During the Second World War, for example, genuinely patriotic Russians and Americans sometimes had to express active hostility towards German, Italian, or Japanese soldiers. During the war in Vietnam, genuine Vietnamese patriots were sometimes compelled by circumstances to shoot their enemies. But we can distinguish the constructive hostility of a soldier motivated by a genuine commitment to fundamental democratic values, including the value of the equality of all nations, from the malignant indignation and resentfulness that results from a weak ego and the need to displace aggression from the moral authorities of the ingroup.

No one would deny the great difficulty of objectively separating genuine patriotism from pseudopatriotism, least of all the Berkeley group, but they were not overwhelmed by them. On the basis of Freudian theory they worked out in detail the differences between genuine and "pseudo" commitment. They presented their results in terms of a contrast between two extreme types of personality, a conformist, punitive, moralistic, and repressed "authoritarian" type, and an independent-minded, tolerant, and liberated "equalitarian" type. The first type is incapable of genuine commitment to moral values, and he shows this by the irrational opinions he adopts. The second type has internalized genuine moral values; he has a well-balanced psyche; his opinions and behavior show that he is an *individual*. The essential difference between these two types is the different ways that they have internalized moral values, and this difference can be related in turn to different degrees of ego strength and to the childhood experiences that produce greater or less ego strength.

The F scale was developed specifically to measure the difference in personality that determines genuine or "pseudo" commitment. When authoritarianism, as measured by the F scale, correlates *positively* with a particular nationalist attitude, the implication is clear: that particular kind of nationalism has little to do with any genuine patriotism—any genuine commitment to the distinctive culture and traditions of the nation—and more to do with the irrational, inhibited, and resentful mode of existence of the authoritarian type. The characteristic basis for such a nationalism must be the anxiety and resentments of the hostile, compulsive conformist, the authoritarian, the "new 'anthropological' type" produced by advanced capitalist society. When there is a clear *negative* correlation between authoritarianism and nationalism, the implications are, of course, just the reverse: that particular kind of nationalism must have little to do with the fearful, inhibited, and resentful mode of existence of the authoritarian type and much to do with the genuine patriotism of the equalitarian with a strong ego and a strong superego.

The studies summarized in the first section of this chapter clearly suggest that American patriotism and nationalism during the past thirty years have been of the fundamentally irrational type. The studies summarized in the second section hint that the nationalisms of the various peoples in revolt during the same period deserve a clean bill of mental health from psychologists.

But what if these conclusions, rather than making us more dubious about American nationalism and more fond of the Vietcong, make us dubious about the theory that produced them? Few may be inclined to press this objection, but defenders of the theory should have a good answer to quiet such doubts.

Several different answers are possible, but one merits special attention at this point: we are dealing here with an *empirical* theory; the correlation between nationalism and authoritarianism among Americans is a *fact;* we should not let our *values* distort our perception of *the way things are;* our task as scientists is *to test empirical hypotheses,* not to accept or reject empirical findings on the basis of our own emotional reactions to them. This is the answer provided by "positivism," and it has obviously had much to do with the wide acceptance of the Berkeley group's theory and methods.

Let us accept this answer, at least provisionally, and let us shoulder our burden, as scientists, of testing hypotheses.

The Canadian Case

What would be involved in testing the Berkeley group's theory in a new country? First we should have to determine whether the nationalism found there was rational or irrational. Until we had made this basic determination, their theory would yield no predictions and could accommodate almost any results. We would next have to determine whether there were in fact the predicted correlations between nationalist attitudes and authoritarianism. If there were, the theory would be vindicated; it would have successfully passed another test. If there were not, that is to say, if an ethnocentric and irrational kind of nationalism failed to correlate positively with authoritarianism, or if a rational and humanitarian kind of nationalism failed to correlate negatively, then the theory would be discredited, and we should have to consider revising or rejecting it.

The studies of Canadian attitudes reported in the next five chapters were designed to test the Berkeley group's hypotheses. It seems essential, then, that we first determine whether the different kinds of nationalism found in Canada are rational/equalitarian or irrational/ethnocentric, for otherwise our statistical results will be equivocal and our tests inconclusive.

How are we to make the necessary classification in the Canadian case? We cannot appeal to the consensus of all informed observers, for there is no such consensus. The different kinds of nationalism in Canada are controversial.[38] The partisans of nationalism believe that their causes are rational and nobly motivated; their opponents, the federalists and continentalists, believe that their own causes have reason and nobility on their side. Both sides have their academic defenders and representatives. Simply putting the conflicting authorities on a scale and weighing them will not settle the question: there are heavyweight on each side.

It is hard to think that such a "balanced" division of opinion is a peculiarity of Canada alone. Where are we to look for a nationalist movement that is not controversial and that does not have its reasonable defenders?

Is it possible for us to determine for ourselves, as scientists, how Canada's nationalisms should be classified? It would be foolish to deny this

possibility, but equally foolish to minimize the difficulties. We would have
to resolve the main differences of opinion between Canadian or Quebec
nationalists and their opponents. Among the questions we would have to
settle are the following: Does foreign direct investment, in the context of
economies like those of Canada and Quebec, produce net economic benefits
in the long run or would incomes be higher, on the average, if the inflow of
foreign capital were restricted? What kinds of restrictions would have what
effects on whom? What differences, if any, are there in this realm between
theoretical possibilities and administratively practical policies? Do the different nations in question (Canada, the United States, Quebec, English
Canada, and French Canada) hold different values and live different ways of
life, or do they have the same values and the same way of life? Similar or
different by comparison with whom? Would free trade and the free movement of labor and/or capital mean assimilation for the smaller nations, or
would it help them to survive as distinct groups? What about common
political institutions? Does economic nationalism open the door for broader
economic and political reforms (comprehensive economic planning, par-
ticipatory democracy, common ownership of the means of production, the
overcoming of the division of labor, the elimination of the commodity
categories, and so on) or does it only promote "fascism"? By the time we
had answered all these questions, and some others that might occur to us in
the course of the research, we might well have lost interest in testing the
Berkeley group's theory. At the very least, we would have traveled a long
detour and we would need a volume as large as the present one just to report
its results. Surely it is clear that any classification I might offer here, and try
to justify briefly, would be only my own partisan prejudices disguised in the
trappings of science. And an even more serious difficulty lurks just beneath
the surface. After all, we would be trying to determine whether particular
nationalist demands are rational or irrational, and whether they spring from
noble or base motives. What if someone should question our standards of
reason and nobility? What is reason, really, and what is nobility? The
Aristotelian account of these things differs from, say, the Christian or the
Nietzschean. Whose should we adopt? Can we, as scientific specialists,
make any such determination? Is it not precisely this sort of judgment that
is being excluded from science, when scientists and philosophers of science
say that science is *value free,* that it deals with what *is* and not with what
ought to be?

It would certainly be far less work simply to use the Berkeley group's
concepts and methods, particularly their E and F scales, to determine
whether Canada's nationalisms are good or bad. If we found strong positive
correlations between the measure of a particular kind of nationalism (e.g.,
anti-American nationalism) and scores on the E and F scales, we would
conclude that this particular kind of nationalism was ethnocentric and

irrational. But if we found strong negative correlations, we would conclude that it was humanitarian and rational.

The difficulty with this strategy is, of course, that it assumes what a moment ago we were obliged to test, the soundness of the Berkeley group's theory. The different nationalisms would be put to the test, not the theory, and the test imposed upon them could be one based upon unsound premises. In accepting it uncritically, we might be demonstrating only that we are in the grip of false consciousness. The whole elaborate Berkeley theory and methodology might be just an obscure way of appealing to our prejudices—an *ad hominem* argument in the strict sense.

We seem to have landed ourselves in a quandary. If we knew that the Berkeley group's theory and methods were sound, we could use them to answer our questions about the character of nationalism in Canada. If we could confidently classify nationalist movements as either rational or irrational, we could then go on to verify (or falsify) the Berkeley group's theory. But it seems that we can do neither. We cannot trust our psychology to throw light on our politics, nor can we trust our political intuitions (or prejudices) to provide the basis for a test of our psychological theory and its associated methods. Neither our psychology nor our politics seem to have the necessary independent foundations.

Why Nationalism?

Nationalism occupies an ambiguous middle ground between something in good repute, patriotism, and something in bad repute, xenophobia. Patriotism—love of one's country and devotion to the best interests of one's people—we are obliged to commend. Xenophobia—unreasonable dislike of outsiders and contempt for their ways of life—we wish to condemn, particularly when we are its victims. But what are we to say about nationalism? Is it ardent, active, virile patriotism, or is it really the worst, most baneful kind of prejudice and fear of foreigners?

We shall turn now to an examination of some detailed facts about nationalism in Canada—facts about correlations between different nationalist attitudes and authoritarianism. Further theoretical discussion will be deferred until after these factual results have been presented.

It may seem pointless to examine a lot of statistical coefficients before working out some definite hypotheses regarding what values to expect. It is worth recalling, however, that this was not how the Berkeley group organized their pathbreaking research, and yet their studies turned up facts that were embarrassing for conventional accounts of racial and religious prejudice and that served to establish a new way of looking at the psychology of ethnocentrism. As Nevitt Sanford pointed out, "a correlation of .83 between a measure of 'prejudice' (E) and a measure of 'deep personality trends' (F) in a group of 154 middle-class women . . . comes as something of a shock to the social scientist long accustomed to considering 'prejudice' as mainly a function of contemporary social and economic factors."[39] Some new and similarly shocking facts would be useful in reopening the debate, closed now for more than a generation, between the Berkeley group and their critics.

Part Two

Empirical

4

Measuring and Testing

One of the most striking features of *The Authoritarian Personality* is the contrast between the narrowness of its empirical base and the breadth of its theoretical concepts. The statistical data that support the book's argument came from three dozen different samples that were chosen mainly, it seems, on the basis of convenience. Almost all of the respondents were white, Christian, native-born Americans; most of them were young and most were middle class; almost all of them were residents of California; and all the data were collected in 1945 and 1946. Nonetheless, the Berkeley group generalized about ingroups, outgroups, ethnocentrism, and personality. Common sense and casual observation bridged the gap between data and theory. The book is an outstanding example of the relation between broad conjectures and narrow but careful empirical research that during the past century has come into the social from the natural sciences.

Following the example of *The Authoritarian Personality*, this study will rely on data from two samples of Canadian high school students (see Appendix A). The main variables in this study will be measured by means of conventional attitude scales. Authoritarianism will be measured by means of a short scale, described in Appendix B, which is essentially a simplification of the F scale originally developed by the Berkeley group. Nationalism, or nationalist attitudes, will be measured by means of fourteen different scales which will be used to distinguish extreme nationalists— those who manifest a particular nationalist attitude to a greater than average degree—from moderate nationalists and antinationalists.

Nationalism in Canada

Nationalist attitudes among Canadians are diverse and contradictory. If we were to examine all the thinkers, writers, and politicians generally called nationalists, we would admittedly see certain common concerns and typical attitudes, but not one thing rightly called nationalism in Canada. We would be struck, above all, by the diferences between French-Canadian nationalists and English-Canadian nationalists.[1]

Nationalism has a long history in French Canada, and it has recently undergone important changes. Since the Conquest in 1759, nationalists have generally been distinguished from other French Canadians by their concern to preserve their own language and customs by limiting the influence of the British government and the English-speaking colonists in the affairs of Canada and particularly Quebec. During the nineteenth century some French-Canadian leaders toyed with the idea of national independence, while others combined nationalist complaints against the English with a desire to become part of the United States. In 1837 there was a small but significant rebellion against the colonial authorities which was suppressed with the loss of about 250 lives. The leaders of this rebellion held ideas not unlike those of the American rebels of 1776. For almost a century after the Confederation settlement of 1867, which gave Quebec control over its own schools and civil law, and which confirmed the internal self-government of Canada as a whole, most French-Canadian nationalists advocated provincial autonomy and respect for minority rights, rather than the independence of Quebec, as the best means of preserving the social, cultural, and religious distinctiveness of their nation. In the 1930s, however, interest in national independence revived, and around 1960, spurred by the example of decolonization in Africa and Asia, a separatist movement of unprecedented strength began to develop in Quebec. This change was associated with two further changes. Nationalists began to define themselves as *Québécois* and their nation as the population of Quebec (which is about 80 percent French-speaking) rather than all French Canadians in Canada (most of whom live in Quebec, but about a million of whom live outside the boundaries of the province). Nationalists also began to put much more emphasis on language and history, rather than religion, when defining their national identity. Until about thirty years ago the principal and one of the most troublesome differences between English and French Canada was the religious difference: French Canadians were almost all conservative Roman Catholics, while most English Canadians were Protestants. Within Quebec there was a close relation between church and state, while at the federal level and in the English provinces the two realms were clearly separate, despite the concessions that had been made to denominational schools in some provinces. But because of the decline in the power of the clergy in Quebec, and in the intensity of devotion among Catholic Quebecers, and because of the heavy postwar migration of Catholic southern and eastern Europeans to the cities of both English and French Canada, religious issues are now much less salient, and religion is no longer seen by French-Canadian nationalists as a defining trait of their nation. Today what distinguishes French Canadians from their English compatriots is language and what may be called, for want of a more precise expression, historical grievances. Thus we find French Canadians today divided between those who claim that the language can be preserved and the grievances allayed within the framework of Confederation, the *federalists,* and those who claim, on the contrary, that the French-Canadian or Québécois nation must have its own state, the separatists or *indépendantistes.*

It is more difficult to describe the main currents of national feeling and the main divisions of opinion among English-speaking Canadians. No one would dispute that Canada's binational character and close historic relations with both Great Britain and the United States have profoundly influenced nationalism among English Canadians. Few would deny that the main focus of English-Canadian loyalty for more than a generation had been Canada as a whole, rather than particular provinces or regions of the country or any larger empire. There is general recognition that French Canada's anti-English nationalism is matched by an English-Canadian anti-French nationalism among English Canadians. Few would deny that the main focus of English-Canadian loyalty for more than a generation has been Canada as a whole, rather than particular provinces or regions of the country or any the diversity of the Canadian population, Canadian nationalism is generally conceded to have a distinctly political character, even though it has not yet been animated by a distinctive political creed, one that would set Canada apart from Great Britain and the United States.

Present-day English Canada traces its roots to the influx of Loyalists following the American revolution. Since that time English Canadians have always felt called upon to justify their independence of the United States. Until fairly recently, the standard justification was Canada's British constitution, its participation in the British Empire and Commonwealth, and the British manners and customs of Canadians: Canada was *British* North America, and it should remain British. This argument is still sometimes heard, but infrequently, because of the growing assertiveness of French Canada, the growing importance of non-British groups in the English-speaking population, and the declining interest in subtle differences in the political institutions of representative democracy. During the past generation English Canadians have had to adjust not only to rapid immigration from southern and eastern Europe, Asia, and the West Indies, but also to the hegemony of the United States in the North Atlantic world to which Canada is so closely tied by interest and tradition. During this period the integration of the Canadian and American economies has steadily advanced. This integration increasingly takes the form of direct ownership and control of Canadian branch plants by American multinational corporations. As a result, business careers more and more often have a continental rather than a national scope. During this period English Canadians have also been drawn more closely into the American world of politics and entertainment through mass periodicals, books, television, and the movies.

Among English Canadians "nationalism" used to mean opposition to British imperialism. The English-Canadian nationalist was the person who emphasized the continental or North American dimension of Canadian life, who preferred American democracy to the aristocratic traditions of Great Britain, who insisted on Canadian autonomy vis-à-vis Great Britain, and who drew attention to the conflicts between British and Canadian interests in foreign affairs. This "liberal" nationalism provided a basis for accommodation between French and English Canadians for more than a generation, from roughly the end of the First World War until about 1960. But today this old nationalism is dismissed as "continentalism." "Nationalism" now connotes, among English Canadians, anti-Americanism and a certain nostalgia for the British connection.

During the 1960s many English Canadians sought to distinguish Canada more clearly from the United States without defining it as British. The war in Vietnam changed the image many Canadians had of the United States and increased demands for a distinctive Canadian foreign policy. The racial violence in American cities further reduced American prestige among Canadians. The New Left's indictment of modern bourgeois civilization was widely accepted as an accurate description of the American way of life. Economists pointed to the increasing American ownership and control of Canadian industry and resources, and some argued that Canadians were in danger of being reduced to poorly paid "hewers of wood and drawers of water." Political economists blamed American investment for the growing tension between English Canada and Quebec. Philosophers lamented the impact of American power on the Canadian mind. Many Canadians concluded that Canada was rapidly becoming a duplicate United States, America North, a nation unwilling, if not unable, to give any real content to its formal political sovereignty. Anxious discussion of the problem of national identity increased greatly during the 1960s. Policies designed to defend Canada's waning economic independence were the subject of widespread public debate by 1970. The Committee for an Independent Canada, established in that year, was one indication of the new public mood. It grouped nationalists from all political parties (though mainly from the Left) to resist continental economic policies and to press for increased governmental support for Canada's cultural industries.

The rise of this "new nationalism" stimulated a more self-conscious, if not much more articulate, continentalism. Suspicious of the leftist inclinations of many nationalists, and uneasy about the possible practical implications of the shibboleths of the movement (e.g., dependency theory, Red Tory, industrial strategy, Canadian content, Harold Innis, and Quebec's right to self-determination), many in the business, educational, and trade-union establishments vigorously opposed nationalist demands. They accused leading nationalists of a variety of sins, ranging from self-indulgent radicalism and economic naiveté to chauvinism and latent racism.

During this same period, as already noted, the separatist movement was growing in Quebec, and the leaders of the Quebec government, while rejecting independence, were demanding a new constitutional settlement between English and French Canada. These developments did not evoke a clear reaction from English Canada, nor did they even create a clear division of opinion among English Canadians. The overwhelming majority of English Canadians were basically content with the constitutional status quo; most were probably willing to make some changes to recognize "French rights" outside Quebec and in the operation of the federal government in Ottawa (though when changes began to be made after 1969, there was bitter opposition from some of those directly affected); some were willing to make fundamental changes to accommodate the demands of Quebec's provincial politicians; and a few contemplated the use of force to compel an unwilling Quebec to remain within Confederation. Behind the irritation, vacillation, and confusion of the English-Canadian response, one could sense the lingering effects of more than a century of struggle to make Canada a British and Protestant rather than a French and Catholic country, a strong emotional resistance to any suggestion that the country be divided, the bad conscience associated with any kind of "racism" today, the fear of the Left that "constitutional reform" might be a cover for dismantling Canada's welfare state, the resentment of many "New Canadians" that the French minority was being given special treatment, and generally, the desire to maintain "national unity" on terms as favorable as possible to unilingual English-speaking Canadians.

The increased emphasis on the distinctive cultural identity of French Canadians in recent years has thrown into stark relief the fundamentally political character of Canadian nationality. The basis for Canadian nationality is not a common language shared by all citizens; it is not a common literary or folk culture, nor a common religion; it is not common historical memories. To the extent that there is a will to remain united among Canadians, it consists of allegiance to common political institutions and the sharing of common hopes for the future of the country. Thus Canada is a *modern* nation: it is large, ethnically diverse, democratic, republican in spirit (though formally a monarchy), and devoted to commercial pursuits. The proudest boasts of its citizens are no doubt the same as those of Americans, that they are free and democratic and that they are rich.

Scales to Measure Nationalism

The scales described in this section measure nationalism as it presents itself to the untutored common sense of Canadians. They are concerned with differences in national identity and with controversial national policies.

They are designed to measure attitudes towards national power and national unity, separatism, bilingualism, Canada's relations with Great Britain and the United States, and the broad problem of international organization and world government. Only in Chapters 6 and 7 will it be necessary to consider more recondite definitions of nationalism derived from reflection on the theories outlined in Part I of this study.

National Power and National Unity

Any study of nationalism in Canada today must begin with the question of separatism. As noted above, French-Canadian nationalism has practically always connoted opposition to English Canada and the federal government, and support for provincial autonomy and the independence of French Canada, but these connotations have become particularly clear during the past twenty-five years. Since 1960 many French Canadians have been persuaded to equate the boundaries of their nation with those of the province of Quebec and to regard the political independence of Quebec as a practical alternative to federalism. In the fall of 1967 the Quebec Liberal party split on this issue, and in 1968 the Parti Québécois was formed. The challenge to the federal regime it represents has dominated Quebec and Canadian politics since that time. Separatist nationalism is, of course, opposed by a federalist nationalism of "national unity." Both English and French Canada are divided on these issues: there are English-speaking separtists and French-speaking federalists, but the divisions are not the same in the two groups. For our French respondents, the basic question had to be which side they favored; for the English, it had to be how much they opposed separatism and what they thought should be done about the problem. Our two groups of respondents were repeatedly asked these questions, in a variety of slightly different ways, and the results were combined to yield scores on two scales:

1. Separatist Nationalism (SN, French questionnaire, 8 items).
2. National Unity (NU, English questionnaire, 5 items).

For further information about the questions used and the statistical properties of these scales, see Appendix B.

Are those who get high scores on these two scales rightly called nationalists? Perhaps the term should more properly be applied to those French Quebecers who support national rather than provincial power (i.e., the opponents of an independent Quebec, who are generally called "federalists") or those few English-speaking Canadians who, from respect for the "principle of nationalities," favour Quebec's independence. The difficulty one has justifying the conventional labeling of the scales illustrates the ambiguity of nationalism in Canada.

Fortunately there is little room for disagreement about the importance of this conflict between separatists and federalists. Any study of nationalism in

Canada that neglected the problem of "separatism" would be as remote from reality as a study of nationalism in the United States that neglected the Cold War. Nor is there much room for argument about the desirability of adapting our measures of nationalistic attitudes to the real cleavages that exist among our respondents. Our scales must distinguish proponents from opponents of Quebec's independence, among both our French-speaking and our English-speaking respondents. The fact that the opposing groups, separatists and federalists, can both be called nationalists, in different senses, is no reason for ignoring the obvious differences between them, and it is no guarantee that any hypothetical "neutral" or "balanced" measure of nationalism, designed to distinguish the nationalists among separatists and federalists from the nonnationalists or antinationalists in each camp, would be anything but an arbitrary confounding of fundamentally different attitudes.

Three additional scales were constructed from questions in the French and English questionnaires to make possible more precise comparisons among our respondents. The first of these is designed to place the French respondents along a quantitative dimension of Québécois vs. Canadian identification, a dimension that is potentially independent of the one measured by the SN scale, since the questions composing the new scale make no reference to constitutional options or the independence movement. The last two scales in this series are designed to measure anti-French attitudes among the English respondents and their attitudes towards national power.

3. Separatism (SEP, French questionnaire, 7 items).
4. Anti-French Feeling (AF, English questionnaire, 7 items).
5. National Power (NP, English questionnaire, 7 items).

"Anti-French feeling" could also be called "English-Canadian nationalism," for the new scale measures the propensity of the English respondents to take a resolutely "English" view of the rivalry between English and French in Canada. The Separatist Nationalism (SN) scale presumably taps a comparable dimension of "anti-English feeling" among the French respondents, but the National Unity (NU) scale, its mate, does not do so to the same extent among the English respondents. Scores on the NU scale are really quite ambiguous with respect to anti-French feeling. Who are really more anti-French, those who want to keep Quebec in Confederation, using force if necessary to do so, or those who do not want the province as part of the country and are willing to see the Québécois separate and form a state of their own? Hence the need for the AF scale. The NU scale also needs to be supplemented by a scale designed to measure the desire for greater national power among our English respondents. The SN scale measures the tendency among the French respondents to demand sovereign power for a state, Quebec, that does not presently enjoy it. The scale thus measures the strength of the desire to *increase* the power and status of Quebec, putting it on a footing of equality with other sovereign states. The NU scale, by contrast, taps only the desire to preserve Canada's existing power and prestige; it does not directly measure whatever inclination there may be among the English respondents to demand *greater* power and status for Canada vis-à-vis foreign nations. Hence the need for the NP scale. See Appendix B for detailed information about these three scales.

National Independence

For more than a century many of the great issues in Canadian politics had to do with Canada's relations with Great Britain. The basic question was whether Canada should remain an integral part of the Empire or whether it should aspire to a separate national existence.[2] On one side were those who valued Canada's British character and its ties with the "mother country" and who wished to see colonial nationalism accommodated within the framework of imperial unity. On the other side were those who decried imperialism and who looked forward to the day when Canada would be completely free of Great Britain. At one time, around the turn of the century, two diametrically opposed conceptions of Canada's future appealed to, and could both claim to express, the national feeling of Canadians. According to the "imperialist" conception, which had powerful support among English Canadians, Canada's destiny was to develop fully as a nation within the Empire and eventually to take a leading role in governing the backward parts of the Empire (India, the African colonies, etc.). According to the "nationalist" conception, which was particularly identified with the Mouvement Nationaliste in Quebec, but which had support in English Canada as well, Canadians should see themselves as a North American rather than a British nation and should strive for complete independence from Great Britain. These "nationalists" preached the development of a purely Canadian nationality based on conciliation between English and French Canadians and the avoidance of any entanglement in Great Britain's imperial wars.

Today these issues are almost forgotten. Contemporary Canada is more or less the Canada the "nationalists" envisioned. For all practical purposes Canada became a sovereign state at the end of World War I, when it achieved separate representation in the League of Nations, and this status was confirmed in 1931 by the Statute of Westminster. In 1968 only the monarchy and the procedure for constitutional amendment remained to remind Canadians of their colonial past. British influence in Canada was less immediately apparent than American influence, at least to English Canadians, and it was not nearly so controversial.

Since World War II the great problem for Canadian nationalism has been Canada's relations with the United States. This problem has many facets— Canada's participation in NATO and NORAD; its attitude towards American policy in countries like Vietnam and El Salvador; the activities of

American multinational corporations, and the policies that should be adopted towards them; restrictions on American immigration and employment in Canada; Canadian content regulations for radio and television; the support that should be given recent immigrants from Europe, Asia, and Africa to stay out of the "melting pot"; the old issues of the tariff and Canadian-American free trade; and finally, the basic question, which is always in the background, of Canada's "joining the United States." These issues have been debated in both French and English Canada, but they have been particularly salient for English Canadians, many of whom believe that in the past generation Canada has reverted to a new colonial status, with the United States taking the place of Great Britain.

Both the French and the English questionnaires contained a number of questions tapping the respondents' attitudes towards British and American influence in Canada. These questions were used to construct two scales:

6. Independence/U.S. (US, both questionnaires, 6 items).
7. Independence/U.K. (UK, both questionnaires, 4 items).

For additional details, see Appendix B.

Internationalism

Both the English and the French questionnaires contained five opinion statements about the United Nations and the ideal of world government. These statements were used to construct a scale to measure the attitude often considered the opposite of nationalism, namely, internationalism.

8. Internationalism (IN, both questionnaires, 5 items).

Although nationalism and internationalism are theoretical opposites, the internationalism measured by this scale may be compatible with nationalist feeling among Canadians, for Canada is a relatively small (in population) and weak country. Institutions like the United Nations, which proclaim the formal equality of all sovereign states, large and small, may be seen by the citizens of a weak one as a tool of national power rather than as a limitation upon such power. Thus "worldminded" acceptance of international organization may reflect nationalist pride and ambition rather than any cosmopolitan rejection of national power or sovereignty.[3]

Validity

There is no way to dispel all reasonable doubts about the validity of these scales as measures of nationalism or any narrower nationalist attitude. A scale to measure attitudes towards separatism, for example, cannot be compared to any criterion measure of this variable. All that can be done to confer some methodological legitimacy on the scales just described is to test their "construct validity" by correlating them with other variables that should be related, according to some plausible theory, to the attitudes being measured. Such correlations can be regarded as tests of the *constructs*, however, as well as tests of the *scales*.

It seems reasonable to assume, for example, that Separatist Nationalism should be related to Separatism (i.e., a Québécois identity) and to support for nationalist parties in Quebec provincial politics. In fact there are such relationships: the correlation between the SN and SEP scales is substantial ($r = .60$), as is the correlation between SN and party preference (table 4.1).

Table 4.1 Provincial Party Preference by Separatist Nationalism (French Respondents Only)

Party Preference	Nationalism Scores			
	0, 1	2–4	5–8	9–11
Separatist Parties[a]	6%	7%	28%	60%
Union Nationale	25	27	20	15
Liberal	34	41	28	14
No Preference	34	24	23	10
(100% =)	(111)	(270)	(205)	(98)

$X^2 = 150.15$ $p < .001$

[a]Rassemblement pour l'Indépendance Nationale, Ralliement National, and Mouvement Souveraineté-Association

These correlations are some evidence of the validity of the SN scale. For the English respondents, it seems reasonable to assume that scores on the National Unity, National Power, and Internationalism scales—three different measures of a single concept, nationalism—should be closely related to each other. In fact, however, the correlations between the three sets of scores are very weak:

NU and NP: $r = +.04$

NU and IN: $r = +.02$

NP and IN: $r = -.02$

These minimal correlations could be used to challenge the validity of all of these scales, but they can also be used to argue that broad concepts like "nationalism" are sometimes confusing when they are used to describe the attitudes of ordinary people. The fault may be in our expectations, and not in the NU, NP, or IN scales. Before it will be possible to choose intelligently between these alternatives, the problem will have to be stated more generally and a wider range of relevant data will have to be considered. It is discussed at length in Chapter 8. For the present it seems necessary to maintain the distinction between attitudes towards national unity, attitudes towards national power, and attitudes towards international organization and world government. The weak correlations do not justify combining the three scales and averaging the scores to get a more comprehensive measure of nationalism among the English respondents, nor do they require that we simply abandon the concept of nationalism and the idea that all these scales, despite their weak intercorrelations, may be called measures of nationalism.

Testing the Hypotheses

Scores on the seven measures of nationalist attitudes just described were correlated with scores on a shortened version of the F scale (see Appendix B for details) in order to test the hypothesis that nationalism is associated with authoritarianism. Table 4.2 shows the basic results. Only four of the eleven coefficients in this table are statistically significant—the negative correlation between authoritarianism and support for national unity (or opposition to separatism), the positive correlation between authoritarianism and anti-French attitudes, the positive correlation between authoritarianism and the demand for national power, and the negative correlation between authoritarianism and anti-British nationalism—all among the English respondents. Only the third correlation is large enough to seem theoretically as well as statistically significant. None of the remaining seven correlations are even statistically significant. Among the French respondents, authoritarianism fails to correlate with any of the five nationalist attitudes we have measured. Among neither the English nor the French respondents is there the expected negative correlation between authoritarianism and internationalism.

Table 4.2 Correlations between Nationalist Attitudes and Authoritarianism

Nationalist Attitude	English Respondents	French Respondents
Separatist Nationalism		− .04
National Unity	− .07*	
Separatism		− .07
Anti-French Feeling	.16***	
National Power	.29***	
Independence/USA	.00	− .06
Independence/UK	− .07*	− .03
Internationalism	.02	.06

* p < .05
*** p < .001

To avoid any misunderstanding of the figures in table 4.2, table 4.3 presents the three most interesting correlations in tabular form. Evidently there is virtually no association whatever between authoritarianism and scores on the National Unity (NU) scale. There is a stronger association between scores on the F and the AF scales, but clearly not a very strong association. The last panel of table 4.3 shows the distributions of scores on

Table 4.3 Three Nationalist Attitudes and Authoritarianism Among the English
                Respondents

	Authoritarianism		
Nationalist Attitude	Low (0–10)	Medium (11–26)	High (17–26)
National Unity			
High (12, 13)	19%	18%	21%
Medium (9–11)	58	55	48
Low (0–8)	23	27	31
(100% =)	(278)	(500)	(217)
Anti-French Feeling			
High (6–13)	19%	24%	35%
Medium (2–5)	53	47	44
Low (0, 1)	28	29	21
(100% =)	(267)	(473)	(214)
National Power			
High (6, 7)	9%	14%	37%
Medium (3–5)	61	64	53
Low (0–2)	30	22	10
(100% =)	(273)	(504)	(217)

the National Power (NP) scale within categories of authoritarianism.
Clearly the authoritarians have a substantially greater tendency to be
nationalists, by this measure of nationalism, than the equalitarians.

Let us try to summarize these results as they bear on the hypotheses
under investigation. A total of eleven correlations have been calculated.
One of these is strong enough to illustrate the personality hypothesis. Three
others are statistically significant, but they are too weak to be considered
evidence of any very intimate connection between nationalism and personality. None of the correlations provide any impressive support for what I
have called the "mirror-image hypothesis." The hypothesis is undoubtedly
true in some circumstances, and the reasoning behind it may have some
relevance for understanding nationalism in Canada, but the correlations in
table 4.2 refute the hypothesis as a description of the relations between
nationalism and personality among our French-speaking as well as among
our English-speaking respondents.

The Problem and a Possible Solution

Significant correlations are abundant, not scarce, in the literature on
nationalism and personality. In the past, the problem has been to find the
best explanation for these correlations. Some writers have speculated about

lawful relations between opinions and personality, arguing that political attitudes resonate with deeper psychological dispositions, so that particular attitudes are naturally linked with particular types of personality. Others have thought that social class, education, intelligence, or response set are more relevant explanatory concepts. But the problem has always been to explain correlations, not to account for their absence.

The results just summarized present a novel problem: Why have we found only one really striking correlation among eleven coefficients?

This same problem was posed by one earlier study of nationalist attitudes in Canada. In 1973 a sample of 667 undergraduates at the University of Toronto were given a questionnaire containing measures of nationalism, internationalism, and dogmatism. Nationalism was narrowly defined as "attachment to or identification with Canada rather than the United States, and as the desire for political, economic, and cultural independence from this metropolis." Canadian nationalism in this sense was measured by means of an 18-item scale covering a variety of relevant topics. Internationalism was broadly defined as "some form of desire for cooperation among nations and peoples of the world," and it was measured by means of a 4-item scale. Dogmatism was conceived as "general authoritarianism," and it was measured by means of a shortened version of Rokeach's D scale. The main results of the study were clear and surprising—no really significant correlations between any of these variables. Nationalism was independent of internationalism, and both were independent of dogmatism. The correlation between nationalism and dogmatism was statistically significant, but so weak ($r = .09$) that it provided no real support for the personality hypothesis.[4]

How are these results to be explained? At first glance the answer seems obvious: there are *different types of nationalism*, and some but not all of these correlate with authoritarianism. The literature on nationalism and personality leads one to think along these lines. The Berkeley group, as noted above, distinguished between genuine and pseudopatriotism. Pseudopatriotism, they suggested, was a part of ethnocentrism and thus related to authoritarianism, but genuine patriotism was nonethnocentric and equalitarian. Other writers, too, have suggested that nationalism can be authoritarian or equalitarian depending upon the circumstances in which it is found. Thus Sartre clearly distinguished the nationalism of national liberation movements from the ethnocentrism of which anti-Semitism is a species. "[The anti-Semite's] hatred of the Jew cannot be compared to that which the Italians of 1830 felt toward the Austrians or that which the French of 1942 felt toward the Germans. In those instances it was a case of oppressors, of hard, cruel, and strong men who had arms, money, and power and who could do more harm to the rebels than the latter could have dreamed of doing to them. In hatreds like these sadistic leanings have no place."[5] On a lower level, the so-called "functional approach," which we shall examine in Chapter 7, distinguishes between different bases of national loyalty or different "modes of commitment" to the "national role," and it implies that nationalism may be ethnocentric and authoritarian, or humanitarian and equalitarian, depending upon the psychological functions it serves for national actors.

It is hardly surprising, then, that the author of the 1973 Toronto study, confident that his scales measured what they were supposed to measure (nationalism, internationalism, and dogmatism), argued that nationalism in Canada represents quite a different type of nationalism than has been analyzed in the American literature on nationalism and personality. He concluded that "nationalist sentiments vary considerably in metropolitan and hinterland countries, both in terms of dimensions emphasized and in social-psychological correlates." In metropolitan countries like the United States nationalism may generally be associated with "conservatism, dogmatism, and anti-internationalism," while in hinterland nations like Canada or Cuba, nationalism may generally mean "the struggle to break away from the conventional metropolitan-hinterland political, economic, and cultural relations," and this may not appeal to "a dogmatic (authoritarian) student body or public."[6]

The present study is designed to investigate whether different kinds of nationalism have different relations to personality. The basic purpose of the study is to test the personality hypothesis in a country where nationalism has different connotations than it does in the United States. The difficulty is: How exactly are we to distinguish nationalism in Canada from nationalism in the United States? Chapters 6 and 8 below present findings from our two surveys, and from a few earlier studies, that will throw some new light on the usefulness of the distinctions just mentioned. Only after we have worked through the details of these results will we be in a position to take a fresh look at the fundamental problem of how to distinguish different types of nationalism. Chapter 10 will present an interpretation of the literature on nationalism and personality based on some rough but serviceable distinctions between the types of nationalism that correlate with F-scale scores and the types that do not.

But is any such elaborate investigation of types of nationalism really necessary? Perhaps there are much simpler ways of reconciling the results of the present study with the results of earlier studies. The next chapter examines six explanatory hypotheses of a "technical" or "methodological" character.

5

Methodological Explanations

Nationalism and authoritarianism are closely related among Americans, but not, it seems, among Canadians. This may be explained by the kind of country Canada is and by the kind of nationalism that is found among Canadians. Before accepting this working hypothesis, however, the reader may wish to examine six explanatory hypotheses that do not involve making any difficult distinctions between types of nationalism. The first of these would resolve the apparent anomaly by distinguishing types of respondents rather than types of nationalism. The next two would attribute our unexpected results to methodological shortcomings of the present study, while the last three would explain away the apparently significant correlations found in earlier studies by pointing to methodological weaknesses in those earlier studies. The six hypotheses are:

1. that there are correlations between nationalism and personality among adults, but not among adolescents;
2. that the failure to observe strong correlations between nationalism and authoritarianism in the present study is the result of poor measurement of the attitude and personality variables;
3. that the failure to observe strong correlations results from the obscuring effect of important "third variables," such as social class, on both nationalism and personality;
4. that the positive results of earlier studies are best understood in terms of "acquiescence response set," while the negative results of the present study are explained by the insensitivity of most of our measures to this response set;
5. that the earlier results were a spurious by-product of differences in education broadly conceived, which is to say, differences in age, intelligence, and general sophistication, while the present results are explained by the homogeneity of our samples with respect to age and education; and

6. that the earlier results are explained by the fact that all the scales involved—the various E, N, and F scales—tapped a single ideological syndrome, conservatism.

Youthful Respondents

Urban high school seniors from central Canada are obviously unrepresentative of the Canadian population, not to mention humanity as a whole, with respect to age, education, and residence. They may also be unrepresentative with respect to the correlation between nationalist attitudes and authoritarianism.

Perhaps the correlations between opinions and personality are generally much weaker among children and adolescents than among adults. Strong correlations between opinions and personality may emerge only after high school, as a result of increased maturity and greater exposure to political controversy. High school students may know significantly less about politics, generally speaking, and take less interest in it, than do college students or adults. They may be less attuned to the "psychological" connotations of different political opinions and less likely, therefore, to hold opinions that harmonize with their personalities. Their opinions may reflect external influences—the views of parents and teachers, for example—rather than deeper psychological needs. If all this were true, then we should not be surprised by the weak correlations shown in table 4.2.

But is it true? A diametrically opposed argument could just as easily be outlined. Adolescents are unusually free of social pressure. Rebelling against parents, without a job or profession, free to choose their own friends, when will they ever be more likely to adopt opinions for ego-defensive reasons? And when do egos ever need more defense, generally speaking, than during adolescence? Surely the adolescent ego must often live in fear of the adolescent id, and it must frequently employ every prop and defense that the culture makes available, including ethnocentric and nationalist opinions.

Past research does not clearly support either of these hypotheses,[1] but three bodies of literature deserve brief examination—the literatures on prejudice in children, on cognitive development during childhood, and on the political knowledge and opinions of high school students. We must also check how a control for interest in politics, which may be the key difference between adolescents and adults, affects the correlations between nationalism and authoritarianism among our respondents.

Sensitivity to ethnic and racial differences and willingness to make favorable or unfavorable judgments of various groups have repeatedly been found in large numbers of preschool children. "In general, research has indicated that ethnic awareness emerges about age 4, with finer discriminative and conceptual skills emerging thereafter."[2] This is an authoritative summary of a large body of research.

Some studies suggest that ethnocentric ideology is well enough developed in middle childhood to be related to differences in personality. An influential study by Else Frenkel-Brunswik yielded impressive evidence of authoritarianism among quite young children and of its relation to hostile ethnic attitudes.[3] This study did not, however, try to measure prejudice or authoritarianism by standard E or F scales, nor did it use standard coefficients to describe the strength of the correlations found, so it is impossible to say whether the correlations among the children were as strong as the correlations generally found in studies of adults. A more recent quantitative study suggests that the authoritarian syndrome generally is clearer among adolescents than among adults, perhaps because the former are less mature intellectually, on the average, and have a less discriminating view of the social order.[4]

Several careful studies by developmental psychologists influenced by Piaget have shown that there are important changes in children's thinking about ethnic and national groups during the primary-school years. These studies suggest that children attain the adult conception of nationality, and begin to understand the "reciprocity" and "relativity" of national memberships and preferences, around the ages of ten or eleven.[5] If so, it may not make sense to use the Berkeley group's distinction between ethnocentric and humanitarian outlooks with children younger than ten or eleven. (It may not make sense, in other words, to interpret unflattering remarks about outgroups as evidence of "contraidentification" unless the individuals being studied are generally capable of understanding the reciprocity and relativity of group memberships and preferences.) But there should be no objection to doing so in studies of older children and adolescents.[6] Their prejudices may still be rooted in various cognitive deficiencies, but these deficiencies might no longer be simply outgrown. They might well have an emotional basis, and they might be quite common even among adults.

Studies of the political knowledge and opinions of high school students suggest that such students are fundamentally the same creatures, politically, as adults. The most thorough study of this question, which was based on a national sample of high school seniors in the United States, found roughly comparable levels of interest, information, and "conceptualization" among students and their parents.[7] A follow-up study eight years later found that the opinions of the students were more changeable, generally speaking, than the opinions of their parents, but the differences were not great.[8] There was no evidence of the kind of instability of opinion among the students that would make it senseless to talk of systematic relations between opinions and personality.

These studies provide little support, as well, for the view that late adolescents simply echo the political opinions of their parents and teachers.

When parents and teachers are all of the same mind, the students will presumably take over their opinions. (In Islamic countries most children become Moslems, and in French-speaking ones they learn to speak French.) But when we turn to controversial opinions, and individual-level correlations, the situation is quite different. Generally speaking, the two studies found little relation between the opinions of the students and those of their parents or social studies teachers.[9] Great numbers of students simply disagreed with their parents, and there was virtually no evidence, in the individual-level correlations, of any influence by teachers. These studies did not specifically investigate nationalism, ethnocentrism, or authoritarianism, but other studies show similar weak correlations between parents and their offspring in this domain as well.[10] In short, high school seniors seem not very different from adults when it comes to making up their own minds about politics.

Our respondents are all roughly the same age and all have approximately the same education, yet we can indirectly test the impact of age and education on the correlation between nationalism and authoritarianism by dividing our respondents according to their interest in politics and then comparing the correlations within these subsamples. Some of our respondents no doubt pay close attention to politics and have a serious interest in political discussion, while others must be still children politically, more oblivious to politics, perhaps, than even the most apathetic adult. According to the hypothesis being considered, the students who were more attentive and more involved should be more sensitive to the deeper meaning of different political opinions and should be more likely to adopt opinions in harmony with the unconscious tendencies of their personalities. It seems reasonable to expect, therefore, that the correlations between F-scale scores and the seven measures of nationalist attitudes should be stronger among those who are more interested and involved in politics.

Both questionnaires contained four questions about interest in politics and attention to political affairs in the media. A simple and reliable index of political involvement can be constructed from these four items (see Appendix B). Table 5.1 shows the correlations between authoritarianism and nationalism, within categories of political involvement. There is no support in these figures for the hypothesized interaction between political interest, authoritarianism, and nationalism. There is no consistent tendency for the correlations in the "High Interest" columns of the table to be larger than the correlations in the "Low" or "Medium" columns.

These calculations are not meant to deny the gross unrepresentativeness of the two samples with respect to many characteristics, but they do discredit the idea that our results would have been completely different if somewhat older and more sophisticated respondents had been chosen instead of high school seniors—if college sophomores had been used, for

Table 5.1 Correlations between Nationalist Attitudes and Authoritarianism, Controlling for Interest in Politics

Nationalist Attitude	English			French		
	Low (N = 226)	Medium (N = 518)	High (N = 249)	Low (N = 135)	Medium (N = 422)	High (N = 170)
Separatist Nationalism				.23**	−.07	−.08
National Unity	−.11	−.08	.10			
Separatism				.23**	−.13**	−.08
Anti-French Feeling	.24***	.09*	.21**			
National Power	.31***	.27***	.34***			
Independence/USA	.00	−.01	.05	.00	−.01	−.15*
Independence/UK	−.01	−.10*	−.14*	.12	−.06	−.06
Internationalism	.04	.07	−.06	−.07	.09*	.05

* p < .05
** p < .01
*** p < .001

example, in order to make it easier to compare the results of the present study with the results of earlier studies of nationalism and personality.

Unreliable Scales

Does poor measurement explain the weak correlations shown in table 4.2? None of our scales consist of more than a few items, and none therefore can be very reliable: random errors of measurement must be important in all the scores derived from these scales. Random errors of measurement attenuate correlations. Our observed correlations between nationalist attitudes and authoritarianism must be smaller than they would have been if the scales had been free of random error. How much smaller? The answer depends upon the reliabilities of the scales.

The attitude and personality scales used so far have coefficients of reliability ranging from .43 to .78 (see Appendix B, tables B.7 and B.8).[11] In other words, random error varies from about 20 percent to about 60 percent of the total variation in these scores. This is clearly substantial. Ten percent error is the maximum usually considered acceptable in tests for counseling or clinical work, where attention is focused on the individual person. In survey work, however, where large groups are being compared, much greater unreliability is acceptable, since random errors of measurement tend to cancel out and sound inferences are possible provided the groups being compared are large enough. Unreliability is offset by large sample size. The same reasoning applies when two quantitative variables are being correlated. The observed correlation may be contrasted with a hypothetical "true correlation" that would have been observed if the two measures in question had had no random error. The observed correlation will be smaller than the true correlation, and the discrepancy will be a simple function of the reliabilities of the measures.[12]

Table 5.2 shows the correlations from table 4.2 corrected for attenuation. These are the correlations we could expect to find, given our sample data, if our measures of attitudes and personality had had no random error whatsoever. Perfect reliability is a theoretical fiction, of course, not a practical possibility. To achieve a reliability of .90 (10 percent error), the various scales would have had to be several times longer than they were. The F scale would have had to consist of at least 30 and perhaps 100 items. The attitude scales would have had to consist of 20 to 60 items each. Thus the correlations shown in table 5.2 are as large as we could ever reasonably expect to observe between these variables. They can be compared with the correlations reported in the most careful previous research.

Table 5.2 Correlations between Nationalist Attitudes and Authoritarianism, Corrected for Attenuation

Nationalist Attitude	English Respondents	French Respondents
Separatist Nationalism		− .07
National Unity	− .13	
Separatism		− .12
Anti-French Feeling	.29	
National Power	.59	
Independence/USA	.00	− .11
Independence/UK	− .14	− .07
Internationalism	.04	.12

NOTE: The correlations shown in table 4.2 have been increased to compensate for the estimated unreliability of the attitude and personality scales. The figures shown in this table are estimates of the correlations that would have been observed if all the scales had been perfectly reliable, that is to say, if there had been no random errors of measurement.

The net effect of the corrections for attenuation is to sharpen the contrast between the two largest correlations in the table and all the other correlations. The figures do not bear out the conjecture that the unreliability of the scales obscures important correlations between the basic variables of interest. The conclusion to draw seems plain. If there is a serious problem of measurement in this study, it is a problem of validity, not of reliability. If the scales are unsatisfactory, it is because they measure something different from what they are supposed to measure, not because they fail to measure anything at all.

Third Variables

A correlation between two variables can be obscured by the opposing effects on these two variables of a third variable. Let us assume that our personality and attitude variables have been adequately measured and that there is, in fact, a correlation between nationalist attitudes and authoritarianism among our respondents. There could still be zero (or very weak) correlations between nationalism and personality because one or more extraneous variables had effects on nationalism that were confounded with the effects of personality. These disturbing factors would have to have a direct relationship with one of the variables (personality or attitudes) and an inverse relationship with the other.[13]

To fix ideas, consider the possibility that nationalism varies *directly* with social status, while authoritarianism varies *inversely* with status. Imagine, in other words, a situation in which nationalism is a middle-class movement, but in which authoritarianism is characteristic of the working class.[14] Other things being equal, nationalists would tend to be middle class; and other things being equal, they would also tend to be high on authoritarianism. But other things would not be equal: those who had high social status would tend to be low on authoritarianism. The result might be a zero correlation between nationalism and personality: the tendency for nationalists to be recruited from the middle class, which tends to score low on the F scale, might exactly offset the natural tendency for nationalism and authoritarianism to go together.

Plausible hypotheses about "third variables" are easy to think up when there is a lot of uncontrolled variation along relevant dimensions. In this study, however, many potentially disturbing sources of variation have been controlled in the selection of the respondents. They do not differ greatly in age: they are all about eighteen years old. They are almost all city dwellers. They differ in intelligence and in prospects, but not as much as a sample of the general population would. They all have roughly the same education. The English and the French respondents differ in many ways, but for this very reason the two groups are analyzed separately.

The students differ greatly, of course, in social class: some are the sons and daughters of affluent and influential business and professional families, while others are the offspring of poverty and deprivation. For the reasons just outlined, these differences may be obscuring significant correlations between nationalist attitudes and authoritarianism among our respondents. Fortunately this hypothesis is easily tested by calculating the partial correlations between nationalism and authoritarianism, controlling for social status.

The students were asked to describe the occupations of their fathers and to indicate the levels of formal education attained by each of their parents.

Occupations were classified in one of seven categories from high to low status according to the method developed by Warner, Meeker, and Eels.[15] Levels of education were converted to years of schooling. With three different indicators of parental socioeconomic status—father's occupation, father's education, and mother's education—and eleven different measures of nationalist attitudes, thirty-three different partial correlations were calculated. Rather than presenting all of these correlations, I shall present only one set of eleven and then present the basic (or zero-order) correlations (a) between SES and F-scale scores and (b) between SES and the measures of nationalist attitudes. These basic correlations will convey essentially the same information the twenty-two additional partial correlations would, and in addition they will throw some light on why the partial correlations have the values they do.[16]

Table 5.3 shows the partial correlations between nationalist attitudes and authoritarianism controlling for father's occupation. The figures in this table and in table 4.2 are virtually identical. Social status seems to have nothing to do with the relations between nationalism and authoritarianism among our respondents. The reason is not hard to find: there is virtually no relation between parental SES and either authoritarianism or nationalism in our samples. For the English respondents the correlations between F-scale scores and the three different measures of SES are as follows:

> Father's occupation   − .09
> Father's education   − .14
> Mother's education   − .11

All of these correlations are statistically significant and all have the expected signs, but all are very weak. For the French respondents the comparable correlations are:

Table 5.3   Correlations between Nationalist Attitudes and Authoritarianism, Controlling for Social Status

Nationalist Attitude	English Respondents	French Respondents
Separatist Nationalism		− .04
National Unity	− .07*	
Separatism		− .07
Anti-French Feeling	.16***	
National Power	.29***	
Independence/USA	− .01	− .06
Independence/UK	− .08*	− .03
Internationalism	.02	.06

NOTE: The control variable is father's occupation scored on a 7-point scale of socioeconomic status.
  * p < .05
*** p < .001

Father's occupation $-.04$
Father's education $-.05$
Mother's education $-.05$

None of these figures are even statistically significant. Table 5.4 presents the correlations having to do with the second leg of the model, that is to say, the links between SES and nationalist attitudes. Again the coefficents are very weak. The largest figures in table 5.4 show, contrary to our hypothesis, an *inverse* relationship between social status and the demand for national power among the English respondents: this nationalist attitude, like the authoritarianism with which it is correlated, is more common among the offspring of low-status families.

Table 5.4 Correlations Between Nationalist Attitudes and Parental Occupation and Education

Nationalist Attitude	English Respondents			French Respondents		
	Father's Occup.	Father's Educ.	Mother's Educ.	Father's Occup.	Father's Educ.	Mother's Educ.
Separatist Nationalism				$-.04$	$-.04$	$.00$
National Unity	$.01$	$.02$	$-.03$			
Separatism				$.02$	$-.01$	$.05$
Anti-French Feeling	$-.06$	$-.10^{**}$	$-.08^*$			
National Power	$-.11^{**}$	$-.13^{***}$	$-.08^*$			
Independence/USA	$-.05$	$-.03$	$-.05$	$-.03$	$-.01$	$.03$
Independence/UK	$-.08^*$	$-.01$	$-.05$	$.08^*$	$.06$	$.03$
Internationalism	$.03$	$.06^*$	$.06$	$-.06$	$-.07^*$	$-.08^*$

$* \ p < .05$
$** \ p < .01$
$*** \ p < .001.$

The main point, however, is clear: all of the correlations with social status are weak. And because both nationalism and authoritarianism are essentially unrelated to SES, controlling for SES can have virtually no effect on the strength of the correlations between nationalism and authoritarianism. The hypothesis that strong correlations between nationalism and personality are being obscured by the confounding effects of social class is not sustained by the data.

What about other social characteristics? One hypothesis springs to mind—that Catholics may be more authoritarian and less nationalist than Protestants, and that these differences may obscure a positive correlation between nationalism and authoritarianism among our English respondents. (Among our French respondents, of course, there is virtually no variation in religion, and no possibility, therefore, of using this hypothesis to explain the results of the French study.) It is a commonplace that Catholics are more authoritarian than Protestants, and in Canada Catholics may also be less nationalist than Protestants, perhaps because of differences in national origin or because Protestants are the dominant religious group in the country and the symbol of political authority, the Queen, is the Defender of another Faith. In fact, however, there are no relevant differences between Catholics and Protestants in our English sample. Table 5.5 shows that the Catholics are no more authoritarian, on the average, than their Protestant compatriots, nor are they any less nationalistic. The only significant differences between the two groups have to do with anti-French feeling (the Catholics tend to be more accommodating towards the French) and anti-British nationalism (the Catholics tend to be more nationalist than the Protestants on this dimension). Taken as a whole, the data provide no support for the idea that religious differences are obscuring the expected correlations between nationalism and authoritarianism.

Table 5.5 Means of Personality and Attitude Variables by Religion (English Respondents Only)

Variables	Protes- tants (N = 560)	Roman Catholics (N = 225)	Critical Ratio
Authoritarianism	13.6	13.6	
National Unity	9.5	9.6	− .46
Anti-French Feeling	4.0	3.4	2.44*
National Power	4.0	4.0	
Independence/USA	6.2	6.0	1.23
Independence/UK	4.7	5.8	− 4.95***
Internationalism	2.8	2.7	1.33

* p < .05
*** p < .001

A third possible confounding variable is the sex of the respondents. Males and females differ in many interesting ways, but when our respondents are classified by sex, there are few significant differences on any of the dimensions of interest.[17] The relevant statistical details can be found in Appendix B, tables B.7 and B.8. Since there are no large differences between male and female respondents on any of the personality or attitude dimensions, there is no possibility of attributing the weak correlations in table 4.2 to differences in the natures or nurtures of boys and girls.

Arguments about the possible confounding effects of "third variables" are always somewhat inconclusive. No matter how many variables have been tested and rejected, the right variable to explain a correlation or its absence may still lurk undetected in the shadows. The number of suspects is reduced, in this case, by the homogeneity of our samples on age and education. It must be left for future investigators to find the right "third variable," if one exists.

Response Set

The F scale developed by the Berkeley group consists of thirty rather ambiguous, aphoristic statements, all of them worded in such a way that agreement implies authoritarianism. The F scale used in this study is a shorter version of the original scale. Its ten statements are simpler than the originals on which they are modeled, but most of them (8 out of 10 items) are still worded in the "positive" direction (agreement implies authoritarianism), and only two are "reversed" (see Appendix B, table B6). Thus both the original F scale and the one used in the present study have a common weakness: to the extent that people have a general tendency to agree or to disagree with broad statements, regardless of their content, this tendency will be confounded with whatever else it is that the F scale measures.

The E scale developed by the Berkeley group to measure ethnocentrism also consists of a series of statements all worded in the "positive" direction. To the extent that people generally tend to agree or to disagree with statements of opinion, therefore, any positive correlation between the E and F scales will be inflated by the response sets they both measure. Critics were quick to point this out: "acquiescence response set," some suggested, is a sufficient explanation for the strong correlations the Berkeley group reported between the E and the F scales.

The same reasoning might be used to explain the results reported here. Six of our eight scales of nationalist attitudes (the SN, NU, SEP, AF, US, and UK scales) are built up from questions with a variety of response formats, so that response sets should play no very significant role in determining scores on these dimensions. The correlatoins between these six scales and the F scale are interesting only because they are very weak. Two of the seven scales—the National Power (NP) scale in the English questionnaire and the Internationalism (IN) scale in both questionnaires—consist of opinion statements with which the respondents agreed or disagreed. All the questions in the NP scale are worded in the positive direction: agreement is the nationalist response. For the IN scale, the wording is the reverse: disagreement is the nationalist response. For the English respondents the raw correlations between these two scales and the F scale are .29 and .02 respectively (table 4.2), and the correlations corrected for attenuation are .59 and .04 respectively (table 5.2).

It is tempting to attribute the one striking correlation, between F and NP, to the effect of acquiescence response set on both measures, and then to explain the lack of any other significant correlations by the absence of any similar effect of response set on the other measures. But should we really dismiss the present results as nothing more than another illustration of the problem of response set in the F scale? The data from this study do not permit any direct test of this "acquiescence hypothesis." It must be judged against the background provided by more than thirty years of empirical research on response sets and styles in a variety of psychological tests.[18] But a few simple calculations based on the two correlations just noted will reveal certain fundamental difficulties with the hypothesis.

Let us begin by trying to explain the F-NP correlation in terms of response set alone, but let us assume, as it seems we must, that the IN scale is sensitive to the same response sets as the NP scale, since both scales consist of simple agree-disagree items. If we assume that no common factor except "acquiescence response set" is influencing the F and NP scores, then we should make the same simple assumption, it seems, when we turn to the F and IN correlation. In short, we must expect a positive correlation between F and IN of about the same strength as the correlation between F and NP, since the common factor, response set, should have roughly equal effects on NP and IN. (See figure 5.1, top panel, for a diagrammatic representation of this reasoning.) In fact, however, the observed correlation between F and IN is essentially zero. We must therefore reject this simple "acquiescence hypothesis." Some other factor must be at work, and we must take it into account in constructing our model. Let us call this factor *authoritarianism*, meaning by this term "something the F scale measures that is uncorrelated with response set."

The simplest model consistent with the observed correlations would postulate two underlying factors, response set and authoritarianism, each with the same influence on F, NP, and IN. The covariation between F and NP would be divided equally between the two underlying factors, while the lack of any covariation between F and IN would be attributed to the equal but opposite effects of response set and authoritarianism on these two variables. This model is shown in the second panel of figure 5.1.

There is, of course, no need to make exactly these assumptions in order to explain the observed correlations in terms of the two factors, response set and authoritarianism. We could, for example, assume that the F scale is a better measure of both response set and authoritarianism than either the NP or the IN scales. We could increase the "loadings" of the F scale on these two common factors up to the point where all the reliable variation in F-scale scores was being attributed to these two factors. In order to fit such a model to the observed correlations, however, we should then have to assume corresponding reductions in the loadings of the NP and IN scales on the same factors. A model of this kind is shown in the third panel of figure 5.1. Obviously a great many different models are possible. All of the values shown in figure 5.1 are purely hypothetical. The point is merely to illustrate a way of reasoning about response set.[19]

A surprising conclusion emerges from the arbitrary details of these examples. If response set is a major determinant of scores on the F, NP, and IN scales, then we must assume that authoritarianism is also an important determinant if we are to explain the observed correlations among the F, NP,

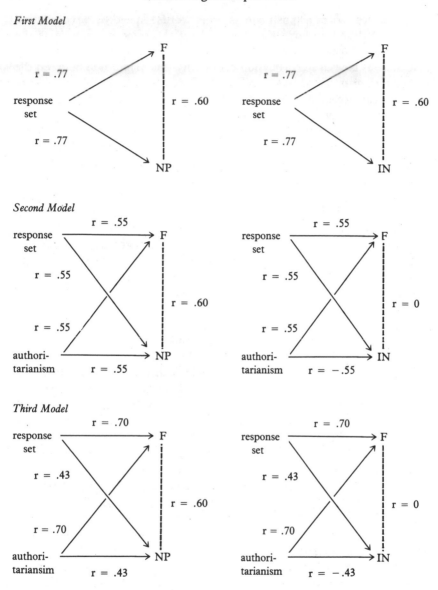

Figure 5.1 Three Models of the Relations between Acquiescence Response Set, Authoritarianism, F-Scale Scores, and Nationalist Attitudes.

and IN scales. We must postulate, in other words, an *underlying* correlation between NP and authoritarianism of about the same magnitude as the *observed* correlation between NP and F. Even more surprising, we must say that there is a *negative* correlation of roughly this magnitude between the authoritarianism factor and scores on the IN scale, even though we do not see the evidence of this correlation we would normally expect to see—a significant negative correlation between F and IN. This correlation is apparently being obscured by the influence of response set. In short, rather than explaining away the observed correlation between F and NP, a more careful consideration of the acquiescence hypothesis brings to light a correlation, between F and IN, that we thought did not exist.

We have not succeeded in showing how the magician had the rabbit concealed up his sleeve; we have only given him the opportunity to pull another one out of his hat.

If there is a weak point in our reasoning, it is the assumption that response set determines a third to a half of the reliable variation in the scores on scales like the F, NP, and IN scales. Are there any grounds for supposing that such a large part of the variation in these scores is due to individual differences in acquiescence response set?

A detailed review of the long controversy about response set is out of the question, but a brief outline of changes in thinking over the past forty years may be helpful. The controversy antedated the appearance of *The Authoritarian Personality* but was given a new point and vitality by the methodological criticism of that work. A large and complex literature developed that was devoted to research on authoritarianism and acquiescence. Today it is mainly of interest as a storehouse of methodological curiosities,[20] but during the fifties and early sixties, proponents of the "acquiescence hypothesis" were clearly on the offense, while those who favored any sort of "personality hypothesis" were on the defense. Opinion changed in the mid-1960s. A scathing review of the literature on response biases did much to kill enthusiasm for the idea that a few simple response sets and styles had a serious impact on most psychological tests.[21] Closer examination of the F scale showed that the early studies of acquiescence had greatly exaggerated the quantitative importance of the acquiescence factor in F-scale scores. It became clear that the most widely used method for estimating this component—the method of directly comparing responses to standard and "reversed" items—was inadequate.[22] Studies during the 1960s brought into clearer focus the basic fact that acquiescence is very hard to measure. Acquiescence is not, it seems, a single basic disposition measured more or less adequately by any and all paper-and-pencil tests that involve agreement or disagreement with statements of opinion or belief, but rather a variety of subtle tendencies that can be assessed only with carefully constructed instruments. As the phenomenon became more complex and elusive, and the concepts to describe it more refined and abstruse, interest declined among psychologists. One of the most prominent researchers concluded in 1972 that "empirical efforts to establish agreement acquiescence as a broad and encompassing dimension underlying individual differences have failed. The field of personality assessment has turned to other concerns."[23]

The implications for the interpretation of F-scale scores are clear. Whatever the proper interpretation of these scores (and it remains a matter of debate what this is), we can be reasonably certain that the F scale does not measure "acquiescence response set" as traditionally understood. "The F scale is, along with all paper and pencil instruments, potentially vulnerable to biases from a variety of sources. But there is little hard evidence for the actual existence of a serious acquiescence bias."[24]

Education and Sophistication

It has long been known that the E scale and the F scale correlate with variables like education, intelligence, and group membership.[25] Two small studies published in the 1950s demonstrated that college students can fake "uneducated" and "neurotic" responses to the F scale.[26] An early and influential review of the literature on authoritarianism summed up the import of these various findings as follows: "In broad terms the authoritarian syndrome reflects adherence to values which run counter to those accepted by liberal and literate citizens of the United States."[27] Some of the most interesting criticisms of *The Authoritarian Personality* have started from this observation. Perhaps the Berkeley group's strong correlations between E and F are to be understood not as evidence of any connection between opinions and personality but as evidence of the pervasive effects, in survey research, of differences in education, intelligence, and general sophistication.

The most important study of anti-Semitic attitudes in the United States since the California studies, *The Tenacity of Prejudice* by Gertrude Selznick and Stephen Steinberg, provides the clearest and most detailed exposition of this line of thought. Its authors report the usual strong correlation between anti-Semitism and authoritarianism ("simplism"), but they interpret it as a spurious result of differences in education, broadly understood, rather than as support for the Berkeley group's theory.[28] They assume that two cultures exist in the United States, an official enlightened culture and a popular unenlightened culture.

> The official culture contains the ideal norms that characterize our society in its public and secular spheres. These norms are derived from scientific and democratic values and represent the cognitive and moral commitments of a society whose political order is a democracy and whose economy is based on technol-

ogy. Scientific and democratic values provide ample grounds for
rejecting prejudice and discrimination. Intellectually and morally, the official culture is enlightened and unprejudiced.[29]

They contrast this official culture with the common culture constituted by
the superstitious beliefs and primitive morality inherited from the past.

> Alongside the official culture is an unofficial or common culture
> which not only differs from the ideal culture but is at odds with
> it. Historically more archaic, the common culture is not only
> prescientific and predemocratic but antiscientific and antidemo-
> cratic. Nevertheless, it is the culture normally taken on by
> Americans unless they acquire criteria for rejecting it.[30]

Selznick and Steinberg regard anti-Semitic opinions as part of the "syndrome of unenlightenment" associated with participation in the common
culture.

> Viewed in their cognitive aspect, anti-Semitic beliefs are intel-
> lectually unenlightened. They are generalizations about an en-
> tire group, usually accepted uncritically on the basis of hearsay.
> When not patently false, they typically involve false inferences
> about Jewish motives and purposes. Viewed in this way, anti-
> Semitic beliefs are a small subset of a very large class of unso-
> phisticated and cognitively primitive beliefs. Among their
> closest relatives are superstitious and magical beliefs, character-
> istic of almost any preliterate or semiliterate group.[31]

The opinions used to test for authoritarianism are also typical manifestations of this syndrome of unenlightenment. "On their face value alone it is
evident that—whatever else they may or may not represent—F beliefs are
unenlightened beliefs and embody a primitive cognitive style."[32] The correlation between anti-Semitism and authoritarianism (as measured by the F
scale) is not to be regarded, therefore, as a correlation between opinions and
personality, but rather as a correlation between two different aspects of the
same network of unenlightened opinions. "That anti-Semitic beliefs are
highly associated with other unenlightened beliefs hardly requires a recondite explanation. The less educated the individual, the less likely he is to
possess the requisite cognitive and ethical criteria for rejecting all such
beliefs, whatever their content."[33] Which culture a person reflects in his
attitudes and beliefs mainly depends upon his exposure to and training in
one or the other culture, not upon his basic personality, for the two cultures
are not presented "cafeteria-style, to be rejected or accepted according to
the individual's personality needs."[34] Among the determinants of exposure
and training, formal schooling is by far the most important. "The enlight-

ened culture is an overlay on the common culture. Generally speaking, one participates in it only to the extent that one ascends the educational ladder."[35]

The Berkeley group's error, from this standpoint, was to misinterpret a correlation that undoubtedly exists, but that is due to differences in education rather than to differences in personality.

> In our view it is an error to regard the relation between F and ethnocentrism . . . as in any sense causal. If anything, the relation has a formal or logical character. . . . What is involved is not a causal chain but . . . a syndrome. This syndrome encompasses a primitive cognitive style, ignorance of democratic norms, a blaming and apocalyptic orientation toward social reality, rejection of civil libertarian principles, intolerance of cultural diversity, and anti-Semitic prejudice.[36]

All these are highly interrelated because they are all common effects of differences in effective exposure to the enlightened culture of the modern world, mainly, though not entirely, due to differences in formal schooling.

This "cultural" or "sociological" interpretation of the authoritarian syndrome clearly provides a possible explanation for the weak correlations shown in table 4.2. The crucial fact about our samples, from this standpoint, is not that our respondents are young rather than old, or inexperienced and immature rather than seasoned and sophisticated, but that they are all more or less *the same* on these dimensions. If education and sophistication are the crucial determinants of both nationalist attitudes and personality (i.e., F-scale scores), then the attitude-personality correlations will be much weaker among groups defined by age and education (e.g., high school seniors, college graduates at age forty, etc.) than among the general population, which is heterogeneous with respect to age and education. By studying only high school seniors, and consequently controlling crucial extraneous sources of variation, we have been able to see the real correlation between opinions and personality, which is very weak, rather than the inflated correlations that result from confusing the effects of education, intelligence, and experience with those of personality.

This explanation is simple, even elegant and parsimonious, and it is plausible, but is it correct? No definite answer is possible, but various considerations ranging from the narrowly factual to the broadly theoretical suggest that it is not.

The narrowly factual considerations are initially the most impressive. Many studies show striking correlations between authoritarianism (as measured by the F scale) and ethnocentrism, despite controls for education. Only two such studies need be cited here. First, Daniel Levinson's exemplary study of nationalism and personality, as noted earlier, reported a correlation of + .60 between nationalism and authoritarianism (above, p. 51). The subjects for this study were not a sample of the general population; they were "two classes in education and one in social relations at the Harvard University summer session. The eighty-four subjects included some college undergraduates, a few graduate students in education, and a considerable number of persons in teaching and related community work." As Levinson noted, the sample showed "some homogeneity in the direction of high education level."[37] Selznick and Steinberg provide the second noteworthy source of strong correlations despite controls for "enlightenment." Table 45 of their book summarizes their main evidence regarding the importance of education as a determinant of both authoritarianism and anti-Semitism. If we disregard the control for education that is used in constructing this table, we find a correlation of + .56 (gamma) between anti-Semitism and "simplism" (i.e., authoritarianism). The comparable correlations within categories of education are:

Grade School:	+ .35	(n = 419)
High School:	+ .53	(n = 816)
Some College:	+ .27	(n = 205)
College Graduate:	+ .69	(n = 184)

Can we conclude from these figures that differences in formal education are what really explain the apparent relation between ethnocentrism and authoritarianism? No. The correlation is essentially the same for the largest subgroup of respondents, those with high school education, as for the sample as a whole. It is weaker for those with only grade school education or some college, but it is stronger for those who graduated from college.

Education or Conservatism?

The "two cultures" theory, simple though it is, can be improved by being simplified. The relevant differences between authoritarians (high scores on the F scale) and equalitarians (low scores) have nothing to do with enlightenment or cognitive sophistication, objectively defined, we could say, and everything to do with political opinions or "ideology." The relevant ideology is indicated by the word *conservatism:* the F scale measures conservatism and it correlates with other scales that measure the same thing. In California in 1945 and 1946 one aspect of conservatism was a suspicious and rejecting attitude towards Jews, blacks, zootsuiters, and Oklahomans. More generally, American conservatism involves ethnocentrism and belligerent patriotism. In discovering a strong correlation between their E and their F scales, the Berkeley group were discovering the obvious. But what is obvious in America need not be obvious elsewhere. In other cultures progressive rather than conservative individuals may be especially unfriendly towards relevant minorities; there may even be socialist syndromes that are ethnocentric. Some African socialist regimes, for example, seem to be quite ethnocentric just under the surface. An African study of the E-F correlation might show that E (defined operationally so as to take the local situation into account—no questions about zootsuiters or Oklahomans) can correlate *negatively* with F (with garden variety American conservatism as indexed by the F scale). The conventional bigots would be Marxists, not Rotarians.

This reasoning can be applied, mutatis mutandis, to explain our findings, and it resolves the empirical difficulties of the Selznick-Steinberg hypothesis about education while preserving its basic insight about "two cultures" and "sophistication." Education no doubt plays some role in determining political opinions (college as a liberalizing experience), but differences in conservatism are the result of a great many influences, not just education. Hence a control for education should not, on the present hypothesis, make the "authoritarian syndrome" vanish. Only a control for the underlying factor of conservatism would reduce the standard correlations to zero.

Much can be said in favor of this simple "ideological" hypothesis. The Berkeley group, it will be recalled, presented the F scale as primarily a measure of ideology and only indirectly and hypothetically a measure of anything else. The need for something like the F scale is first discussed in Chapter 5 of *The Authoritarian Personality*, which analyses the relation between ethnocentrism and conservatism. To make possible a quantitative study of this relation, a new scale, the Politico-Economic Conservatism (or PEC) scale, was constructed. A high score on this scale indicated "support of the *status quo* and particularly of business; support of conservative values; desire to maintain a balance of power in which business is dominant, labor subordinate, and the economic functions of government minimized; and resistance to social change" (AP, 157). About three-fifths of the items in the scale dealt with economic issues and labor-management conflict. But when scores on this PEC scale were correlated with scores on the E scale, the results were disappointing. The Berkeley group had reasoned that ethnocentrism should be associated with conservative politico-economic ideology, and the data generally supported their hypothesis, but not as strongly as they had expected: most of the correlations were in the range .5 to .6. An examination of the scatter diagrams revealed that the essential problem was the variability of conservatives (high PEC) on ethnocentrism. This discovery led them to distinguish two kinds of conservatism, one that was nonethnocentric because it was based on a firm commitment to American values,[38] and the other that was ethnocentric and proto-fascist because it had more "psychological" roots.[39] They called the former *genuine conservatism* and the latter *pseudoconservatism*. The pseudoconservative, they said, is the "the E-PEC 'correlation raiser' because . . . his politico-economic views are based on the same underlying trends—submission to authority, unconscious handling of hostility toward authority by means of displacement and projection onto outgroups, and so on—as his ethnocentrism" (AP, 182). The pseudoconservative also represented, they claimed, "the greatest psychological potential for antidemocratic change" since his needs disposed him "to the use of force and oppression in order to protect a mythical 'Americanism' which bears no resemblance to what is most vital in American history" (AP, 182). They concluded "that political ideologies do not fall neatly along a simple liberalism-conservatism dimension; that the relation between ethnocentrism and 'conservatism' is extremely complex; and the individual's receptivity to political ideology, as to 'group relations' ideology, is based to a large extent on deep-lying personality trends" (AP, 183).

The F scale was developed to measure more precisely the pseudoconservative and antidemocratic ideological trend and to show its close connection with ethnocentrism. The theoretical background to this effort has already been discussed. A comparison of the F and PEC scales shows that the statements in the former are similar to the noneconomic statements in the latter. The F scale is thus, on the surface, a test of conservative social attitudes, less oriented than the PEC scale was to class conflict and economic interests, and more to general problems of changing values.

Critics of *The Authoritarian Personality* were quick to emphasize the ideological content of the F scale. Edward Shils, for example, described the scale's statements as "illiberal opinions which are the stock in trade of the xenophobic fundamentalist, the lunatic fringe of the detractors of the late President Roosevelt" and as "clichés abominated by 'progressive intellectuals'."[40] The F scale, he concluded, was a measure of "right authoritarianism" and not of authoritarianism per se. More recently John Ray has written that the "the so-called right-wing 'bias' in the F scale is in fact the whole of what the scale measures."[41]

Numerous studies since 1950 have shown strong correlations between authoritarianism, as measured by the F scale, and other conservative attitudes, for example, general conservatism,[42] political conservatism,[43] religious orthodoxy,[44] traditional family ideology,[45] acceptance of the "Protestant work ethic,"[46] conservatism regarding the treatment of juvenile delinquents and mental patients,[47] and various kinds of pessimistic alienation from modern society.[48] Most of these attitudes have little to do directly with preserving the privileges of the wealthy. The people who receive high scores on these various scales of conservatism are expressing dissatisfaction with a society that is becoming more urban, more bureaucratic, more cosmopolitan, more secular, more hedonistic, and more permissive. The common element in the different attitudes might well be called traditionalism, to designate a preference for old-fashioned customs and values over contemporary ones, but it can equally well be called conservatism. Perhaps the best single measure of this preference, and of the worldview usually associated with it, is the F scale.

The difficulties with the "ideological" hypothesis are conceptual rather than empirical. They come to light when we consider the broad conclusion to which it points, namely, that the relations between "opinions" (the E scale and its derivatives) and "personality" (the F scale and its derivatives) are conventional rather than natural. The hypothesis implies that there are no natural laws relating opinions to personality: "personality" is ultimately just opinion, and in the realm of opinion, anything goes. *Autres temps, autres moeurs.* Such conventionalism is not without its attractions, but not without its difficulties as well, and to see what these are in the present context, we can do no better than to turn back to *The Tenacity of Prejudice*. The "ideological" hypothesis is the real heart of Selznick and Steinberg's criticism of *The Authoritarian Personality*, yet they do not state it as clearly nor push it as hard as they might have. Why not?

Tenacious Prejudices?

How are we to understand the relations between opinions and personality? Do motivational factors, or structures of personality, have a role in determining beliefs? Is there any lawful relation between the content of opinions and the structure of personality? Is a purely "cultural" or "sociological" interpretation of political opinions consistent with what we know about ourselves and others from introspection and casual observation? Selznick and Steinberg insist that differences in opinion are essentially the result of differences in education rather than in personality, but they are unwilling to deny altogether the role of personality factors and to say that people simply echo the cultural traditions to which they have been exposed. The result is considerable ambiguity in their analysis, and in the end, conclusions that differ very little from those of the Berkeley group.

The main novelty of *The Tenacity of Prejudice* is its emphasis on socialization. Its authors talk about two different cultures and about the processes by which individuals are inducted into one or the other of these cultures. They deny that any significant number of people choose their opinions to fit their personalities. Life is no "cafeteria" where one chooses beliefs according to one's personal tastes, and where ethnocentrism is the dish that appeals to the authoritarian palate. They find it "difficult to accept the implication that our heterodox [heterogeneous?] culture is presented, cafeteria-style, to be rejected or accepted according to the individual's personality needs."[49] Beliefs are prior to personality, they say, and education—or "integration into enlightened social institutions"—is prior to both. "Authoritarian personalities do not choose the unenlightened cul-

ture; rather the unenlightened culture creates authoritarian personalities."[50] In short, the unenlightened are no more to blame for their
primitive and unsophisticated beliefs than are the members of some savage
tribe in New Guinea. We are all the hapless products of our education and
cultural background, and the savages amongst us have just not had the
benefit of a high school or college education.

Now if education is the crucial variable, education is what we must strive
to understand. How exactly are we to understand the differences between
the educated and the uneducated? Both, it seems, are cultured, though
their cultures differ—just as the French and the Germans, the Algonquins
and the Navahos, all have cultures, even though their cultures differ. Is
enlightenment, then, just conformity to a distinctive set of cultural norms?
Are scientific and democratic values merely the cognitive commitments an
ambitious youngster should make if he wishes to earn his badge of sophistication? Do the differences between the enlightened and the unenlightened
come down, in the end, to the fact that different opinions prevail in
different strata of society? Selznick and Steinberg sometimes answer these
questions affirmatively, and much of the force of their critique comes from
such affirmations. They say, for example, that "the significance of education for prejudice is that it brings people into contact with the official norms
and values of our society" and that "the uneducated are cognitively and
morally unenlightened because they have never been indoctrinated [sic]
into the enlightened values of the larger society and in this sense are
alienated from it."[51] Such remarks are in harmony with the whole tenor of
their analysis, with its emphasis on *cultures, values,* and *socialization.* But
Selznick and Steinberg also sometimes sense that they are teetering on the
brink of a precipice and they sometimes deny that tolerance is merely
outward conformity to respectable opinion. "More is involved in education," they declare flatly, "than learning that prejudice is not respectable."[52]

When Selznick and Steinberg try to explain what more is involved, they
return to the ideas of the Berkeley group. Cognitive sophistication is not the
result, it seems, of echoing sophisticated opinions, but of repressing unsophisticated errors. "As both Freud and Durkheim recognized, the enlightened culture is an inhibiting culture; it is designed to restrain and
discipline the more primitive impulses of man."[53] Education strengthens
the ego, they say, and it counteracts man's natural tendency, in his "natural
state of cognitive innocence," to resort to primitive modes of coping with id
impulses, including "distortions of reality."

> In the absence of strong countervailing influences, [such distor-
> tions] are routine responses of the ego to the restrictions placed
> on the id by man's life in society. It is part of man's nature to
> externalize and project, and this accounts for the emergence of
> projective and paranoid belief systems in whole cultures. . . .
> Only a high level of cognitive sophistication—as embodied in

science with its relentless pursuit of the reality principle—can counteract the natural tendency of man to resort to primitive modes of coping with his id, including his impulses to aggression.[54]

Selznick and Steinberg, like Freud and the Berkeley group, see the rejection of prejudice as one result of a strong and mature ego. What surprises them, in the Berkeley group's treatment of this theme, "is the failure . . . to connect the development of the rational ego with the educational process."[55] But perhaps they should not have been surprised, for they routinely assume that educational differences should be interpreted *culturally* rather than *psychologically,* and at one point they even state that "there is no reason to believe that the basic psychological needs and basic psychodynamics of the uneducated differ from those of the educated."[56]

The equivocations of Selznick and Steinberg are best understood as the result of unresolved internal conflict. They scorn the Berkeley group's bold hypotheses—that ethnocentrism is naturally linked to conservatism, and that the conservative-ethnocentric ideological syndrome is naturally linked to psychopathology—because such hypotheses are sociologically unsophisticated ("too psychological" and "biased"). But they also dimly recognize that the Berkeley group's problem of "receptivity" or "susceptibility" is a genuine problem, and that the sociological interpretation of authoritarianism does not do it justice. They cannot bring themselves to deny that different people have different personalities, or that differences in personality are related to the differences of opinion that interest them, and when it comes to matching opinions with personalities, they adopt the Berkeley group's theory. They present themselves as iconoclasts, but in the end they endorse the orthodox view that "the 'true' authoritarian is a pathological personality in the sense that he has an emotional investment in rigid, punitive, and 'paranoid' beliefs" and that "some people seek out such beliefs and score high on F (and similar measures) for reasons of personal psychopathology."[57]

Selznick and Steinberg thus join the chorus of critics who say, in effect, that the Berkeley group made some methodological mistakes, and exaggerated the role of personality, but still provided valuable insights into the psychology of ethnocentrism and conservatism. By joining this chorus they are spared the ungrateful task of explaining it. If there were nothing more to *The Authoritarian Personality* than suggested by the "ideological" explanation of the correlation between the F scale and other attitudinal variables, then the Berkeley group's most eloquent and influential critics would clearly have been remiss in not saying so. They would be vulnerable to the criticism that they were almost as gullible as the outright defenders of the book. We might have to speculate about possible political and professional prejudices that numbed their critical faculties and blinded them to the book's real defects. But this would surely be unfair. The critics were clearly

right to think that *The Authoritarian Personality* advances a novel theory and
to insist that this theory be judged on its own merits, apart from the
methodological strengths or weaknesses of the Berkeley group's empirical
studies.

None of our six simple hypotheses have provided a satisfactory explanation
of our anomalous findings. The correlations between nationalism and authoritarianism are undoubtedly somewhat different among high school
students, college students, and adults, but there is no reason to believe they
are zero among high school seniors and full strength among college students
and adults. Random errors of measurement have undoubtedly attenuated
the correlations between our variables, but not enough to explain the
striking differences between our results and the results of earlier studies.
Some "third variable" may be obscuring significant correlations between
our measures of nationalism and personality, but if so, this variable remains
to be found. A variety of response sets and styles have undoubtedly affected
the correlations we have observed, depressing some and elevating others by
comparison with what we would have observed had we had pure measures
of our variables, but there are no grounds for attributing the one significant
result in the present study, and all the positive findings of earlier studies, to
"acquiescence response set." The nature of this "set" is obscure, as is its
quantitative importance. The differences in "enlightenment" and "intellectual sophistication" associated with large differences in age and education may well inflate the apparent correlation between opinions and personality in many studies, but not in all. The "sociological" interpretation of
authoritarianism cannot be dismissed out of hand, but there are a variety of
reasons, briefly indicated above, for thinking that it provides a fundamentally incomplete account of the psychology of ethnocentric opinions.
The "ideological" hypothesis is the most interesting of the six, and it may
provide the simplest and best explanation of our findings. Authoritarianism
is in principle a kind of conservatism, and the F scale is at best a measure of
right-wing authoritarianism. But the hypothesis must be held in abeyance
until we have examined more evidence about the correlates of F-scale
scores.

The correct explanation, it seems, will be found in the direction first
indicated: we must distinguish different types of nationalism, some of
which will be related to authoritarianism while others are not. The weak
correlations reported in this chapter are puzzling only if we assume that our
opinion variables are essentially the same as the opinion variables in previous studies of nationalism and personality. This assumption may be false.
It may be necessary to distinguish different types of nationalism with
different relations to personality.

6

Negative Attitudes towards Outgroups

Differential evaluation of ingroups and outgroups is an essential part of ethnocentrism as conceived by the Berkeley group. The original E scale was built up from more specific measures of attitudes towards diverse ethnic groups, and according to Daniel Levinson's concise definition of the basic concept, "ethnocentrism . . . involves stereotyped negative imagery and hostile attitudes regarding outgroups and stereotyped positive imagery and submissive attitudes regarding ingroups" (AP, 150). Many studies demonstrate strong correlations between ethnic prejudice and authoritarianism, not just in the United States, but in many other countries as well. The relation of authoritarianism, as measured by the F scale, to racial and religious prejudice is one of the best established in social psychology.[1]

Perhaps the anomalous results reported in Chapter 4 can be explained by saying that the measures of nationalism used so far have not directly tapped ethnocentrism. Perhaps the fundamental connection, in the whole field of ethnic attitudes and personality, is between authoritarianism and negative attitudes towards outgroups. What distinguishes the authoritarian from the equalitarian, we could say, is his greater tendency to repress aggression and then to displace it onto innocent scapegoats who lack the power to retaliate, a tendency that is manifested in his uncritical evaluation of ingroups and his disparagement of ethnic and national outgroups.

Measures of Imagery and Evaluation

A variety of methods can be used to measure attitudes towards groups. The most widely used method involves asking subjects to agree or disagree with controversial statements about the groups in question and their relations with other groups. The opinion statements themselves can be scaled to clarify the differences in attitudes that are being measured. Attitudes can also be inferred from the adjectives used to describe a group, or from answers to a "social distance" questionnaire. Open-ended questions have been used, as have a variety of indirect or projective techniques. But finally, and most simply, attitudes can be inferred from judgments about groups elicited by means of the "semantic differential" rating scales made familiar by Osgood, Suci, and Tannenbaum.[2]

The measures to be described here are based upon semantic differentials. Both questionnaires contained five pages of rating scales which respondents used to describe Canada and the national or ethnic groups most important to Canadians—English Canadians, French Canadians, Americans, British people, and Frenchmen. For example:

CANADA

beautiful __:__:__:__:__:__:__ ugly

For each group there were three or more rating scales that all asked, in effect, for the respondent's judgment of the overall goodness or badness of the group—the so-called "evaluative dimension of meaning." Ratings on these scales were given numerical values from 1 (least favorable) to 7 (most favorable). The average of these ratings for each individual indicates his generally positive or negative attitude towards the group. High numbers correspond to positive attitudes, low numbers to negative attitudes. A score of exactly 4 would represent the middle position between positive and negative feeling.

Tables 6.1 and 6.2 show the scales used to measure attitudes towards Canada and towards the ethnic or national groups. English Canadians and French Canadians were rated on all five scales shown in table 6.2; Americans were rated on the first four, and the British or French on the first three, the former by the English respondents, the latter by the French respondents. The respondents rated Americans first, then Canada, then English and French Canadians, and finally British people or Frenchmen.

Table 6.1 Evaluative Scales Used for Rating "Canada"

English Questionnaire	French Questionnaire
Beautiful—Ugly	beau—laid
Fair—Unfair	juste—injuste
Dull—Exciting	terne—fascinant
Honest—Dishonest	honnête—malhonnête
Success—Failure	succès—échec
Selfish—Generous	égoïste—généreux
Interesting—Boring	intéressant—ennuyeux

Table 6.2   Concepts and Scales Used to Measure Attitudes Towards National Groups

CONCEPTS	SCALES
ENGLISH CANADIANS	Friendly—Unfriendly (amicaux—hostiles)
FRENCH CANADIANS	Fair—Unfair (justes—injustes)
AMERICANS	Dull—Exciting (ternes—fascinants)
BRITISH PEOPLE[a]	Selfish—Generous (égoïstes—généreux)
FRANCAIS DE FRANCE[b]	Dishonest—Honest (malhonnêtes—honnêtes)

[a]English questionnaire only.
[b]French questionnaire only.

The main advantage of semantic differentials, in the present context, is that they help to make clear the distinction between attitudes towards groups and attitudes towards policies. A semantic differential keeps the attention of the respondent focused on the group and its characteristics, not on policy questions having to do with the group's relations with other groups. It makes no reference to the practices that prevail or ought to prevail in relations between groups—domination, subordination, segregation, discrimination, equality, independence, and so on. Opinion statements, by contrast, can hardly avoid such topics. Thus conventional measures based upon opinion statements tend to blur the distinction between (a) hostility towards outgroups and (b) militancy in pressing the demands of one's own group upon other groups for status and respect. This distinction may be crucial, because hostility may spring from ego-defensive personality needs, while militancy may be independent of such needs or may even be evidence of an unusually strong ego.

Two other advantages of the method should also be noted. First, measures based upon semantic differentials are easy to construct and quick to administer. These are important virtues when it is necessary to measure attitudes towards several different groups. Second, by using the same rating scales, it is easy to ensure that roughly the same attitudes are measured among different respondents and towards different groups.

Correlations with Personality

Table 6.3 shows the correlations between authoritarianism and favorable or unfavorable attitudes towards groups. A positive coefficient implies that those with high scores on the F scale tended to have unusually positive

Table 6.3 Correlations between Attitudes Towards Groups and Authoritarianism

Group Evaluated	English Respondents	French Respondents
CANADA	.05	.08*
ENGLISH CANADIANS	.08*	.01
FRENCH CANADIANS	−.12***	.09*
AMERICANS	.05	.08*
BRITISH PEOPLE	.04	
FRENCHMEN		−.02

  * p < .05
*** p < .001

attitudes towards the group in question. As expected, there is a negative correlation between authoritarianism and attitudes towards French Canadians among the English respondents. There are four other statistically significant correlations, and one of them— the positive correlation between authoritarianism and attitudes towards Americans among the French respondents—might be compared with the results of earlier studies of minority-group authoritarianism (above, pp. 55-56). But the most striking thing about all the correlations is their weakness; they are no stronger, on the average, than the correlations between authoritarianism and nationalism discussed in the last two chapters (cf. table 4.2). Taken as a whole, these results, like the earlier results, are contrary to expectations. By shifting from opinions about policies to images of groups, we have not revealed any stronger correlations between nationalism and personality. There are some significant correlations, to be sure, and some of these have the expected signs, but all of them are weak by comparison with the correlations typically found in previous studies of nationalism and personality.[3] Rather than confirming a plausible explanation for the earlier anomalous results, the data just summarized add to the anomalies demanding explanation.

One possible explanation may be dismissed immediately. Several of the groups in question—particularly "English Canadians" and "French Canadians"—were ingroups for some of the respondents and outgroups for others, but this ambiguity does not explain the anomalous results. The data from the French study provide a good illustration of this point. Table 6.4 presents the relevant correlations for the French respondents, controlling for subjective national identity.[4] The figures in the first column of the table are the correlations between authoritarianism and the semantic differential evaluations among the respondents who called themselves "Canadiens"; in the second column, the comparable figures for the "Canadiens français"; and in the last column, the "Québécois." Now the correlations between attitudes and personality are almost exactly the same within categories of

Table 6.4 Correlations between Attitudes Towards Groups and Authoritarianism, Controlling for Subjective National Identity

Group Evaluated	Whole Sample (N = 700)	National Identity		
		Canadian (N = 195)	French Canadian (N = 320)	Québécois (N = 165)
CANADA	.08*	.13	−.01	.11
ENGLISH CANADIANS	.01	−.02	.01	−.03
FRENCH CANADIANS	.09*	.06	.09	.21*
AMERICANS	.08*	.06	.00	.20*
FRENCHMEN	−.02	−.04	−.06	.09

NOTE: "Subjective National Identity" refers to the respondents' answers to three questions used in the separatism scale (below, pp. 201–202). Scores of 1 and 2 are grouped as "Canadian"; a score of 3 as "French Canadian"; and scores of 4 and 5 as "Québécois."
* p < .05

national identity are as they are in the sample as a whole. It makes no difference, in other words, whether the respondents are judging, say, "English Canadians" as an ingroup (the *Canadian* respondents) or as an outgroup (the *Québécois* respondents); the correlations are still essentially zero.

One or more of the "methodological" explanations discussed in Chapter 5 might be adapted to these findings, but some new data from four independent studies of attitudes towards French Canadians and French Americans suggest a better approach. These studies, which are summarized in the next section, suggest that we distinguish between the "ethnocentrism" measured by the Berkeley group's E scale and the "ethnocentrism" measured by scales of attitudes towards French Canadians.

Ethnocentrism or Ethnocentrisms?

Among our English respondents there is a correlation of − .12 between authoritarianism and attitudes towards French Canadians (table 6.3). Authoritarianism is associated with a negative view of French Canadians, as expected, but the association is very slight, which was not expected. This weak correlation does not seem to be a fluke of sampling: our sample is reasonably heterogeneous; the number of observations summarized by the coefficient is large (n = 1029); and other studies have reported similar results.

The other studies whose results are directly comparable were done by Robert Gardner and Wallace Lambert around 1960.[5] Gardner and Lambert were more interested in the influence of attitudes and motivation on success in learning French as a second language than in the influence of personality on attitudes towards outgroups, but in order to test their hypotheses they had to measure attitudes towards the groups whose language was being learned (French Canadians or French Americans), general ethnocentrism, and authoritarianism, and fortunately they published complete correlation matrices for all the variables in their studies. It is easy to compare their results with ours because they used very similar measures of attitudes and personality and because their subjects were also high school students.

The first of the relevant studies was done in Montreal in the late 1950s. The subjects were English-speaking high school students who were studying French. During 1960–61 similar studies were done with high school students in three places in the United States—in Lafayette Parish, Louisiana, near Lewiston, Maine, and in Hartford, Connecticut. In all of these studies data on attitudes and personality were gathered by means of self-administered questionnaires. Attitudes towards French Canadians or French Americans were measured by means of semantic differentials. In the Montreal study the measure consisted of three rating scales, while in the American studies it consisted of twenty-three scales. The questionnaires also included conventional measures of ethnocentrism (in the Montreal study, an adaptation of the Ethnocentrism Scale for Children developed by Else Frenkel-Brunswik, and in the American studies, seven slightly reworded items from the standard E scale) and authoritarianism (twenty-seven items from the original F scale in the Montreal study and thirteen items in the American studies).

Table 6.5 puts the correlation of −.12 that summarizes the relation between authoritarianism and attitudes towards French Canadians among our English students beside the four comparable figures from the studies just described. Our weak negative correlation seems to be of roughly the same magnitude as the others. The studies by Gardner and Lambert produced one significant positive correlation between authoritarianism and

Table 6.5 Comparison of Correlations between Authoritarianism and Attitudes Towards French Canadians or French Americans

Source of Data	Corre-lation	N =	95% Confidence Interval
Quebec-Ontario-Manitoba	−.12	1029	−.18 to −.06
Montreal	.22	83	+.01 to +.42
Louisiana	−.17	96	−.36 to +.03
Maine	−.01	145	−.17 to +.15
Connecticut	−.04	142	−.20 to +.13

SOURCE: The correlations for the Montreal, Louisiana, Maine, and Connecticut samples are taken from Gardner and Lambert, *Attitudes and Motivation*, pp. 206, 167, 170, and 173 respectively.

favorable attitudes towards French Canadians ("identification with the aggressor"?) and three very weak negative correlations. The last column of figures in the table are the lower and upper bounds, respectively, of the 95 percent confidence intervals determined by the sample data. Although there is no single value that is enclosed by the intervals from all of the studies, one might guess that the common underlying correlation—assuming that it is sensible to speak of such a correlation—would be a value on the negative side of zero, but not very far away from it.[6]

Gardner and Lambert also measured attitudes towards French Canadians (or French Americans) by means of conventional opinion statements. The questionnaire used in the Montreal study included an attitude scale consisting of twenty positively-worded statements; the American questionnaires contained a similar sixteen-item scale. These more traditional attitude scales correlated relatively strongly, though imperfectly, with the attitude measures based upon semantic differentials. For the Montreal, Louisiana, Maine, and Connecticut samples the correlations were .54, .73, .52, and .33 respectively (all significant at the .001 level).[7] Such values do little to strengthen the claim to validity of the semantic differential measures, but neither do they provide any grounds for doubting their validity. They are roughly the values one would expect between different and not very accurate measures of closely related dimensions, and they leave open the possibility that the more conventional measures may have a much stronger relation to authoritarianism than do the semantic differential measures.

Table 6.6 shows two new sets of correlations with authoritarianism (as measured by the F scales used by Gardner and Lambert) that bear on the hypothesis being investigated. The figures in the first column are the correlations between authoritarianism and attitudes towards French Canadians or French Americans when these attitudes are measured by conventional opinion statements. These correlations are remarkably similar to the

Table 6.6 Correlations of Authoritarianism with Attitudes Towards French Canadians or French Americans and with Ethnocentrism

Source of Data	Correlations		N =
	Attitudes	Ethnocentrism	
Montreal	.24*	.30**	83
Louisiana	−.13	.33**	96
Maine	−.07	.39***	145
Connecticut	−.04	.33***	142

SOURCE: Gardner and Lambert, *Attitudes and Motivation*, pp. 167–74 and 204–6.
  * p < .05
 ** p < .01
*** p < .001

correlations shown in table 6.5. In short, whatever the differences between opinion statements and semantic differentials as methods of attitude measurement, they seem to have no effect on the strength of the correlations with personality. The figures in the second column summarize the relations between authoritarianism and ethnocentrism as measured by the E scale. These correlations are not very strong, but they are all stronger than the comparable figures in the first column. All are positive and all are statistically significant. They can be regarded as further evidence of the well-known relationship between F-scale scores and prejudice. But a comparison of the two columns raises the question, how can authoritarianism have a different relation to ethnocentrism than it has to anti-French attitudes?

Table 6.7 provides the answer: there is practically no relation between ethnocentrism, as measured by the E scales used by Gardner and Lambert, and anti-French attitudes, no matter whether these attitudes are elicited by means of semantic differentials or by means of conventional opinion statements. In the first column we find the correlations between the E scales and the semantic differential measures; in the second, between the E scales and the more conventional measures. Only one of the eight correlations is statistically significant. In short, hostility towards French Canadians or French Americans does not seem to be part of the syndrome of ethnocentric attitudes measured by the E scale.

Table 6.7 Correlations between Ethnocentrism and Attitudes Towards French Canadians or French Americans

Source of Data	Attitude Measures		N =
	Semantic Differentials	Opinion Statements	
Montreal	− .03	− .14	83
Louisiana	− .29**	− .18	96
Maine	− .12	− .02	145
Connecticut	.04	− .06	142

SOURCE: Gardner and Lambert, *Attitudes and Motivation*, pp. 167–74 and 204–6.
** $p < .01$

But how can this be? Ethnocentrism means the tendency to criticize and reject outgroups—all other groups, no matter what characteristics may distinguish them from the ingroup (see above, pp. 22–26). How can ethnocentrism as measured by the E scale be unrelated to the tendency to reject French Canadians or French Americans? The puzzling fact that ethnocentrism and anti-French attitudes are unrelated may be our best clue to why there are only very weak correlations, generally speaking, between nationalism and authoritarianism among Canadians.

Recapitulation

Ethnocentrism is a complex concept, and the attitude scales described in Chapter 4 may have failed to measure the dimension of ethnocentrism that is invariably related to authoritarianism. Such was the hypothesis with which we began this chapter. If repression and the displacement of aggression are the underlying processes that link nationalism and personality, then the nationalist attitudes that correlate with authoritarianism may be, not identification with one's nation and determination to defend its legitimate interests, but only chauvinism and the rejection of other nations as outgroups.

To test this reasoning, we needed to measure our respondents' evaluations of important ingroups and outgroups. We had to distinguish those who tended to hold stereotyped negative images and hostile attitudes regarding outgroups, and stereotyped positive images and submissive attitudes regarding ingroups, from those who manifested the opposite tendencies. This chapter presented six scales of such attitudes towards groups all based on "semantic differentials." The new scales seem to be good operational definitions of the relevant concepts.

In fact, however, the correlations reported in this chapter are quite similar to the correlations reported in Chapter 4. Broadly speaking, these new scales do not correlate in the expected ways with the F scale, just as the earlier scales of nationalist attitudes did not. Among the English respondents, negative attitudes towards French Canadians seem to be associated with authoritarianism to a statistically significant degree, but the association is unexpectedly weak. None of the correlations reported here is as strong as the correlation between F-scale scores and scores on the National Power scale among the English respondents discussed in Chapter 4. We must conclude, therefore, that the distinction between attitudes towards policies and attitudes towards groups contributes nothing to clarifying the relation, whatever it is, between nationalism and personality in Canada.

7

The Functional Hypothesis

The Berkeley group hypothesized that ethnocentric ideology is a consequence of authoritarianism in personality. Most readers of *The Authoritarian Personality*, following its example, have equated ethnocentrism with the moralistic rejection of particular outgroups and have assumed that the Berkeley group's theory is tested by correlating such rejection with relevant personality variables. A positive correlation between, say, antiblack attitudes and authoritarianism as measured by the F scale has been regarded as support for the Berkeley group's conjectures. But their theory lends itself to a quite different interpretation requiring more complex statistical procedures. Hostile attitudes towards particular groups are not, according to the alternative interpretation, a sure sign of ethnocentrism, for humanitarians too can harbor such attitudes. Only a particular style of ingroup glorification and outgroup rejections, or a particular syndrome of intergroup attitudes, approximating what Daniel Levinson called "a pervasive and rigid ingroup-outgroup distinction" (AP, 150), should count as ethnocentrism, and our task should be to determine whether this particular style or syndrome is generally associated with authoritarianism. This may be called "the functional hypothesis" because of its close relation to certain ideas popularized by "the functional approach" to the study of attitudes.

The Functional Approach

During the fifties, as the threat of a fascist takeover in the United States slowly receded and as the Cold War became part of everyday life, American social scientists turned their attention to new problems. Instead of trying to measure susceptibility to fascism, they tried to find ways to make people more democratic. The problem that had preoccupied the Berkeley group—how to evaluate the latent support for fascism in the general population—

114

gradually lost its practical relevance. The urgent need was for effective techniques to make people accept the reforms demanded by genuine respect for other people's opinions.

The most efficient way to change an attitude clearly depends upon the psychological basis of that attitude. A hostile attitude towards an outgroup, for example, may be held by one person because he has mistaken beliefs about the characteristics of the group, by a second because he wishes to identify with prejudiced leaders, and by a third because he needs a scapegoat upon whom to heap his surplus aggression. The first person should change his opinions in light of the new facts brought to his attention by an information campaign designed to destroy mistaken stereotypes, but the other two might not change at all, because mistaken beliefs are not really the basis for their negative attitudes. The second person might change as a result of being told that those in authority—powerful politicians, respected writers, famous scholars, creative theologians, great actors—all endorse the cause of democracy. The third person's attitude might be more rigid, yielding only to prolonged analysis, under the guidance of a psychotherapist, designed to reveal its ego-defensive function. Clearly, then, any attempt to manipulate opinions requires some knowledge of the different functions that the same opinion can serve for different individuals. Some social scientists concluded that the best way that science could serve democracy would be by developing better techniques for manipulating opinions.

The second important reason for the development of the functional approach during the fifties was the need for a constructive response to the charges, already noted, that the work of the Berkeley group was "too psychological" and "biased." Critics had argued that *The Authoritarian Personality* neglected the social, political, and economic factors that are crucial for understanding antidemocratic behavior. Conceding that psychodynamic conflicts and unconscious motives can sometimes explain the sentiments of fear and hostility in people's minds, they had denied that such factors could explain actual patterns of intergroup relations, since social structures and "social facts" are largely independent of individual psychology. Only rarely, according to these critics, do men act out, in the public sphere, their own private fantasies and neurotic conflicts. In particular, conflicts between nations are usually realistic rather than imaginary; they are not just the result of "psychological tensions."[1] The problem for constructive critics of *The Authoritarian Personality* was to moderate its excessively "psychological" orientation, which could be used tendentiously, without abandoning its important insights. They had to develop a more balanced account of the motivation for opinions and behavior, one that recognized rational motives and conformity to social norms as well as unconscious processes of ego defense.

The first full statement of such a constructive response was *Opinions and Personality* (1956) by Brewster Smith, Jerome Bruner, and Robert White, three eminent psychologists from Harvard. This "Harvard group" argued that any given attitude can serve different psychological functions for different individuals and that three basic functions of any attitude should be distinguished: object appraisal, social adjustment, and externalization— very roughly, sound common sense, conformity, and pathological ego defense.

To illustrate the usefulness of these distinctions, the Harvard group conducted a very detailed study of American opinions about Russia. They spent some thirty to forty hours with each of their subjects—ten fairly average Bostonians—accumulating data by means of questionnaires, some of the main objective tests of aptitudes and personality, and a variety of projective tests of personality (the TAT, etc.). After analyzing these data they reached two broad conclusions: first, that it is hard to generalize about the psychological determinants of opinions ("The impression left by a series of intensive case studies is one of almost boundless individual variation")[2] and second, that differences in attitudes towards Russia and Russians could not be directly linked to any differences in personality ("There is no rigid or one-to-one relationship between the opinions a person develops and the underlying needs or dynamics of his personality").[3]

It was particularly significant, as the Harvard group noted, that the limited role of externalization (pathological ego defense) was made clear in a study of attitudes towards Russia. "Remote and affect-laden as Russia was to most Americans, the topic doubtless afforded more opportunities for externalization than others that might have been selected."[4] Nonetheless both realistic object appraisal and social adjustment processes were very important in determining their subjects' predominantly negative attitudes.

> In this respect our topic contrasts sharply with that of antisemit-ism, the focus of the California studies of "the authoritarian personality." In the nature of the case, the more extreme forms of prejudice are overwhelmingly irrational, that is to say pro-jective, externalized in content. The dynamic account given by the California authors of the correspondence they found be-tween *extreme* prejudice and a particular configuration of personality is an excellent instance of what we mean by externalization.[5]

What was true of ethnic prejudices within nations was not true, apparently, of hostile attitudes between nations.

Be that as it may, the functional approach makes it easy to recognize that not all patriotism is pathological or intellectually unsophisticated. The same attitude (e.g., a positive attitude towards Americans or a negative attitude towards Russians) may serve different functions for different individuals, and what may rightly be condemned as chauvinism and ethnocentrism in one person may be praised as loyalty in another. There are clearly different ways of being a patriot—different modes or styles of national loyalty or commitment—and not all forms of patriotism are to be condemned out of hand. The difference between an ethnocentric and a cosmopolitan form of loyalty should not be confused with the difference between loyalty and hostility. Nationalists are not the only loyal citizens, and the opponents of nationalism (those who denigrate chauvinism, xenophobia, ethnocentrism, etc.) are not necessarily disloyal or alienated from the national role.[6] The relation between patriotism in politics and authoritarianism in personality is more complex than sometimes supposed: there is not a simple linear relation, implying that the authoritarians are the patriots, the equalitarians the cowards or the traitors (cf. above, pp. 22-27). The functional approach clarifies the Berkeley group's point that one can oppose nationalism (i.e., pseudopatriotism) and still be a patriot (a *genuine* patriot). It concedes the value and limited validity of the California studies, which showed that nationalism and ethnic prejudice often have irrational, emotional roots, but it insists that these early studies were mistaken insofar as they implied that such attitudes can have no other psychological basis. Nationalism and ethnocentrism, like any political attitudes, can serve quite different needs for different people. Nationalism and national loyalty are today normal, not deviant, ways of behaving, and they should be found among those who are psychologically normal (reasonable and conforming), and not just among neurotics and psychopaths (with their propensity to adopt political opinions for ego-defensive reasons).

The Functional Hypothesis

The broad hypothesis associated with the functional approach, that the same attitude may have very different properties depending upon its psychological basis or the functions it serves for the individual, may take an interesting or a trivial form, depending upon how we specify properties and functions. The simplest "functional" theory about attitudes would consist of the familiar distinction between reason and emotion as bases for attitudes, and reasonable and emotional as the corresponding properties of attitudes. But this little theory has no virtue other than simplicity. It would surely be foolish to doubt, or to try to demonstrate, that an attitude (e.g., favoring capital punishment or abortion on demand) based on reason will be more reasonable, and backed by better reasons, than the same attitude based on emotion. Once we concede that a particular attitude can be based on reason, it is surely obvious that it will be more reasonable if it is. As regards nationalism, we could easily distinguish two types, one based on

reason, the other on emotion. But casual observation suffices to establish
that the nationalism of intelligent, informed, prudent, moderate and emotionally stable people differs from the nationalism of unenlightened cranks
and neurotics. Emotional nationalism based upon emotion differs *by definition*, we can say, from reasonable nationalism based upon reason and
reflection.

The Berkeley version of functionalism is more interesting. If we distinguish authoritarianism (or a weak ego and ego-defensive personality needs)
as one possible basis for nationalist attitudes, and equalitarianism (or a
strong ego and a healthy balance between the different components of the
psyche) as another, then we can hypothesize that *ethnocentric* describes the
distinctive characteristics, or style, of the national ideology based on authoritarianism. This hypothesis is testable because we have a means of
distinguishing authoritarians from equalitarians (the F scale) and a fairly
clear conception of the intercorrelations among different nationalist attitudes that constitute ethnocentrism (above, pp. 20-22). The hypothesis is
worth testing because it represents a plausible interpretation of the Berkeley
group's ideas about nationalism and authoritarianism.[7]

The simplest and most common interpretation, as already noted, equates
nationalism with ethnocentrism (the one is a species of the other), and
assumes that ethnocentrism is an attitudinal dimension measured by the
E scale, thus leading to the hypothesis that nationalistic attitudes, as
by-products of ego-defensive personality needs, correlate directly with
authoritarianism as measured by the F scale. In short, the higher a person's
score on the F scale, the higher he should be on any measure of nationalism
(national-mindedness, isolationism, jingoism, chauvinism, separatism,
etc.). This is the "personality hypothesis" that was tested in the previous
chapters by simply correlating measures of nationalism with a measure of
authoritarianism. The alternative interpretation leads to more complex
empirical procedures, but it may be truer to the Berkeley group's thinking,
for it avoids simply equating all nationalist attitudes with ethnocentrism.
Only a particular combination of such attitudes, equivalent to a particular
way of playing the national role or a particular "mode of commitment,"
would be equated with ethnocentrism and related to ego-defensive personality needs. The influence of personality variables will be observed, according to this interpretation, not in the *covariation* between authoritarianism
and nationalist attitudes, but in the *interaction* between authoritarianism
and different nationalist attitudes. Authoritarianism is to be regarded, not
as a determinant of the individual's total "consumption" of nationalist
attitudes, but rather of his way of combining different such attitudes—his
style of thinking about nations and nationalism. The hypothesis to be tested
holds that the nationalist attitudes of authoritarians are combined in a
pseudopatriotic and ethnocentric way, while those of equalitarians are
combined in more diverse ways.[8]

Statistical Results

To test the interaction between personality and the structure of attitudes, both the English and the French respondents were classified according to their scores on the F scale. Table 7.1 shows the scores that define the three categories to be used—authoritarians, a middle group, and equalitarians— and the proportions of each sample in each of these categories. In what follows we shall be concerned only with the differences between the extreme groups, which are approximately the top and bottom quartiles of the distributions. All the measures of nationalist attitudes were intercorrelated for both "low" and "high" authoritarians. The result is four sets of correlations, two sets for the English respondents and two for the French respondents (see Appendix C). Are there different patterns of correlations among the "high" and the "low" groups due to the greater tendency of the "highs" to employ an ethnocentric way of thinking about groups and intergroup relations?

Table 7.1   Grouping of Respondents by F-Scale Scores

Groups	Range of Scores	No. of Cases	Percentage Distribution
English Respondents			
Low F	2–10	291	28%
Medium F	11–16	524	50
High F	17–26	228	22
Totals		1043	100%
French Respondents			
Low F	1–11	142	20%
Medium F	12–18	416	58
High F	19–29	158	22
Totals		716	100%

Table 7.2 gives four comparisons from the English data that illustrate the kind of differences we are looking for. The correlation between the first pair of variables, evaluation of Americans and evaluation of British people, is stronger among the authoritarians than among the equalitarians, in line with the hypothesis that authoritarians tend to develop general attitudes towards outgroups, rather than specific attitudes towards specific groups. The second pair of variables, evaluation of English Canadians and evaluation of French Canadians, are positively correlated among the equalitarians, but negatively correlated among the authoritarians. Neither correlation is very strong, but the difference between them supports the hypothesis that authoritarians are more "ethnocentric." The third and fourth pairs of correlations in the table might also be used to support the claim that

Table 7.2   Selected Comparisons of Correlations between Nationalist Attitudes for Author-
              itarians and Nonauthoritarians

Variables Correlated	Low F	High F	Difference
AMERICANS and BRITISH	.20	.29	− .09
ENGLISH CANADIANS and			
FRENCH CANADIANS	.10	− .03	.13
Independence/US and			
FRENCH CANADIANS	.11	− .05	.16
Independence/UK and			
CANADA	− .27	− .03	− .24

NOTE: See Appendix C for the full matrices of correlations from which these examples have
been selected.

"ethnocentrism" is a better description of the organization of attitudes
among authoritarians than among equalitarians. Even though these correlations are weaker among the authoritarians than among the equalitarians,
they are perhaps closer to what we would expect if consistent rejection of
outgroups were combined with glorification of ingroups.

The figures in table 7.2 have been selected to illustrate the hypothesis we
wish to test. They are only 4 of the 55 correlations from the English data.
There is no easy way to summarize all the relevant data for testing our
hypothesis—the two sets of 55 correlations. The best methods would
probably be complex multivariate techniques such as factor analysis or
principal components analysis that relatively few social scientists understand clearly. Before applying any such statistical treatment to the data,
therefore, we must first satisfy ourselves that there are differences between
the two sets of correlations worth summarizing and interpreting.

The most striking thing about table 7.2 is the smallness of the differences
between the figures in the first column, for the equalitarians, and those in
the second column, for the authoritarians. The first three of the four
comparisons seem to involve correlations of almost the same magnitude.
Even the fourth comparison does not reveal a very large difference. Before
we can use any of these differences to support a complex theory about
nationalism and personality, we must first show that they are not simply the
result of sampling variability.

It may seem that we should begin by testing each of the 55 differences
separately for significance, eliminating the insignificant differences and
considering only the statistically significant ones as evidence for (or against)
our hypothesis. In fact, however, we must look at all 55 correlations as a
group, and not at each one separately. We must determine whether the 55
correlations describing the attitudes of the authoritarians differ from the 55
correlations describing those of the equalitarians by more than can be
attributed to sampling variability. Only if we can reject the null hypothesis,

that the two groups, authoritarians and equalitarians, are random samples from the same population, can we legitimately try to interpret particular "significant" differences according to our hypothesis about nationalism and personality.

To fix ideas, imagine that we wanted to test the hypothesis that there were two different types of nationalism, one characteristic of people born on even-numbered days (or under particular signs of the Zodiac), the other characteristic of people born on odd-numbered days (or under different signs), and that we could not directly measure the presence or absence of this type of nationalism, but only infer its presence or absence from the intercorrelations among diverse nationalist attitudes. We could test this "astropolitical" hypothesis by dividing a sample into "even" and "odd" subsamples and then intercorrelating all the measures of nationalist attitudes for these two groups. Comparing these two sets of correlations, skeptics would not expect to find many statistically significant differences, but they should be prepared to find a few that seem "significant" when examined out of context. Even if the comparison were between two groups known to be random samples from a common population, a few large differences would be expected, since the random assignment of individuals to groups should produce a few large differences, as well as many small differences, between the two groups. Imagine now that a study has been carried out and that a few "statistically significant" differences between "odds" and "evens" have been found. Should these few relatively large differences be counted as evidence that nationalism has different characteristics among "even" and "odd" people? Only if there are a *surprising number* of such large differences, or in other words, if there are more of them than can easily be explained by chance processes. If there were relatively few large differences—only as many as would be expected if the two groups were random samples from the same population—then chance, or sampling variability, would be the appropriate explanation for *all* the differences, even the apparently "significant" ones.

Plainly we must be concerned here with the entire distribution of observed differences, and not just with the relatively large differences considered individually. We must compare (a) the observed distribution of differences with (b) the distribution of differences we would expect from random sampling.

Given the size of the English samples (about 220 authoritarians and 285 equalitarians), the null hypothesis of random sampling from the same population yields a theoretical distribution of the differences that is approximately normal with mean zero and standard deviation of .09.[9] Now the observed distribution of differences is a very close approximation to this theoretical distribution; the mean of the 55 differences is .001 and their standard deviation is .094. As these figures suggest, the null hypothesis of random sampling provides an adequate description of these data.[10] The only reasonable conclusion to draw in light of the data, and in the absence of any compelling reasons for focusing our attention on only a few of the correlations to the exclusion of all the rest, is that the two samples are drawn from the same population—as regards the organization of nationalist attitudes. The results are precisely what we would expect under the null hypothesis: a large number of small differences and a few relatively large differences.

A similar analysis of the data from our French respondents points to the same conclusion. Again we have two sets of correlations, one for the authoritarians, the other for the equalitarians, and we are mainly interested in the overall similarities or differences between these two sets of correlations. Thus we must first calculate all 45 differences (45 rather than 55 differences since the French data consist of scores on only 10 attitudinal variables) and then compare the distribution of these differences with the distribution we would expect if the two groups, those "high" and "low" on the F scale, had been drawn at random from the same population. Since the French samples of authoritarians and equalitarians are smaller than the English samples (see table 7.1), the distribution of differences expected under the null hypothesis has a slightly larger standard deviation, namely, .119. The mean of the 45 observed differences is − .014, only very slightly below the theoretically expected mean of zero. The standard deviation of the observed differences is .129, almost the same as the theoretical value of .119. The conclusion to draw is the same as for the English data: there are no grounds for rejecting the null hypothesis that, as regards the organization of nationalist attitudes, authoritarians and equalitarians are random samples from the same population.

Conclusion

Evidently "ethnocentrism" does not provide any better description of the pattern of nationalist attitudes among authoritarians than among equalitarians. Whatever the best simplification of diverse nationalist attitudes should be, it should be the same, it seems, for both authoritarians and equalitarians. No one would dispute, of course, that the nationalist attitudes based upon emotion, or adopted for ego-defensive reasons, must differ in many ways from the nationalist attitudes based upon reason, just as the nationalism of optimistic people will tend to be optimistic, of democrats to be democratic, of bigots to be bigoted, of monks to be monkish, and so on. But the nationalism associated with authoritarianism does not seem to be any more ethnocentric than the nationalism found in the absence of authoritarianism. There seems to be no interaction between authoritarianism and the organization of nationalist attitudes.

8

The Descriptive Hypothesis

The personality hypothesis—that nationalism and ethnocentrism covary with authoritarianism—has always been controversial. Since 1950 it has been investigated in a great many empirical studies. In its strong form, asserting that individual differences in prejudice are mainly due to differences in personality, the hypothesis is now generally rejected. In its weaker forms, asserting that authoritarianism is one source of ethnocentrism, or that the analysis of the authoritarian personality reveals the psychological cause or characteristic motive for racism and ethnic prejudice, the hypothesis is now generally accepted. Whatever the real merits of the hypothesis, one must recognize that the current consensus is based on expert evaluation of the results of many careful factual studies.

The functional hypothesis has received far less attention and has never, so far as I am aware, been subjected to such a direct test as the one reported in the last chapter. The hypothesis, which has been more influential than visible, has a strong affinity with the functional approach to the study of attitudes and has been carried along on its coattails.

By the descriptive hypothesis I mean the idea that differences in attitudes towards ethnic and national groups are reducible to variation along a single dimension of greater or less ethnocentrism. This novel hypothesis has been accepted with scarcely a cavil. All the evidence seems to support it, and little attention has been given the evidence that might possibly refute it. Scholars today generally take for granted that this particular way of ignoring detail and simplifying an admittedly more complex reality is the right way, the way that defines the interesting questions.

The descriptive hypothesis, and not the personality hypothesis, represents the boldest innovation and the real distinctiveness of the psychological literature on nationalism and ethnic prejudice. The hypothesis sets the problem—to explain ethnocentrism. It draws attention away from the characteristics of groups as relevant explanatory factors. It leads us to formulate, and almost requires that we entertain, hypotheses about *the* connection between personality and prejudice. In short, the descriptive hypothesis is the foundation for the whole "psychological" approach to nationalism, ethnocentrism, and intergroup conflict. Clearly the hypothesis deserves criticism, if only to show more clearly the grounds for its validity.

The Descriptive Hypothesis

Quantitative studies of ethnic attitudes before 1950 made a single basic discovery, namely, that hostile attitudes towards any particular ethnic outgroup tend to be associated with similar attitudes towards other outgroups and with vociferous national loyalty. The research of the Berkeley group provided additional evidence of this pattern of ethnic attitudes, which they called ethnocentrism. Their E scale clarifies the meaning of their concept: it consists of unfavorable statements about Jews, blacks, Mexicans, Filipinos, zootsuiters, and Oklahomans. It was designed to measure the tendency to reject outgroups in general and to submit to ingroups. Subsequent studies supported the hypothesis that ethnic prejudice is general, rather than specific, and that it is associated with intense national involvement.[1]

An article in the *Handbook of Social Psychology* summarizes the basic claims associated with the descriptive hypothesis:

> It seems to us essential for the understanding of intergroup attitudes to keep firmly in mind the existence and importance of a general factor (tolerance versus ethnocentrism) and group factors (degree of favorability or unfavorability toward Negroes, Jews, Turks, etc.) *and* a variety of specific factors (for example, beliefs about Jewish power and influence, acceptance of Negroes in close personal relationships, and so on). At times we need to focus on the fine details, and at other times we need to stand back to see the big picture.[2]

In other words, whatever the groups in question, the correlations between different prejudices, favourable or unfavorable, will be strong enough to justify talking about a "general factor," and this general factor will be "tolerance versus ethnocentrism." For some purposes we shall have to focus on the fine details (that is to say, the specific attitudes towards particular groups), but when trying to "understand intergroup attitudes," it will be important not to forget that there is also a big picture, the overarching contrast between those who are tolerant and those who are ethnocentric. If we "stand back," this is the big picture we shall see.

The main argument of *The Authoritarian Personality* was, of course, that the basic contrast between tolerance (or humanitarianism) and ethnocentrism was also a contrast between types of personality (equalitarian and authoritarian) and that only by studying authoritarianism could we gain any real understanding of the psychology of intergroup relations.

Chapter 4 presented some relevant data in the section on the validity of the nationalism scales. The weak correlations between the NP, NU, and IN scales cast doubt on the basic assumption that there is an important general factor in nationalist attitudes among Canadians. In fact, there are only very weak correlations between some of the main measures of nationalism among both the English and the French respondents. (The relevant statistics are in Appendix C.) These weak correlations suggest that differences in nationalism should not be treated as part of a single dimension of variation, no matter whether this be called nationalism or ethnocentrism. The correlations between the nationalism scales and the evaluative measures based upon semantic differentials, and the intercorrelations among the latter, must also be considered, however, before drawing any conclusions about the organization of nationalistic attitudes among our respondents.

Table 8.1 presents the intercorrelations among the semantic differentials for both the English and the French respondents, the former above the diagonal, the latter below. Some of these correlations are quite strong; others are virtually zero. The most interesting feature of table 8.1, however, is that all the correlations are positive. Our respondents seem to judge all groups, ingroups and outgroups alike, in a consistent way, either favorably or unfavorably. The Berkeley group's concept, however, requires some significant *negative* correlations, for "ethnocentrism" implies that positive attitudes towards ingroups are generally associated with negative attitudes towards outgroups. Only such negative correlations would justify contrasting the ethnocentric person, who disparages all outgroups while glorifying his ingroup, with the nonethnocentric (or humanitarian) person who judges each group separately and does not draw sharp distinctions between ingroups and outgroups. Table 8.1 suggests that we should contrast, not ethnocentrists and humanitarians, but philanthropes and misanthropes, or boosters and knockers, those who have a favorable opinion of all groups as against those who are generally negative and disparaging.

Table 8.1 Correlation Matrix for Measures of Attitudes Towards Groups (English Above the Diagonal, French Below)

Variable	1	2	3	4	5
1. CANADA	—	.49	.23	.14	.33
2. ENGLISH CANADIANS	.37	—	.08	.26	.41
3. FRENCH CANADIANS	.44	.12	—	.09	.09
4. AMERICANS	.31	.37	.19	—	.22
5. BRITISH PEOPLE					—
6. FRENCHMEN	.06	.07	.28	.06	

To evaluate all the evidence bearing on the descriptive hypothesis, we need better summaries of the relevant data than tables such as these provide. Principal components analysis provides what we need. It yields a simple quantitative measure of the importance of the general factor in a set of variables, and thus the amount of detail that must be ignored in constructing a composite measure from a series of more specific measures, and it also yields a clear indication of the nature of this general factor or, in other words, the overall pattern of the intercorrelations among the basic variables. In the case at hand, it will help us to see whether the general factor should be considered tolerance versus ethnocentrism or some other broad dimension, such as philanthropy versus misanthropy or liberalism versus conservatism.

Principal Components Analysis

Principal components is a method for analyzing the intercorrelations among a set of variables and for representing all of the variables by a smaller number of underlying components. These components are simply linear functions, or weighted averages, of the original variables. The weights are chosen so as to produce components, themselves uncorrelated, that are correlated as strongly as possible with the original variables. The stronger the intercorrelations among these variables, the more faithfully they can be represented by the best average of them all, the *first* principal component. The weaker the intercorrelations among the original variables, the weaker will be the relation between any one component and all of the variables, on the average. We shall be mainly interested in the amount of variation accounted for by the first principal component in each set of data. This statistic is the best measure of the overall strength of the intercorrelations among the variables.[3]

Table 8.2 shows the basic results of the two analyses, one of the eleven measures of nationalist attitudes among the English respondents, the other of the ten such measures for the French respondents. It is of course no real criticism of the descriptive hypothesis simply to point out that the correlations between different ethnic attitudes are less than perfect, and that the first principal components therefore explain less than 100 percent of the variation in each set of variables. But it is pertinent to note how much detail would be ignored were we to construct a composite measure, analogous to the E scale, from our series of more specific measures. The figures in table 8.2 suggest that a great deal of information would have to be ignored. The first components account for only about 23 and 33 percent of the reliable variation in the English and the French variables respectively. In other words, roughly two-thirds to three-quarters of the "true" variation in the variables could not be associated with these "best averages" of the vari-

Table 8.2 Eigenvalues and Variance Explained by Principal Components of English and French Variables

	English		French	
Component	λ	% Var.	λ	% Var.
1	2.57	23	3.30	33
2	2.04	19	2.07	21
3	1.63	15	1.07	11
4	1.11	10	.96	10
5	.99	9	.80	8
6	.85	8	.68	7
7	.61	6	.53	5
8	.46	4	.30	3
9	.31	3	.18	2
10	.27	2	.11	1
11	.15	1		

ables. There seems to be more than one underlying dimension of variation in each set of scores.[4]

Principal components analysis can throw a clear light on the *pattern*, as well as on the overall *level*, of the intercorrelations among a set of variables. In this particular case, it can help us to decide whether the general factor is "tolerance versus ethnocentrism" or some other broad dimension such as philanthropy versus misanthropy. The relevant statistics are the correlations between the original variables and the first principal components. These correlations (or "loadings") describe the components in terms of the original variables; they allow us to infer what a composite of all the scales would measure, if that composite were constructed, as the first principal component is, to maximize the overall correlations between itself and the original scales. For the English data, the loadings on the first principal component are as follows:

National Unity	.00
Anti-French Attitudes	.03
National Power	.05
Independence/U.S.	−.27
Independence/U.K.	−.44
Internationalism	−.12
CANADA	.77
ENGLISH CANADIANS	.83
FRENCH CANADIANS	.26
AMERICANS	.57
BRITISH PEOPLE	.78

This first component seems to represent a contrast between (a) those who accept British and American influences in Canada and who tend to rate the various groups, and Canada as a whole, more favorably, and (b) those who demand independence of Britain and the United States and who tend to denigrate all the groups, particularly English Canadians and British people. Perhaps we should think of it as a dimension of acceptance versus rejection of Canada, its people, its allies, and its historical ties with Great Britain and the United States. More broadly, we could say that this component contrasts negativism and alienation, on the one hand, with conventional enthusiasm and positive thinking, on the other hand. Four of the most important nationalist attitudes—measured by the National Unity, National Power, Anti-French, and Internationalism scales—have virtually no correlation at all with this component. Evidently it does not represent ethnocentrism (or nationalism) as this syndrome is usually understood. For the French study, the comparable figures are as follows:

Separatist Nationalism	.72
Separatism	.81
Independence/U.S.	.57
Independence/U.K.	.59
Internationalism	$-.16$
CANADA	$-.53$
ENGLISH CANADIANS	$-.78$
FRENCH CANADIANS	$-.15$
AMERICANS	$-.72$
FRENCHMEN	.02

Plainly this first component is a dimension of separatist nationalism. The Separatist Nationalism and Separatism scales correlate strongly with it, as do the two Independence variables. Internationalism is negatively related to the component, as the descriptive hypothesis requires, though rather weakly. There are strong negative correlations with the evaluations of Canada, English Canadians, and Americans. The component brings out the contrast in the data between (a) those who support Quebec's independence, who oppose British and American influence in Canada, and who rate Canada, English Canadians, and Americans relatively unfavorably, and (b) those who oppose independence, express unconcern about British and American influence, and who rate all the groups more favorably. The interpretation is straightforward except for one oddity, the weak negative loading of "French Canadians" on the component. According to this analysis, then, negative attitudes towards French Canadians must be considered evidence of French-Canadian nationalism, and not of its absence.

These two sets of results suggest that "ethnocentrism" is not always a natural simplification of ethnic attitudes. "Ethnocentrism" does not describe the contrast between "boosting" and "knocking" among the English respondents, nor does it accurately describe the separatist-federalist contrast among the French respondents. "Ethnocentrism" may of course describe the first principal component in other situations, using other scales, with other respondents. But if so, this is simply a fact, and not a necessary result of the way human beings at all times and in all places organize their thinking about ethnic and national groups. The "big picture" varies, it seems, depending where you look, and sometimes it may be pretty hazy.

Some Evidence from France

A study of French university students demonstrates that "ethnocentrism" can sometimes be a quite misleading description of the main dimension of variation in nationalist attitudes.[5] The study was based on data from a questionnaire that contained sixteen scales to measure a variety of relevant attitudes, including anticommunism, militarism, demands for national sovereignty, national pride, strength of national identity, cultural nationalism, and anti-American and anti-German nationalism. The measures were intercorrelated and four factors were extracted from the correlation matrix. We shall be concerned with only the first unrotated factor, which accounted for 69 percent of the common variance and 36 percent of the total variance in the measures. It is the only factor that is easily interpreted, and it clearly summarized differences of opinion on a single basic issue.

This first factor (table 8.3) contrasts right-wing anticommunists with left-wing anti-Americans. The three largest positive loadings are for the

Table 8.3 First Unrotated Factor from an Analysis of the Attitudes of French University Students, 1962

Variables	Loadings
Anti-Communism	.83
Imperialist Nationalism	.81
Militarism	.73
Defence of National Sovereignty	.67
Ethnic Prejudices and Racism	.61
Antidemocratic Attitude	.65
Religious Conservatism	.71
Strength of National Identity	.66
Political Pessimism	.52
European Outlook and Identity	.46
Evaluation of France	.52
Pride in French History	.49
Cultural Nationalism	.38
Anti-Americanism	− .28
Anti-Germanism	− .36
Pro-Socialism	− .82

SOURCE: Michelat and Thomas, *Dimensions du nationalisme*, p. 47. The names of the variables have been modified or expanded to indicate as clearly as possible what the scales measure.

measures of anticommunism, imperialist (or colonial) nationalism, and militarism. The measures of anti-American and anti-German sentiment and of positive attitudes towards socialism correlate negatively with the factor. The main dimension of variation in nationalist attitudes among the French students evidently corresponds to the left-right dimension in French politics. The monograph from which these results are taken establishes this point beyond reasonable doubt.

The extremes of the first factor represent two types of nationalism: neither extreme can be thought of as nationalism (or ethnocentrism) *tout court;* neither extreme represents a general rejection of foreign nations in favor of the French nation. Antagonism towards one group of foreigners tends to be combined with favorable attitudes towards another group, who are their enemies. The factor implicitly contrasts right-wing nationalists (anti-Soviet) with left-wing nationalists (anti-American). The contrast between all Frenchmen and all foreigners had apparently given way, in the thinking of these students, to the more striking contrast between the Left and the Right. It was as if France herself were two warring nations, the "left French" and the "right French," and foreigners were judged according to whether they were enemies or allies of these factional nations. Ethnocentrism, as a general dimension, did not exist.

Multidimensional Factor Analysis

"Ethnocentrism" should not be abandoned, however, before considering another possibility, that our statistical results inconsistent with the concept are merely a consequence of trying to represent multidimensional domains unidimensionally. What would happen if we tried to represent our basic variables in terms of three or four underlying dimensions? Would we find a clear dimension of ethnocentrism cutting across dimensions of separatist nationalism, anti-American nationalism, and so on?

The *Handbook* article quoted earlier suggests that ethnocentrism is a "general factor" in the sense that it is the most important factor statistically (i.e., the first principal component). This broad claim may be rejected and a slightly different interpretation of the claim, which is much more plausible, may be proposed. In any set of ethnic attitudes, we could say, there will be a general factor of ethnocentrism (a factor defined by an appropriate pattern of loadings of the original variables on the factor) and this factor will emerge after the influences due to various "group factors" and "specific factors" have been removed. The authors of the *Handbook* article may have been mistaken about the statistical importance of the ethnocentrism factor, we could say, but they were right that there is always such a factor in any set of variables having to do with ethnic attitudes. This new descriptive hypothesis is more plausible because it is really a tautology. It asserts only that "ethnocentrism" is a linear combination of different measures of ethnic and national attitudes—a claim that no person who understands the concept will dispute. Nonetheless this new formulation does suggest a procedure that may throw some light on the questions at issue.

Let us try to represent the intercorrelations among each set of variables, not by their relations to a single underlying component for each set, but rather by postulating as many such components (or "factors") as necessary to represent all the correlations adequately, and let us define these factors so that they are as simple and easy to interpret as possible. Let us shift, in other words, from principal components analysis, focussing on only the first principal components, to classical factor analysis.[6]

The English Data

The principal components analysis of the English data showed that four components had eigenvalues greater than one, hence four factors will be used to summarize the intercorrelations among the eleven variables. Table 8.4 shows the Varimax solution for these data. The first factor here is very similar to the first principal component discussed above, except for the reflection of signs. It is a general evaluative factor. It has to do with the respondents' generally positive (enthusiastic, trusting, sanguine) or negative (alienated, misanthropic, choleric) reaction to others, whether ingroups or outgroups. The second factor represents attitudes towards French Canadians: it results from and "explains" the relatively strong correlations between the AF scale and the semantic differential ratings of French Canadians (Appendix C, line 2-9). The third factor represents attitudes towards the United States and Americans. One extreme of this dimension groups those who value national power or independence, who

Table 8.4 Varimax Rotated Factor Loadings, English Data

	FACTORS				
Variables	I	II	III	IV	h^2
National Power	.22	−.12	**.44**	.10	.26
National Unity	−.03	.24	.16	−.12	.10
Anti-French Feeling	.10	**−.97**	−.04	−.03	.95
Independence/US	−.06	.16	**.93**	.04	.90
Independence/UK	−.15	−.08	−.06	**.90**	.84
Internationalism	−.05	.02	.04	.09	.01
CANADA	**.73**	.17	.08	−.13	.59
ENGLISH CANADIANS	**.83**	−.05	−.07	−.11	.70
FRENCH CANADIANS	.22	**.80**	−.08	.11	.71
AMERICANS	**.43**	−.08	**−.57**	.04	.52
BRITISH PEOPLE	**.61**	−.01	−.03	−.37	.51

support efforts to increase Canadian independence of the United States, and who tend to rate Americans unfavorably, while the other extreme brings together those who are less inclined to demand national power or independence, less concerned about American influence, and more favorably disposed towards Americans. The fourth factor represents a similar dimension of nationalist feeling, but directed against the United Kingdom and "British people." The communalities (the last column of figures) show that three variables are poorly "explained" by the four factors postulated in this analysis. Internationalism and National Unity evidently have virtually no relation whatever to the other variables in the analysis, or to each other, and so they must be considered completely independent "dimensions" of nationalist attitudes. The remaining variable with a low communality is the one that, on the face of it, seems to be the single best measure of nationalist sentiment, the National Power scale. Roughly three-quarters of the reliable variation in this variable is specific variation and cannot be associated with variation along the four dimensions that account for the intercorrelations among the variables in the analysis.

It is perhaps surprising that the National Unity scales does not load more strongly on the second factor, which has been interpreted as a factor of positive or negative feeling towards French Canadians. The explanation is to be found, in one sense, in the weak correlations between this variable and other variables (Appendix C, p. 214), and in a more interesting sense, in the ambiguity of scores on the National Unity scale. A high score on this scale indicates that the respondent in question was concerned about national unity and opposed to the separation of Quebec. But such concern and opposition could go along with either favorable or unfavorable attitudes towards French Canadians as a group. It could be based on a positive evaluation of them as a group and a desire to keep them as compatriots, or it could be based on contempt for them and determination to frustrate their movement for national liberation. The questions composing the National Unity scale do not really tap the policy conflict associated with positive or negative attitudes towards French Canadians. That conflict has to do with the acceptance of French Canadians as one of two "founding races" in Canada and of the various public policies that would express the equality of French and English in Canadian life ("bilingualism and biculturalism"). The scale of Anti-French Attitudes is made up of questions that touch on these matters, and consequently it helps to define the dimension of anti-French nationalism or prejudice against French Canadians.

In short, there seem to be at least three independent dimensions of nationalist attitudes, each associated with a different nationalist issue—the issue of the status of English and French in Canada, the issue of economic and cultural independence from the United States, and the issue of cultural and symbolic independence from Great Britain. It is easy to think of factors II, III, and IV as dimensions of nationalist attitudes, but it is difficult to think of any *one* of them as "ethnocentrism." Each of them represents nationalist feeling focused on a single outgroup, not a general nationalist or ethnocentric sentiment applying to all outgroups equally.

The French Data

Three factors were extracted because the principal components analysis showed that there were three components in these data with eigenvalues greater than one. Table 8.5 shows the Varimax rotation of these three factors.

Table 8.5   Varimax Rotated Factor Loadings, French Data

	FACTORS			
Variables	I	II	III	h^2
Separatist Nationalism	.05	.80	.12	.66
Separatism	−.03	.90	.19	.85
Independence/US	−.04	.23	.83	.74
Independence/UK	.01	.54	.13	.31
Internationalism	−.04	−.14	−.03	.02
CANADA	.81	−.24	.00	.71
ENGLISH CANADIANS	.44	−.56	−.16	.54
FRENCH CANADIANS	.79	.26	−.10	.69
AMERICANS	.50	−.30	−.55	.64
FRENCHMEN	.30	.20	−.05	.13

The first rotated factor, like the first factor from the English data, seems to define a dimension that has little to do with nationalism or ethnocentrism. The variables that have substantial loadings on this factor are the evaluative variables based upon semantic differentials. The factor distinguishes those who tend to rate Canada and all the ethnic and national groups positively from those who tend to rate them all negatively. It represents the variation in attitudes towards groups that is uncorrelated with variation in attitudes towards nationalist policies and that is also unrelated to any "ethnocentric" tendency to differentiate between ingroups and outgroups. The positive or negative attitudes summarized by this factor seem to be quite general. It is tempting, therefore, to describe the factor in terms of personality traits or character types, but the relevant difference seems to be that between a positive, trusting attitude towards others (faith in people, etc.) and a misanthropic and distrustful attitude.

The second factor is a purified version of the first principal component discussed earlier. It clearly represents the separatist-federalist cleavage as commonly understood. It defines a contrast between (a) those who support Quebec independence, think of themselves as Québécois, oppose American influence, demand Canadian independence vis-à-vis Great Britain, evaluate Canada, English Canadians, and Americans relatively unfavorably, and French Canadians and Frenchmen from France relatively favorably, and (b) those who oppose separation, think of themselves as Canadians, are relatively unconcerned about American influence, accept British symbolism and British influences in Canadian life, rate Canada, English Canadians, and Americans relatively favorably, and French Canadians and Frenchmen relatively unfavorably. The first set of attitudes constitutes what is generally called "French-Canadian nationalism" or "Québécois nationalism," while the second set represents a kind of "Canadian nationalism" or "federalism," though it might also be described as continentalism.

This main dimension of nationalism differs in two important respects from what researchers have usually understood by ethnocentrism. First, it is only weakly related to Internationalism, suggesting that some types of nationalism may have little to do with attitudes towards foreigners in general or with the problem of world government. Second, there is an admittedly weak but noteworthy positive correlation between this factor and attitudes towards Frenchmen from France. "Frenchmen from France" must be considered an outgroup for French Canadians, and the correlation is directly contrary to the descriptive hypothesis associated with "ethnocentrism." (Only from the standpoint of language are Frenchmen an ingroup for French Canadians; the dimension is perhaps one of *lingocentrism* rather than *ethnocentrism*.)

The third factor clearly represents attitudes towards Americans and American influence insofar as these attitudes can be distinguished from the overall tendency to evaluate groups positively or negatively and from the specific tendency to support or oppose Quebec independence. The factor results from the relatively large negative correlation between demands for independence from the United States and evaluation of Americans (Appendix C, line 3-9).

The last column of figures in table 8.5 shows the communalities for the ten variables. The extremely low communality of Internationalism stands out. Internationalism evidently should be regarded as an independent "dimension" of variation in nationalist attitudes, unrelated to the other dimensions measured in the study. The same is true, though to a lesser extent, for the evaluation of Frenchmen from France.

Some Generalizations

The intercorrelations among our measures of nationalist attitudes seem to be explained by two types of factors, (a) a general factor of evaluation of groups, which has little to do with policies or with the distinction between ingroups and outgroups, and (b) one or more "nationalism" factors that link support for particular nationalist demands with negative attitudes towards particular, relevant outgroups. The general evaluative factor does not represent a tendency to evaluate ingroups differently than outgroups, but rather the tendency to evaluate all of them either favorable or unfavorably. It reflects the fact that the correlations between the evaluative measures are all positive (table 8.1). The existence of the general tendency represented by this factor may explain why there are correlations between negative attitudes towards ethnic minorities and personality traits such as misanthropy and low self-esteem.[7] The "nationalism" factors suggest that there is normally a closer relation between support for nationalist demands and dislike of relevant outgroups (e.g., between Separatist Nationalism and negative evaluations of English Canadians) than between support for such demands and praise for the relevant ingroup (e.g., Separatist Nationalism and positive evaluations of French Canadians). The analysis does *not* produce a factor corresponding to *patriotism* in the sense of love of the national ingroup unadulterated by hostility towards outgroups. We do not find that positive evaluations of the national ingroup load on one factor, along with a propensity to make nationalist demands, while negative attitudes towards outgroups load on another, uncorrelated factor (or factors). What we find, after we remove the covariation due to the general evaluative factor, are factors that represent easily understandable combinations of demands and sympathetic or antipathetic (especially antipathetic) attitudes towards relevant ingroups and outgroups.

Nationalists regularly recommend their policies by saying that they are "pro-X, not anti-Y" and the Berkeley group seem to have had some such distinction in mind when they separated genuine patriotism from pseudo-patriotism. The results just presented, however, suggest a certain artificiality in divorcing the study of national loyalty from the study of hostile attitudes towards relevant outgroups. To be sure, (a) positive attitudes towards one's own nation (patriotism, defensive nationalism, national loyalty, etc.) are not the same as (b) negative attitudes towards outgroups (xenophobia, aggressive nationalism, chauvinism, etc.), but "nationalism" should not be defined in such a way as to suggest that these are independent dimensions of variation.[8]

"Ethnocentrism," it seems, will be a misleading description of nationalist attitudes to the extent that it suggests the existence of a single, dominant dimension of variation in such attitudes. In general, there seem to be several dimensions. In our English data, there are three common factors with equal claim to being considered dimensions of nationalism. In the French data, attitudes towards the United States and Americans are partially independent of the main nationalism factor. In both sets of data, the Internationalism scale was unrelated to the more important dimensions of nationalist attitudes. Among the English respondents, finally, the two scales that had the best claims to being considered omnibus measures of nationalism, the National Power and National Unity scales, were only weakly related to each other and to any of the common factors.

Types of Nationalism

It is difficult to make sense of the various dimensions of nationalism among our respondents without taking into account a simple fact sometimes forgotten in psychological studies of nationalism and ethnocentrism, namely, that the characteristics that distinguish one group (nation, race, ethnic group, etc.) from another group may not be the same characteristics that distinguish the first group from a third group. Group A may speak the same language as Group B, but cherish different religious beliefs, while Groups A and C may speak different languages but have the same religion. And so on for any number of groups and characteristics. If people's "ethnocentric" opinions were generally a reaction to the real differences between groups, and if people were not all equally concerned with all such differences (some people being more religious than others, some more concerned with language, others with politics, etc.), then there would be nothing puzzling about our failure to find a single general factor of "ethno-centrism."

Language divides English Canadians and French Canadians, but language does not distinguish English Canadians from Americans or French Canadians from Frenchmen from France. These facts may help to explain some of the correlations noted above. Among the English respondents, there is a significant correlation ($r = .26$) between attitudes towards English Canadians and attitudes towards Americans, who share the same language, but only very weak correlations ($r = .08$ and $r = .09$) between attitudes towards English Canadians or Americans and attitudes towards French Canadians (table 8.1). Among the French respondents, there is a similar relatively strong correlation ($r = .37$) between attitudes towards English Canadians and Americans, and also a fairly strong correlation between attitudes towards French Canadians and attitudes towards Frenchmen from France ($r = .28$), but only very weak correlations ($r = .07$ and $r = .06$) between attitudes towards Frenchmen and attitudes towards English Canadians or Americans. To understand these facts, it helps to notice that French Canadians are distinguished from English Canadians and Americans by one of the same characteristics, language, that distinguishes Frenchmen from the latter groups; that language differences are generally salient among Canadians; and that they are particularly salient among French Canadians.

This example suggests a general rule: "ethnocentrism" has to do with the real differences between groups. It is not just a by-product of any merely formal distinction between ingroups and outgroups. The differences that create ethnocentrism are differences in language, customs, institutions, values, and political principles—in short, differences in culture, ethnicity, or way of life. An outgroup becomes a focus of ethnocentric attitudes because it represents a challenging alternative to the ingroup's way of life.

To fix ideas, consider once again the study of nationalist attitudes among French university students mentioned above. It showed that anti-Soviet and anti-American feelings tend to be negatively correlated, not positively correlated as "ethnocentrism" would require. This result is easy enough to understand: given the Cold War, given France's military weakness vis-à-vis the superpowers, and given the strength of the revolutionary and conservative traditions in French politics, the contrasts (whatever they are) between all Frenchmen and all foreigners pale before the contrast between the Soviets and the Americans. Soviet communism and American capitalism represent distinct but related challenges to the French way of life. The two countries provide alternative models for the organization of an advanced, technological society. Hence the existence of a general factor of "nonethnocentric" nationalism. The end-points of this dimension represent two types of nationalism—a right-wing type (anticommunist and procapitalist) and a left-wing type (anticapitalist, antiimperialist, and procommunist).

In general, there should be as many types of nationalism as there are salient contrasts between the national ingroup and other groups. If the members of a nation are preoccupied with the differences between progressive and reactionary regimes, then foreign countries will tend to be judged according to their location along the left-right continuum, and there will be two antithetical types of nationalism, as in France. If language differences are salient, then humanity will be divided into two groups, those who speak the national language and those who do not, and there will be a linguistic type of nationalism, as in French Canada. To the extent that no single contrast is of overriding importance, there will be several independent types of nationalism, as in English Canada. People will act as if each foreign nation represented a different challenge to the national ingroup, and there will be little correlation between different types of nationalism.

Consider for a moment why there were separate dimensions of anti-British and anti-American nationalism in our English data. These two dimensions need not have been found. With different respondents (recent immigrants from the United Kingdom, perhaps, or from the West Indies), attitudes towards Britain and the United States could have been part of a single dimension of variation, either because of strong positive or negative correlations between the attitudes. If there had been strong *positive* correlations between attitudes towards Britain and attitudes towards the United States, we could have attributed these correlations to an underlying dimension of proimperialist or antiimperialist sentiment among Canadians. Conversely, if there had been strong *negative* correlations between the two sets of attitudes, we could have focused attention on the differences between Britain and the United States. Britain, we might have said, represents order, aristocratic rule, high standards, privilege, and snobbery, while the United States represents the opposite set of virtues and vices—democracy, freedom, equality of opportunity, and vulgarity. Such imagery would explain negative correlations and lead us to treat the underlying dimension as one of aristocratic versus democratic sentiment. In fact, of course, there is virtually no correlation whatever between attitudes towards Britain and attitudes towards the United States. This result is presumably explained by the variety and confusion of ideas about Britain and the United States among English Canadians. There is no consensus about what the two countries represent. Some Canadians see them as very similar, while others emphasize the differences. British imperialism is still salient for some Canadians, despite the collapse of the British Empire. For others "imperialism" means "American imperialism" and the dominant role of the United States in maintaining the international order. Many Canadians equate Britain with the Royal Family and they associate democracy and equality with the United States. But for other Canadians the most important difference between the two countries is the existence of a socialist party in Britain and the election of socialist governments there, compared with the absence of such a party in the United States. Racial prejudice and racial violence have tarnished the image of American democracy in Canadian eyes, but the image of Britain as a bastion of high culture and civilized behavior has been compromised in recent years by its racial troubles and its important contributions to pop culture. It is hardly surprising, in light of all these considerations, that the net effect of the various influences should be judgments of Britain and the United States that are statistically independent, on the average. In other words, it is hardly surprising that there should be two dimensions of variation in attitudes towards Britain and the United States and two corresponding types of Canadian nationalism, anti-British and anti-American.

A Missing Type

Anticommunist nationalism qualifies as a distinct type. If different contrasts and different challenges produce different types of nationalism, then surely the contrasts and challenges underlying the Cold War should produce a distinct type of nationalism, not just among French university students in 1962, but among Western Europeans and North Americans generally.

Casual observation suffices to establish its existence among Canadians. Most Canadians, like most Americans, are concerned about the military power and ideological influence of the communist countries. Many Canadians are strongly anticommunist, as many Americans and Frenchmen are. Staunch cold warriors may be a smaller proportion of the Canadian population than of the American, but they are certainly not a negligible proportion. Procommunists are a negligible fraction of Canadians, but a significantly minority of Canadians regard the refusal to say anything nasty about the Soviet Union as evidence of intellectual sophistication.

Anticommunist nationalism was overlooked when the questionnaires for these studies were put together. They contained no direct questions about the Soviet Union or communist China, and this fact may explain our failure to find strong correlations between nationalism and authoritarianism. The latter may correlate best with anticommunist nationalism and not with most types of nationalism. The measures of nationalism used in previous research on nationalism and personality may have correlated with authoritarianism because they were largely measures of anticommunist sentiment.

Daniel Levinson's early and exemplary study provides a particularly good illustration of this point.[9] About half the items in his Nationalism-Internationalism scale make more or less direct reference to the communist threat and the need for Americans to make a firm if not a truculent response to it (e.g., "We need more leaders like MacArthur, who have the morals and the strength to put our national honor above appeasement"). Of course some of the items might be regarded as having nothing whatever to do with communism, for example, the following two:

3. In the long run, it would be to our best interest as a nation to spend less money for military purposes and more money for education, housing, and other social improvements.
5. The only way peace can be maintained is to keep America so powerful and well armed that no other nation will dare attack us.

But to understand the attitudes evoked by these more ambiguous items, we must consider when the study was carried out and what the great issues of the day were. The study was done in 1951, at the height of concern about communist aggression, and the great issue in the background was, of course, America's response to that aggression. Those who demanded more military spending did so in order to have military forces better able to defend America against communism. Those who feared attack from other nations feared attack from the communist nations. Almost all of the statements in the scale are straightforward expressions of common right-wing opinions about the communist threat. For Levinson, nationalism = anticommunism.

The same principle of interpretation must be used to understand the results of other studies of nationalism and personality, based upon other measures of nationalist attitudes. We must examine these scales with an eye to the issues of the day. When we encounter a broad statement like "We must be willing to fight for our country without questioning whether it is right or wrong," we have to ask ourselves, "Fight against whom?" A statement like "There is no room in our country for people who find fault with it," should elicit from us the question, "Who is inclined to find fault?" If we follow this principle of interpretation, which relates questions and answers to the important issues of the day, we shall see, I think, that in the American literature on nationalism and personality, nationalism means essentially anticommunism.

The Canadian studies that have shown correlations between nationalist attitudes and personality (above, p. 53) used scales that tapped anticommunist sentiment among Canadians (e.g., Levinson's Nationalism-Internationalism scale). The one earlier study that defined nationalism operationally as anti-Americanism produced quite different results (above, p. 79).

In the present study only one nationalist attitude was clearly associated with authoritarianism, the attitude measured by the National Power scale in the English questionnaire. Does this scale measure anticommunist nationalism, and are high scores on the scale associated with authoritarianism for this reason? No definite answers are possible. We know, of course, that the scale also measures anti-American nationalism—the factor analysis suggests that about one-fifth of the reliable variation in the scores might be attributed to the anti-American factor. But we have other, better measures of anti-American nationalism, and they do not correlate even moderately with authoritarianism. When trying to explain the correlation between the National Power scale and the F scale, it seems reasonable, therefore, to disregard the component of anti-American nationalism and to focus attention, instead, on attitudes that may have been measured by the nationalism scales known to correlate with authoritarianism. Anticommunism is the obvious candidate.

Summary and Conclusions

The descriptive hypothesis asserts that people's clashing opinions about different ethnic and national groups can legitimately be boiled down to differences along a single underlying dimension of greater or less ethnocentrism, but the nationalistic attitudes of our respondents are not organized as this hypothesis requires. Many of the correlations between different attitudes are so weak that it would be scarcely meaningful to speak of their relation to any common factor. The best averages of the different measures, the first principal components, are able to account for only a quarter to a third of the reliable variation in the scores, and these best averages are not measures of ethnocentrism as this concept has usually been understood. When multidimensional factor analysis was used, the "general

factor" was one of favorable or unfavorable attitudes towards people generally—a factor of philanthropy vs. misanthropy, rather than humanitarianism vs. ethnocentrism. The factor analyses also suggest that there may be
many different types of nationalism, depending upon local circumstances—
Québécois nationalism, anti-French nationalism among English Canadians, anti-British nationalism, and so on.

A French study has shown quite clearly that the main dimension of
variation in nationalist attitudes need not be ethnocentrism; it can be a
simple left-right dimension. This finding suggests that we could distinguish
between a right-wing, anticommunist type of nationalism and a left-wing,
anti-American type—at least among French university students in the early
1960s.

If our questionnaires had included scales to measure attitudes towards
communism, the Soviet Union, and communist China, we would almost
certainly have found that they constituted an independent dimension of
nationalism. The neglect of this type of nationalism may explain our failure
to find strong correlations between nationalist attitudes and authoritarianism. Earlier studies may have found such correlations because they equated
nationalism with anticommunist nationalism.

But why should anticommunist nationalism have a special relationship
with authoritarianism? Of all the possible types of nationalism, is anticommunist nationalism really the acme of irrationality? Why should it, and not
other types, be the characteristic expression, along with anti-Semitism and
race prejudice, of ego weakness?

Social Science
and Critical Theory

Here it occurs to me that in conversation on aesthetic matters we use the
words: "You have to see it like *this*, this is how it is meant"; "When you
see it like *this*, you see where it goes wrong"; "You have to hear this bar
as an introduction"; "You must hear it in this key"; "You must phrase
it like *this*" (which can refer to hearing as well as to playing).

Wittgenstein, *Philosophical Investigations*

Durability is one of the outstanding features of *The Authoritarian Personality*. It has survived more than thirty years of attacks, and it stands today as one of the acknowledged classics of social science. The flood of research it stimulated during the 1950s has abated, and each year now adds only a small and slowly diminishing number of new studies to the mass of research designed to throw light on its hypotheses. Some of these new studies support the old hypotheses, others contradict them, but none seem to have much effect on the critical consensus about the book's main strengths and weaknesses that developed a generation ago. In the textbooks and reviews of the literature one still reads that the California theory of authoritarianism is "too psychological," that it may be "biased," but that when the exaggerations are pared away, it offers insights of enduring value.

This critical consensus is unlikely to be shaken by a few awkward facts. The great strength of *The Authoritarian Personality* plainly has more to do with its basic theory than with either the accuracy or practical usefulness of its empirical generalizations. No sensible person, therefore, would expect such a monumental study suddenly to be demolished by statistical results, however unexpected, from questionnaires given to 1,825 Canadian high school seniors in 1968. Any adequate criticism of the Berkeley group's work must start from a proper appreciation of its evident strengths and must somehow come to grips with its underlying theory. It will be helpful to begin by reviewing some simple points in the philosophy of social science.

An introductory course on methodology is part of the training of almost all social scientists. Different courses and different instructors emphasize different themes, of course, but there is nonetheless an orthodox view of empirical science that is strengthened and refined by almost all such courses. The standard textbooks of methodology teach that it is the job of the scientist to develop and test hypotheses. A typical hypothesis is an assertion about the correlation to be observed between phenomena: E goes with F. The scientist tests his hypothesis by collecting and analyzing relevant data. Does E in fact go with F? If it does, the scientist's hypothesis has been confirmed or verified, and he can be pleased and proud that he has added to the stock of human knowledge. If it does not—if his hypothesis is falsified by his data—he should still be pleased and proud, for as a famous historian once said, "If we cannot lay the foundation, it is something to clear away the rubbish—if we cannot set up the truth, it is something to pull down error."[1]

A falsified hypothesis, according to the orthodox view, should be a stimulus to new theoretical thinking. When phenomena are found that are inconsistent with a particular hypothesis, then the theory from which the hypothesis was derived is discredited, in whole or in part, and the scientist's task is to develop a new hypothesis on the basis of a more comprehensive theory, which will in turn be subjected to testing and possible falsification. According to the orthodox view, then, the results presented above, assuming they can be replicated, require that we qualify some of the Berkeley group's hypotheses and that we turn our minds to revising their theory.

There is an almost irresistible temptation, given the tangled history of research on authoritarianism and the obscurity of the basic concept, to accommodate the anomalous findings of earlier chapters by adopting a simple methodological hypothesis—by speaking, for example, of extraneous variables like social class, agreement response set, or education and cognitive sophistication. The most tempting explanation of all is perhaps the one that makes the least demands upon the reader's credulity, namely, the debunking hypothesis that the F scale measures nothing more than unsophisticated traditionalism or conservatism, and that it will correlate with other scales when these scales also tap the same ideological syndrome (above, pp. 98-101). This hypothesis promises a simple and plausible explanation for the results of the present study, reconciling them with the results of earlier studies while depriving them of any theoretical significance. Nationalism, we could say, will correlate *positively* with authoritarianism (i.e., conservatism) when the nationalism in question is conservative nationalism; it will correlate *negatively* with authoritarianism when it is anticolonial nationalism, with revolutionary and anticapitalist overtones; and it will have very weak or zero correlations with authoritarianism when it belongs neither to the Right nor to the Left, but is just nationalism. The results of the present study could be used, along with the results of earlier studies, to illustrate these simple rules about nationalism and authoritarianism. Since the rules are so simple and obvious, the whole literature is of no great interest. All it really demonstrates, according to this interpretation, is the great difficulty of finding convincing evidence of any connection between ideology and personality.

Reasons have already been offered for resisting this temptation. It must suffice for the present to repeat that the debunking hypothesis makes the respectful reception given *The Authoritarian Personality* by its first readers, and the enduring fame of the book, very puzzling. Scientists are not fools, and there must be some good reason for the refusal of the scientific community to dismiss *The Authoritarian Personality* as an obvious example of pseudoscience.

The orthodox view of science promoted by introductory courses in methodology is challenged by a rival view (sometimes offered in advanced courses) that puts more emphasis on the autonomous role of theory in the scientific enterprise. According to this rival view, broad theories are not just collections of empirical generalizations, to be tested one by one and refuted by a few contrary examples, but rather conceptual frameworks, or ways of seeing the world, that are prior to testable empirical generalizations. To adopt a theory is to put on a set of "conceptual spectacles" that provide an overview of the phenomena of interest. The details of that larger picture may then be investigated by the scientist in narrow empirical studies, but the broad picture can be rejected only by replacing it with an alternative, equally comprehensive overview, and this change resembles the experience of religious conversion more than it does the experimenter's (or the quality controller's) acceptance or rejection of a statistical hypothesis in the light of his data. Historians and philosophers of science sometimes employ examples from Gestalt psychology to clarify what they mean by a shift in theoretical perspective: the "facts" remain the same but they are seen differently. Seeing, they sometimes say, is a "theory-laden" activity. A theory creates a language, one might also say, that makes possible the formulation of precise empirical hypotheses and that favors some hypotheses while drawing attention away from others. The truth or falsehood of the favored hypotheses must influence our acceptance or rejection of the basic theory, but acceptance or rejection must also involve metaphysical and pragmatic, or even aesthetic and ethical, as well as strictly empirical, considerations. For it is always possible to save a threatened theory from refutation by adopting appropriate auxiliary hypotheses.

The past dozen years have witnessed a major controversy about the role of empirical research in social psychology and related disciplines. Ideas trickling down from continental philosophy have undermined confidence in the orthodox positivist account of scientific method. Many minds have been opened to previously ignored criticisms of empiricism by disappointment with the results of past research.

A leading contemporary writer in this vein speaks of a decay of empiricism. In the heyday of logical positivism, he notes, almost all researchers assumed "that general theoretical statements are subject to empirical evaluation." But experience belies the earlier confidence in testing and falsification: "Virtually no theory has been discarded as clearly falsified, and no theory sustained because of the clarity of its support or its robust resistance to falsification. From the present perspective there is little reason to suspect that empirically based decisions will ever occur." He concludes that "the major generalizations contained within the traditional repositories of social psychological knowledge (the textbook, the handbook, the research monograph and the journal contribution) [must be viewed] not as empirically based knowledge, nor as the results of an empirical winnowing process, but as representing the commonly favoured opinions of certain subcultures of the discipline. They represent 'appropriate' or 'reasonable' views of certain groups with vested interests in a particular conceptual vocabulary or intelligibility system." He calls for greater theoretical audacity—for theories that challenge "dominant interpretative modes in society," for "antagonistic theorizing" and "generative theory" that will expand the range of human potential. "*The generative theory is one that challenges the guiding assumptions of the culture, raises fundamental questions regarding social life, fosters reconsideration of that which is 'taken for granted' and thereby furnishes fresh alternatives for social action.*"[2] Generative theory, as he recognizes, is similar to what others have called critical theory.

The enormous attention to methodology and factual detail in *The Authoritarian Personality* and the paucity of theoretical discussion suggest that its authors accepted the orthodox positivist view of science. Some of them no doubt did, and no one who has ever glanced at the book is unaware of its heavily empirical style. But we should not judge a book by its cover, and it is worth recalling that the philosophically sophisticated members of the Berkeley group, Max Horkheimer and Theodor Adorno, were pioneers of audacious, antagonistic, generative, *critical* theory.

In a famous essay of 1937 outlining the differences between the traditional positivist and his own "critical"conceptions of theory, Horkheimer gave broad theories clear priority over narrow empirical research. He argued that particular elements of his own "critical theory of society" might be subject to testing, verification or falsification, and practical application in the traditional manner, but not the theory as a whole.

> From the fact that the representation of a unified object is true as a whole, it is possible to conclude only under special conditions the extent to which isolated parts of the representation can validly be applied, in their isolation, to isolated parts of the object. The problem that arises as soon as particular propositions of the critical theory [of society] are applied to unique or recurring events in contemporary society has to do not with the truth of the theory but with how suitable the theory is for traditional kinds of intellectual operation with progressively extended goals.[3]

Horkheimer was saying that a broad theory cannot be judged true or false simply because particular factual propositions or hypotheses derived from the theory are sound or misleading in practice. The traditional conception of theory rests, as Horkheimer explained, on the uncritical acceptance and overgeneralization of the pragmatic view of science that is a necessary and inherent part of a certain stage in the development of society's productive forces. The one-sidedness of this view must be overcome not just by a clearer understanding of the social functions of science, but also by a clearer perception, derived from the practice of science itself, of the relativity of the relation between facts and the conceptual ordering of facts and, finally, by a deeper appreciation of man's nature as both subject and object of a vast historical process. "What is needed is a radical reconsideration, not just of the scientist alone, but of the knowing individual as such."[4] The key to the proper understanding of science was to put scientists in their social context, as understood in the critical theory of society. The theory of ethnocentrism and authoritarianism was itself part of that larger critical theory.

Critical theory, a complex body of thought about difficult questions, defies brief presentation. Those who do not fully understand its appeal should probably refrain from trying to summarize it. Even sympathetic commentators are frustrated by the convoluted irony and deliberate obscurity of its principal sources, especially the more ambitious writings of Theodor Adorno. "It is often not apparent whether Adorno is offering, for example, an explanation of a phenomenon, or an elaborately spun metaphor, or a deliberate hyperbole to stir political action. The problem—a severe problem for anyone who seeks to come to grips with Adorno's thought—is to know what kind of assessment Adorno's work requires."[5] The writings of Max Horkheimer, generally more accessible than those of Adorno, have an equally frustrating tendency to avoid the fundamental questions that concern anyone attempting a systematic exposition of his thought. "Horkheimer had an unfortunate tendency to avoid these questions or to treat answers to them as self-evident."⁶ The result, in most expositions of critical theory, is an emphasis on origins and outward features. No simple formula that claims to penetrate to the heart of the matter—e.g., "Heideggerian Marxism"—is likely to be much help to the uninitiated.

Some brief comments on critical theory's relation to orthodox Marxism may be helpful, however, particularly since it is "Marxism" that some critics have detected behind the Aesopian language of *The Authoritarian Personality*. Like Marx, Horkheimer and Adorno believed that the development of productive forces under capitalism, including the development of modern science and technology, had brought mankind to the threshold of a new, radically different, and fundamentally better way of life than had ever existed in the past. But unlike Marx, they did not believe that there was anything inevitable about the transformation of capitalism into socialism or communism. Indeed they thought that man might be fated never to cross the threshold into the new and better world. Bourgeois civilization might so deaden the hearts and darken the minds of its victims that they might never rebel against its ugliness and exploitation, and socialism might never come into being. Like Marx, they hated and feared the business class, or capitalism, because of its power to distort the current of history and to turn the achievements of mankind into means for defeating mankind's historic hopes of freedom and reason. Modern natural and social science, harnessed to the narrow interests of a selfish, insecure, and neurotic ruling class, might end by destroying all that is most valuable in human life, if not life itself. Unlike Marx, Horkheimer and Adorno knew that the antagonism between business and labor could be at least temporarily suppressed, and perhaps permanently overcome, through the manipulation of consciousness.

Orthodox Marxists must find critical theory merely the pale shadow of a vanished faith. Like denominations that blend Christianity and Voltaire, critical theory blends the German Left and the German Right. And like those denominations, it is held in contempt by the true believers. Nonetheless its synthesis—or amalgam—of materialism, idealism, optimism, pessimism, snobbism, and egalitarianism is the most potent form of Marxism among Western academics and underlies much contemporary radicalism.

Critical theory concerns us here as a critique of false consciousness. It claims to be a comprehensive critique. It deals with every manifestation of human creativity, from the most ephemeral products of the culture industry to the most profound meditations on the human condition, and everywhere it finds hidden tendencies and the subtle poison of class interest. The most impressive demonstrations involve middle-range cultural phenomena, between Tin Pan Alley songs and astrology columns, say, which no sensible person expects to encourage critical self-consciousness, and philosophical treatises like Hegel's *Phenomenology* or Heidegger's *Being and Time*, where the demonstration of bias is hard to follow. Social science is the favored testing ground for critical theory's critique of false consciousness.

How a society understands its own fundamental problems is of more than purely scientific interest. Science is often perverted, critical theorists recognize, by practical motives for presenting a false picture of reality. This is especially true in times of crisis, as Horkheimer said, "when relationships have so far developed and conflicts of interest have reached such an intensity that even the average eye can penetrate beyond appearances to what is really going on."[7] Then a conscious ideological apparatus in the full sense usually makes its appearance. As the danger of conflict increases, so also does the energy devoted to maintaining the ideology of the status quo, and finally the weapons are readied for supporting it with violence.

> The more the Roman Empire was threatened by explosive inner forces, the more brutally did the Caesars try to revitalize the old cult of the State and to restore the lost sense of unity. The ages which followed the Christian persecutions and the fall of the Empire supply many other frightful examples of the same recurring pattern. In the science of such periods the ideological dimension usually comes to light less in its false judgements than in its lack of clarity, its perplexity, its obscure language, its manner of posing problems, its methods, the direction of its research, and, above all, in what it closes its eyes to.[8]

Part Three

Theoretical

Conformity, Diversity, and Authoritarianism

There is a story told of Democritus, that one day he was eating a cucumber that seemed to have a honey-like taste, and, struck by this, he began to speculate about the possible causes of its unusual sweetness. He was about to rise from the table to examine the garden where it had grown, when his serving girl, informed of his perplexity, laughingly told him that he need not trouble himself any longer about it, for the fact of the matter was that she had accidentally put the cucumber in a honey-jar. Democritus pretended anger on receiving this information, saying that it deprived him of an opportunity for research and robbed his curiosity of matter to work on. "Go along," he said to her, "you have done me no favour, and I shall pursue my inquiries, as if this sweetness had a natural explanation." And it is said that he did not fail to find some natural cause for the unusual sweetness of the cucumber.[1]

Unusual results usually have simple explanations. But let us try to develop an account of ethnocentrism and authoritarianism that, even if it lacks simplicity, does justice to the widespread intuitive confidence in the intuitive powers of the Berkeley group. Let us begin by reviewing the principal facts at this stage of the argument.

The Facts to Be Explained

1. Most studies of nationalism and personality have produced evidence favoring the personality hypothesis. There are some three dozen studies, most done in the United States, showing moderate to strong positive correlations between authoritarianism, as measured by the F or D scales, and measures of nationalist attitudes.

2. The present study produced only one really substantial correlation between nationalism and authoritarianism: the English respondents who

received high scores on the National Power scale also tended to receive high scores on the F scale. None of the other measures of nationalist attitudes correlated with authoritarianism. A series of statements about national power was used to test support for Quebec independence among the French respondents, but in this case there was only an insignificant correlation between authoritarianism and Separatist Nationalism (as the variable was called in this context). There were no substantial correlations between authoritarianism and any of the other six measures of nationalist attitudes in either the English or the French studies.

3. Most studies of ethnic prejudice and personality have produced results favoring the personality hypothesis. A great many studies, from about a dozen different countries, have shown correlations between authoritarianism, as measured by the F scale, and various measures of hostility against both domestic minorities and foreign nations. The published studies are probably only a fraction of the studies that have been carried out, and most of these must have turned up evidence confirming the orthodox hypothesis about prejudice and personality.

4. The present study found no really substantial correlations, in either the English or the French data, between authoritarianism and attitudes towards Canada, English Canadians, French Canadians, Americans, British people, or Frenchmen from France.

5. Most studies of the personality correlates of nationalism and ethnic prejudice have proceeded on the assumption that ethnocentrism, though complex and multidimensional in detail, can be treated as a single basic dimension of variation. This assumption is supported by many studies showing strong correlations between anti-Semitic and antiblack prejudice among Americans.

6. The present study provides no support for the descriptive hypothesis that different nationalist attitudes are best seen as slightly different aspects of an all-embracing ethnocentrism. There seem to be different types of nationalism; these types seem to correspond, not to differences in personality among nationalists, but to different possible contrasts between ingroups and outgroups; and the real differences between national or ethnic groups— the differences having to do with the substance of their "nationality" or "ethnicity"—seem to be relevant for explaining people's reactions to them.

The facts summarized under 2, 4, and 6 cast doubt on the standard theory used to explain the facts summarized under 1, 3, and 5. To make sense of all these facts and similar ones, we must clarify the status of authoritarianism as a personality variable. This is partly a problem of clarifying what the F scale measures and partly one of clarifying what kind of ego weakness is naturally linked to ethnocentrism.

The F Scale, Authoritarianism, and Psychopathology

When thinking about the F scale, there are two things to keep in mind it does *not* measure, "authoritarianism" and psychopathology.

"Authoritarianism"

If "authoritarianism" is defined as what the F scale measures, then of course the F scale measures it. But if it is defined as "the desire or tendency to impose one's will on others," a sensible definition consistent with contemporary usage, then it seems that the F scale does not measure "authoritarianism."

The main studies supporting this generalization employ a "directiveness" scale developed by John Ray.[2] It consists of 26 items in behavior inventory format, that is to say, items which ask the respondent direct questions about his own behavior rather than his opinions on controversial social and political questions. Typical items, answered yes or no, are the following: "Are you the sort of person who always likes to get his own way?" "If you are told to take charge of some situation does this make you feel uncomfortable?" "Do you tend to dominate the conversation?" There is relatively good evidence that the answers to these questions are a valid measure of assertiveness or the tendency to dominate others; the scale seems, in fact, to distinguish the bossy from the submissive. Several studies employing this new scale have also included one or another version of the F scale, allowing correlations between "directiveness" and F-scale authoritarianism. The basic result of these studies is no positive correlation, or even a slight negative correlation, between the two measures.[3] These findings, which are in line with the results of at least two earlier studies using comparable measures,[4] raise the difficult question of which scale has the better claim to the term "authoritarianism." Ray not surprisingly favors his own. However the competing claims are eventually resolved, one thing is clear: the relation between attitudes conventionally called authoritarian and behavior conventionally called authoritarian is at best loose and problematic.

Admittedly there are more than two defensible ways of defining authoritarianism—the term is used to cover a multitude of sins—and it would be a monumental task to evaluate the F scale from the standpoint of all the possible definitions. For the present it suffices to note that high scores on the F scale are no guarantee of a domineering manner.

Psychopathology

Rupert Wilkinson assures us that "most American authoritarians are probably not overt homosexuals."[5] (But what about all those authoritarians who are *latent* homosexuals?)[6] Larry Spence, in a show of nonpartisan objectivity, allows that "communists and fascists are not consistently neurotic, sexually repressed, or psychopathic."[7] (But what about a characteristic *tendency* of fascists to be psychopathic?) In short, the exception proves the rule: authoritarians are generally thought to have more wrong with them than simply a propensity to hold the wrong political opinions.

How abnormal is the authoritarian? Are those who get high scores on the F scale any closer, on the average, than those who get low scores to any of the boundaries that separate the healthy-minded from the mentally ill? The answer seems to be no. The relevant research consists of studies that correlate F-scale scores with scores on tests of proven diagnostic validity (e.g., some of the MMPI scales). Considering the political interest of the results, and the ease of doing such studies, it is perhaps surprising how few of them there are. So far as I know, only eight have been published.[8] These studies raise complex methodological and interpretive issues, but their main result seems clear: there is no good evidence that authoritarians are any sicker mentally than equalitarians. Thus the best of the earlier studies found that there was no relation between F-scale scores and "degree of psychopathological tendency as measured by MMPI elevation."[9] The best of the more recent studies have correlated F-scale scores with the neuroticism scale of the Eysenck Personality Inventory and found insignificant or negative correlations; a study in Munich, for example, led to the conclusion that "pro-authoritarian . . . responses [to a balanced F scale] were signs of good mental health."[10]

The main significance of these negative findings is to break up the complex of associations surrounding the term *authoritarian* and to encourage a fresh consideration of how the portrait of the prejudiced personality should be drawn.[11] In what follows I shall argue that conventionalism, conformism, or submissiveness, are what must be emphasized if we are to understand "the authoritarian personality."

One of the standard criticisms of *The Authoritarian Personality* is, of course, that it neglects conformity to cultural norms as an explanation for ethnic prejudice. Many bigots, we are told, may be neither ideopaths nor psychopaths, but only "cultural parrots, repeating the idle chatter they have heard."[12] Without in any way denying the truth of this generalization, I shall argue that it misses the mark as a criticism of the California studies of nationalism, ethnocentrism, and personality. They went astray, not by neglecting, but by distorting conformism as a cause of ethnocentrism.

Authoritarianism and Conformism

The first in the Berkeley group's list of nine defining traits of the authoritarian personality is conventionalism, "rigid adherence to conventional, middle-class values" (AP, 228). Conventionalism, they say, is the result of a basic disposition to yield to social pressure. They contrast "adherence to conventional values [that is] an expression of a fully established individual conscience" with adherence that is "determined by [yielding to] contemporary external social pressure" (AP, 230). It is this second type of adherence that they claim is strongly related to ethnocentrism and "antidemocratic receptivity." In short, *conformism* is one of the most important traits of the authoritarian personality as the Berkeley group conceived it.

The Berkeley group paid little attention, however, to actual *conformity* to "norms of prejudice" as an explanation for prejudice. Perhaps they regarded this explanation as too obvious to deserve comment. Who, after all, doubts that humans are sociable creatures and that they tend to imitate their associates? Who disputes that we can explain the prejudices of many individuals simply by pointing to the prejudices of their families and friends? Who denies that "cultural norms" of prejudice exist? But so what? Do any of these facts help us to explain why there are these norms or what they are? If it is the "norms of prejudice" we wish to understand, as it surely is, then conformity to these norms is of little interest, and attention must turn to the determinants of the norms—in the Berkeley group's terminology, to the factors that govern the production of ideology and the character structures, or fundamental variables of personality, that govern its consumption.[13]

It is a clear implication of the Berkeley group's portrait of the ethnocentrist, though not one they highlighted, that conformism is such a basic motive, not just for conformity to "norms of prejudice," but for greater than average prejudice, and hence that it is one of the determinants of the norm itself. They pointed, in other words, to a connection between conformism and ethnocentrism that is more interesting than the simple connection between conformism and conformity to social norms.

Subsequent studies have supported the Berkeley group's hypothesis that conformism is related to both ethnic prejudice and authoritarianism. The first correlation is not so well documented as the second, but it is the better known of the two. It has been frequently misinterpreted.

Conformism and Ethnic Prejudice

Eight different studies report correlations between ethnocentrism and a conformist disposition to yield to social pressure. In a very influential study of the attitudes of South African whites, Thomas Pettigrew found fairly strong correlations (about $r = .45$) between a paper-and-pencil test of conformism, or conformist values, and a measure of prejudice against black Africans: the respondents who were above average on conformism also tended to be above average on prejudice.[14] Using the same two scales, J. M. Nieuwoudt and Elizabeth Nel found almost the same correlation,[15] while

Christopher Orpen found an even stronger correlation (r = .61).[16] Using a
different measure of antiblack prejudice and the same measure of conformity, John Ray and Patrick Heaven report weaker but still significant correlations between conformism and prejudice.[17] Using the Berkeley group's E
scale as a measure of prejudice and a behavioral measure of conformism
(yielding to group pressure in the sort of experimental situation made
famous by the work of Solomon Asch), Milton Maloff and Albert Lott
found essentially the same relation between prejudice and conformism in a
study of American students.[18] Edwin Lawson and Ross Stagner found a
similar relation between nationalist attitudes and conformity in an Asch-
type situation.[19] Eugene Nadler reports correlations between ethnocentrism
and two different measures of conformism—actual yielding and a paper-
and-pencil test of conformist attitudes.[20]

The concept of "conformity to norms" is sometimes pressed into service
to explain these correlations. The reasoning is as follows: (a) conformists,
that is to say, those high on measures of conformism, tend to conform to
social norms; (b) ethnic prejudice is a social norm, at least in some cultures;
therefore (c) conformists in these cultures should be more prejudiced than
nonconformists.[21]

This reasoning is defective. It overlooks the elementary fact that the
"social norm" is a *certain amount* of prejudice, not prejudice per se or the
greatest possible amount of prejudice. If the eight empirical studies just
cited demonstrate anything, they demonstrate that more is involved in the
relation between conformism and ethnocentrism than is taken into account
in the usual remarks about conformity and social norms. Whatever the
conformist subjects in these studies were doing, they were *not* successfully
conforming to the average opinion of their group.[22] If conformism simply
increased actual conformity to "norms of prejudice," then those with the
strongest tendency to conform would tend to be average on prejudice, not
above average. Comparing conformists and nonconformists as groups, we
would find an inverse relation between conformism and the variance of
scores on the prejudice scales; the conformists would all be about average on
prejudice, while the nonconformists would diverge towards very high or
very low prejudice, depending upon other factors in their experience or
makeup (cf. AP, 125). This is not what we find, however. There seems to be
a simple linear relation between conformism and ethnocentrism. From the
standpoint of the usual ideas about "conformity to norms," this linear
relation is an anomaly.

No one would deny that "conformity to social norms" is extremely
widespread and extremely important. Plainly it must be part of any complete explanation of individual differences in prejudice. But it cannot
explain why conformism is associated with *extreme* rather than *average*
prejudice. This puzzle may have interested the Berkeley group, and it
should interest us.

Conformism and Authoritarianism

The relation between conformism and authoritarianism (as measured by the F scale) is even better documented than the relation between conformism and ethnic prejudice. At least a dozen different studies, which have employed several different methods to measure conformism, have supported the hypothesis that authoritarianism correlates with conformism.[23] But surprisingly little attention is given these studies in almost all the literature on authoritarianism. They are discussed in some detail in only two of the reviews of the literature and even there given little prominence.[24] Generally speaking, conformism is downplayed in presentations of the Berkeley group's concepts and theories.

Why has more attention not been given conformism in discussions of authoritarianism? Two simple reasons may be suggested immediately; a more complex one will be discussed in the following sections.

First, some researchers have failed to find significant correlations between conformism and authoritarianism. There is some doubt, therefore, about the reality of the correlation. An examination of the ten negative studies reveals, however, that they provide little real evidence against the hypothesized link between authoritarianism and conformism. Eight of the ten can be dismissed because of methodological weaknesses and failure to operationalize the relevant variables.[25] The one exceptionally good study, which will be discussed in detail in the next section, demonstrates just the opposite of what it is usually thought to demonstrate.

Second, the popular image of the authoritarian has little in common with the popular image of the conformist. Conformism suggests conformity. David Riesman's *The Lonely Crowd*, for example, an influential book published the same year as *The Authoritarian Personality*, depicts the conformist as a bland, timid, chameleon-like creature with his "radar" busily scanning the opinions of others so that he can echo whatever they are thinking.[26] If this "other-directed" person follows politics at all, it is only because he enjoys "inside dope" about politicians. At heart, he is neither progressive nor reactionary; he simply goes along with the crowd. But "authoritarianism," as already noted, suggests a domineering, authoritative manner. The ideal authoritarian should like to exercise authority; he should be bossy and pigheaded. When dealing with superiors, to be sure, he will stifle his aggressive impulses in order to maintain a facade of mildness and tractability, but with subordinates he will show his true face. He will expect them to bend silently to his will; any show of independence will provoke outraged insistence on absolute obedience. He is the natural extremist, the passionate bigot, the cranky and cantankerous radical rightist, the fanatical anticommunist, the superpatriot and persecutor of minorities, the McCarthyite and Bircher angrily attacking honorable civil servants, public-spirited local politicians, and cowering librarians. He does not simply repeat what others are saying.

How can these two images possibly be reconciled? Perhaps by distinguishing, as I have already suggested, between the tendency to conform, or
conformism, and success in conforming, or *conformity.* Those with a stronger
than average tendency to conform may become, in some circumstances and
on some issues, nonconformists precisely because of their conformism.[27]
The processes that may be at work are nicely illustrated by the study
mentioned a moment ago, which I shall now summarize.

Two Experiments

A study designed to investigate the relation between authoritarianism and
conformity, and which is usually cited as showing that "the authoritarian is
not necessarily a conformist," clearly illustrates some interesting links
between conformism, authoritarianism, and ethnocentrism.[28]

For the naive subjects of the study (students in an introductory course in
psychology), its purpose was apparently to test ability to make simple
perceptual judgments. But bogus "social norms" contrary to personal
convictions (or what could be presumed to be the students' personal convictions) were created by testing each student with three others, two of whom,
though they were presented as other subjects, were actually confederates of
the experimenters. These confederates gave their answers before the naive
subjects, and they sometimes gave false answers. Conformism was measured by counting the number of times the naive subjects yielded to the false
"norms" of the confederates.

The researchers arranged three different experimental situations and to
each one assigned twenty-five students at random. The purpose of the
experiments was to compare the behavior of authoritarians and equalitarians in these different situations of social pressure. All the students completed Form 45 of the California F scale. The researchers correlated differences in the students' behavior with differences in their personalities as
measured by the F scale.

The results from two of the three series of experiments are particularly
interesting because the experimental situations differed greatly in the kinds
of social pressure they put on the naive subjects. In the first situation
(Experimental Group I. Agreeing Confederates) the experimenters' confederates rarely disagreed among themselves (only 4 out of 32 trials) and
quite frequently agreed on a wrong or unpopular answer (9 out of 32 trials).
In the second situation (Experimental Group II. Disagreeing Confederates)
the confederates frequently disagreed among themselves (22 out of 32 trials)
and never both chose a wrong or unpopular answer. Thus in the first
situation the naive subjects presumably experienced some conflict between
their own opinions or perceptions and the frequently misleading but unani-
mous reports of the other "subjects," and in this situation, the conformists
among the naive subjects should tend to yield to these bogus "norms." In

the second situation, by contrast, there was considerable disagreement among the confederates and thus neither cause for conflict nor any "norm" to which to conform.

Table 10.1 summarizes the main results of these experiments. The first column of the table shows the correlations between authoritarianism and various aspects of the behavior of the naive subjects in the first situation. The figures show that the more authoritarian subjects, by comparison with the less authoritarian, were more likely to yield to the bogus norm provided by the confederates ($r = +.42$) and less likely to be made anxious by the situation ($r = -.51$), that is to say, by the conflict between the "social norms" and their own perceptions.[29] The figures in the second column summarize the differences between authoritarians and equalitarians in the second experimental situation. Here we find no correlation between authoritarianism and "total conformity," since it is impossible even for conformists to conform to people who disagree among themselves, and equally impossible for them to distinguish themselves from the independent-minded if social pressures never conflict with personal convictions. The authoritarians did, however, distinguish themselves from the equalitarians by their greater tendency to conform to one or the other of the disagreeing confederates, as shown by the correlation of $+.58$ between authoritarianism and "inequality of conformity." Authoritarians also tended to be more aware of the disagreements between the confederates, as shown by the correlation of $+.44$ between F-scale scores and the subjects' estimates of the number of disagreements between the other subjects being tested (i.e., the confederates). Finally, the negative correlation between authoritarianism and anxiety disappears: those high and low on authoritarianism seem to have been affected in the same way, on the average, by the various conflicts in this second situation.

The interpretation of social psychological experiments is a hazardous business, but these results can be taken as evidence that authoritarians (i.e.,

Table 10.1 Correlations between Authoritarianism and Response to Pressures to Conform

	Experimental Treatment	
Response Measure	Group I	Group II
Total Conformity	$+.42$*	$-.16$
Inequality of Conformity	$-.09$	$+.58$**
Perception of Disagreement	$-.12$	$+.44$*
Anxiety	$-.51$*	$-.01$

SOURCE: Steiner and Johnson, "Authoritarianism and Conformity," p. 29. The labeling of the third dependent variable, awareness of disagreements between the confederates, has been changed to simplify the explanation of the results.
* $p < .05$
** $p < .01$

those who score high on the F scale) tend to be conformists. They are unusually disposed to agree with others. If they are put in a situation where their own opinions conflict with the opinions of their associates, they will tend to resolve this conflict by changing their own opinions rather than by trying to change those of their associates. Yielding seems to ward off anxiety—presumably anxiety that faithfulness to personal convictions, if it were to produce disagreement with others, would lead to isolation and loneliness.

In this, authoritarians may be like everyone else, only more so. Yielding, which is remarkably common in Asch-type experiments, is presumably more common still, among equalitarians as well as authoritarians, outside the psychological laboratory, where the stimuli are more ambiguous, the "confederates" more numerous, and the rewards and punishments they control more important.

But simple yielding depends upon agreement among associates. If a conformist's associates disagree among themselves, then he is in a quandary, for he cannot simultaneously please them all. The second series of experiments represents this possibility. Here too the authoritarian, or conformist, seems to display a common way of coping to an unusual degree. He is more aware than the equalitarian of the disagreements among his associates (the confederates), but rather than being liberated by these disagreements, he immediately takes sides and acts as if the opinions of the side he chose were unquestionably correct.

The second experimental situation is a model of the modern world of increasing contact between different nations and cultures. The authoritarian in this situation is the ethnocentrist who magnifies the differences between his own group and other groups, and who then takes sides, accepting uncritically the institutions and values of his own group and insisting that others do likewise. He avoids contact with outsiders and tries to ensure that others do so as well, in order that their consensus not be weakened by disruptive contacts with alien customs and values.

From this perspective, ethnocentrism is the conformist's response to the conformist's dilemma in a world of diversity—with whom is one to conform? On questions having to do with ethnic loyalties and ethnic prejudices, then, conformism finds expression, not in conformity to "norms of ethnocentrism," whatever these may happen to be, but in greater than average ethnocentrism. When it comes to ethnocentrism, the conformists take the lead.

How the F Scale Works

This account of authoritarianism and ethnocentrism differs from the debunking "ideological" explanation outlined earlier in one key respect: it assumes that the F scale measures conformism directly and not just through conservatism. The point at issue will be clearest if we examine three causal diagrams.

According to the Berkeley group's theory (first panel of figure 10.1), ego weakness leads to acceptance of various odd opinions (or "F beliefs"), which reflect personality dynamics, and also to a tendency to reject all possible outgroups ("ethnocentrism"). The relevant internal dynamics are measured by the F scale; ethnocentrism is measured by the E scale. There is a strong correlation between scores on the two scales because both are

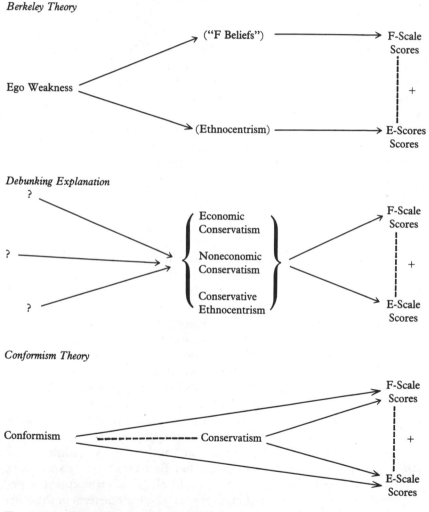

Figure 10.1   Three Theories of Authoritarianism

ultimately caused by ego weakness. Authoritarianism is not an *ideological* but rather a *psychological* syndrome.

According to the debunking explanation (second panel of figure 10.1), the E and F scales are just different ways of tapping a single conservative ideological syndrome. A variety of different personality variables may help determine acceptance or rejection of conservative beliefs, and conformism may be among these determining variables, but there is no need to invoke any recondite hypotheses about personality structure to explain the observed correlation between E and F—nor, for that matter, to explain the *absence* of such correlations when they are not found. The F scale does not measure any basic structure or dimension of personality, and certainly not the elusive quality of "ego weakness," but only the acceptance or rejection of conservative opinions. It is not a test of personality disguised as a public opinion questionnaire; it is a test of opinion that has been disguised (for psychologists) as a test of personality. Similarly, the E scale does not measure ethnocentrism as defined by the Berkeley group; it measures only *conservative* ethnocentrism. A convention exists according to which *cosmopolitan* ethnocentrism (i.e., identification with minority groups, criticism of dominant groups, support for liberal or radical factions, hostility towards their opponents, and so on) is called "genuine patriotism" or "militancy," rather than "ethnocentrism," so that negative correlations between these prejudices and F-scale authoritarianism can be regarded as support for the basic theory.

Substituting "unenlightened culture" for "conservatism," and adding the hypothesis that differences in conservatism are mainly the result of differences in formal education, we have Selznick and Steinberg's account of authoritarianism (see above, pp. 95-97). The substitution is tendentious, and the hypothesis, as noted earlier, is refuted by the evidence they cite. Otherwise Selznick and Steinberg provide a simple and appealing theory of authoritarianism.

The theory of authoritarianism developed in this chapter (and summarized by the third panel of figure 10.1) assumes that at least one personality variable, conformism, has a direct relation with both ethnocentrism and F-scale authoritarianism. The argument for assuming a connection between conformism and ethnocentrism has already been made; it remains to outline an argument for thinking that conformism has an effect on F-scale scores not fully explained by the "conservative ideological content" of the F scale.

No one should doubt, of course, that conformism has an effect on F-scale scores because of the "ideological content" of the scale. Conformism and conservatism are in a sense indistinguishable. Both are shown by acceptance of the conventional opinions or "dominant ideology" of a particular country or period. It is often a matter of indifference whether one term or the other is used to label the dimension of individual differences in acceptance or rejection of such opinions.[30] Only in cross-cultural studies are the two things—conservatism as a set of opinions and conformism as a personality trait—easily separated. Such studies make clear that there are differences between, say, Leninist conservatism and Jeffersonian conservatism, and they help us to recognize that there is no contradiction in saying that a particular individual may accept, from conformist motives, the demands of groups or nations constituted on the basis of liberal, radical, or generally nonconservative principles. There is probably no connection, in general, between conformism and acceptance of the principles favored by conservative Americans today, but there is almost certainly an empirical correlation among contemporary Americans. It is somewhat Byzantine, therefore, to quarrel about how much of the variance in F-scale scores should be attributed to conformism and how much to conservatism.

Nonetheless the Byzantine literature on response sets and styles suggests one reason for thinking that something broader than tough-minded garden-variety noneconomic (Western) conservatism is measured by the F scale. The relevant argument is the one offered by those who think that the F scale is a good measure of authoritarianism because it is a good measure of acquiescence response set. Acquiescence, they say, is precisely the "conventionalism" and "authoritarian submission" of the authoritarian syndrome.

> We may use the theory of authoritarianism itself to predict that "authoritarians" will tend to agree. It [follows] that a scale designed so that the authoritarian can both like its attitudinal [or ideological] contents and can *also* fulfill his yen to agree—such a scale [e.g., the original F scale] should be extra discriminating.[31]

Or as a later group of writers put it:

> Psychologically, disagreeing requires more "ego strength," "emotional security," and "self-confidence" than does the act of agreeing. . . . Psychologically, agreeing may mean yielding to the authority of the printed word or a similar submission to the power and plausibility of the social context in which the test is given. . . . The psychological meaning of acquiescence resembles that of authoritarianism, conformity, [and] low ego strength.[32]

The researchers who made these statements demonstrated, through their operational definitions of acquiescence and authoritariansim, that there is indeed a connection between the two. Where they went astray, it seems, was in their theoretical characterization of the "stimulus situation" that elicits the authoritarian's tendency to agree.

"Acquiescence response set" is defined as a tendency to agree with all statements found in questionnaires regardless of the content of these statements. As noted earlier (above, pp. 91-95), there is no good reason to think that most people depart very far from "average" on such a dimension. The psychologists who studied acquiescence were surely on the wrong track when they speculated about "the authority of the printed word" or "submission to the power and plausibility of the social context in which a test is given" (whatever that means). There is simply no evidence for such a broadly conceived "acquiescence response set."

There may, however, be substantial individual differences in reactions to sweeping generalizations about human nature and society—differences that are not wholly accounted for by the "ideological content" of these statements. If the statements are *aphorisms* or *apothegms* or *bromides* or *clichés* or *commonplaces* or *maxims* or *platitudes* or *saws*, agreement may reveal something broader than, and in a sense prior to, ideological commitment, namely, a person's tendency to find the grain of truth in popular generalizations. Disagreement may indicate the opposite: a settled tendency to react critically to conventional wisdom and to search for its limitations and weak spots. Consider for a moment two different reactions to two opposite proverbs:

"He who hesitates is lost."

"Look before you leap."

Confronted with the first proverb, the "acquiescent" authoritarian might think of situations where immediate action saves time and money in the long run ("a stitch in time saves nine"), and hence agree, while his "critical" cousin might think of situations where "haste makes waste" and it is necessary to "look before you leap." Confronted with the second proverb, the "acquiescent" subject might again agree, thinking of situations where the right action will be found only after long thought and reflection, while the "critical" one might again disagree, this time thinking of situations where "he who hesitates is lost." This difference, between a "critical" and an "acquiescent" temperament or attitude of mind, may be one of the main things measured by agreement or disagreement with a large number of commonplaces with diverse content.

Studies of acquiescence have shown (a) that scales consisting of such statements reliably measure individual differences along some dimension and (b) that this dimension correlates significantly with authoritarianism as measured by the F scale.[33] It is not clear that these differences have anything to do with conformism, but it is plausible to suppose that they do.[34]

It seems, in short, that when the F scale worked, it did so partly because it measured conservatism (its statements were not just any clichés, but as

Edward Shils put it, "clichés abominated by 'progressive intellectuals'") and partly because it measured conformism (its statements were clichés, and agreement was always the authoritarian response). If this explanation is sound, the formula for generating new F-scale items is very simple. It has a little to do with "conservative ideology," a lot to do with conventionalism, and nothing whatever to do with "authoritarianism" or psychopathology. The rule is: assemble a large collection of conservative-sounding clichés; sum or average the number of times subjects agree; and the result will be a reliable measure of authoritarianism.

Ego Weakness vs. Conformism

Why then did the Berkeley group put so much emphasis on "authoritarianism" and "ego weakness," with all their misleading connotations? If their great achievement was to see the connection between ethnocentrism and conformism, why did they not present their insight more clearly? Why was their empirical research not more clearly designed to test its validity and to provide supporting evidence?

A moment's reflection provides an answer. The conformism-ethnocentrism hypothesis just outlined coexisted uneasily in their thought with another radically different hypothesis, namely, that ethnocentrism is essentially a "psychological" problem and that it has nothing to do fundamentally with ethnic groups or ethnic differences. The fame of the California studies, and their significance for sociology and social psychology, rests on their success in popularizing this second hypothesis, which took the ethnicity out of ethnocentrism.

The fundamental cause of ethnocentrism, the Berkeley group suggest, is the fear and hostility of the ethnocentric person, not the variations in culture that distinguish one ethnic group from another. Ethnocentrism, Levinson says at one point, has to do "primarily with psychological trends within the ethnocentrist rather than with the actual characteristics of the outgroups" (AP, 149). Adorno was of the opinion that "prejudice, according to its intrinsic content, is but superficially, if at all, related to the specific nature of its object" (AP, 612). According to this line of thought, differences in customs and values are important only because they formally mark off one group from another; the differences themselves have no real significance. The Berkeley group never stated this unconventional view unequivocally, but it clearly dominated their thinking.

To establish these conclusions the Berkeley group tried to show that ethnocentrism is a single, undifferentiated disposition and that it results from a pathological structure of personality. Ethnocentric attitudes could represent a more or less realistic reaction to the real characteristics of other groups (rather than an irrational use of purely formal distinctions between ingroups and outgroups, having nothing to do with the substance of ethnicity) only if bigots were selective in their antipathies and if they were typically people who had strongly internalized the norms and values of relevant ingroups. If bigotry is general, and if bigots are typically those who have no real understanding of or respect for the values of their ingroups, then ethnic differences must not be the basic cause of ethnocentrism, but only pretexts for behavior that has other motives.

The Berkeley group spent relatively little time establishing the generality of ethnocentrism, but they never denied the difficulty of showing its relation to moral weakness and psychopathology. They devoted the bulk of their research to working out, on the basis of Freudian theory, within a Marxist framework, the detailed differences between genuine and "pseudo" loyalties. The key consideration, not surprisingly, was the strength of the ego.

To show that ethnocentrism is essentially the result of a defect in personality, and not of genuine commitment to moral values, the Berkeley group had to show that ego weakness can be assessed independently of ethnocentric attitudes, and then that it is, in fact, associated with ethnocentrism. The F scale is the first method of assessment they presented, and it provided their most impressive supporting evidence. The second method is implicit in Part II of their book, which shows how data from clinical interviews can be analyzed objectively and quantitatively to yield an indication of the relevant trends in personality. Regardless of the method of assessment, there seem to be strong correlations between ethnocentric attitudes and personality. The implication is clear: ethnocentrism has little to do with the characteristics of the groups against which hostility is directed, and much to do with the irrational, inhibited, and resentful mode of existence of the authoritarian personality type. The California studies culminated in a contrast between two extreme types of personality, the weak and resentful authoritarian type and the strong and compassionate democratic type. The essential difference between these two types was the different ways that they had internalized moral values, due to differences in ego strength. The most essential feature of the authoritarian personality, it seemed, was "a lack of integration between the moral agencies by which the subject lives and the rest of his personality" (AP, 234). In short, the democrat equalitarian, with the strong ego, was the genuinely moral person, while the authoritarian, with the weak ego, was the envious and unreliable hypocrite.

The studies reported here provide no support for this line of reasoning. Indeed, the more we ponder the results of these studies, the more we shall see merit in the opposite theory about ethnocentrism—that it has something to do with ethnicity.

A Conjecture

If the "ego weakness" characteristic of the bigoted personality is essentially conformism, then F-scale authoritarianism may correlate with nationalism only when the nationalism in question is directed against outsiders whose customs and values differ in important ways from those of the national ingroup. Contact with such outsiders tends to disrupt the consensus among national or ethnic ingroups that conformists value. Nationalist policies (national independence, restrictions on travel and immigration, discrimination against foreigners, loyalty tests, indoctrination in schools, military power, economic autarky, etc.) provide some real protection against this disruption. Nationalism directed against such outgroups should appeal to conformists, or authoritarians, and they should gravitate to the nationalist camp. When a nationalist movement is itself seen as a source of disruptive change—the anticolonial movements of the third world and the mininationalist movements of the first world may provide examples—then authoritarianism should correlate *negatively* with support for the movement. If the customs and values of the relevant ingroups and outgroups differ only slightly, in ways that most people consider unimportant and that do not raise fundamental moral or political issues, or if much more important moral and political differences cut across the formal distinction between ingroup and outgroup, then authoritarians should be no more likely than others to make nationalist demands or to support a nationalist movement. Under these circumstances, nationalism and authoritarianism should be unrelated variables.

These hypotheses provide a possible explanation for what have hitherto been unexplained facts, namely, that authoritarianism, as measured by the F scale, correlates with nationalist attitudes among Americans but not, generally speaking, with nationalist attitudes among Canadians.

As suggested earlier, the American studies show a correlation between authoritarianism and anticommunist nationalism. The correlation was found, we could say, because the communist countries were just the right sort of "outgroup" to evoke the ethnocentric reaction of conformists. Communist revolution has been the great symbol for new beginnings during the past hundred years. It represents, as does any revolution, the overthrow of existing governments, but it also represents the violent establishment of a wholly new order, the liquidation of the old ruling class, official atheism and the suppression of religion, the liberation of envy and other previously repressed passions, the abolition of private property, the weakening of the family, and generally the most rapid possible advance towards absolute freedom and equality. During the past twenty years, to be sure, popular images of communism have changed somewhat. The Western countries have moved steadily left, and the communist bloc has lost most of its revolutionary élan. The communist giants, the Soviet Union and communist China, have dedicated themselves to economic growth and mutual vilification rather than to world revolution. Coexistence and détente have tended to make communism merely another "industrial system." Nonetheless "communism" still symbolizes for the unsophisticated all that threatens to disrupt the consensus that authoritarians value, because of their sensitivity to external cues, and that critical intellectuals and nonconformists scorn.

The present study shows essentially no correlations between authoritarianism and the kinds of nationalism—except perhaps for anticommunist nationalism—found in Canada and of most interest to Canadians. No correlations were found, we could say, because the relevant outgroups—English and French Canadians, Americans, Britons, and Frenchmen—simply do not differ in any fundamental or disturbing ways from the relevant ingroups—English and French Canadians. And when there are no important differences between ingroups and outgroups, so that contact between them does not raise any serious moral or political issues, then we should not expect any correlations, either positive or negative, between authoritarianism and nationalism. Nationalist demands that result from a desire to preserve more or less trivial differences between nations, or that reflect the narrow economic interests of a local bureaucratic elite, should have no special appeal to authoritarians.

These conjectures suggest a simple hypothesis, *that the authoritarian's involvement in national or ethnic conflict is proportional to the gravity of the issues at stake*. Admittedly there is something paradoxical in this way of speaking about nationalism and personality, but it is not contradictory. Authoritarianism, in the sense of rigid orthodoxy and compulsive conformity to tradition, is practically the definition of irrationality in political and social thinking. Yet the types of nationalism with a real ethnic or cultural basis, and with a strong appeal, therefore, to the close-minded and conventional authoritarian, may generally make more sense politically than the empty nationalisms that get a clean bill of health from the psychologists. The apparent contradiction is resolved by recognizing that the demands of the intellectual life sometimes conflict with the legitimate demands of society. Only those who are open-minded can rise above common opinion, but a country demands and is protected by a certain close-mindedness among its citizens.

Conclusions

The Berkeley group addressed themselves to all reasonable men willing to be persuaded by a systematic analysis of facts. Their portrait of the bigot was unflattering, but they obviously meant it to be value-free in the sense of objectively valid. They did not present it as merely the expression of their own feelings, nor did they present it in the spirit of partisanship, as merely a clever caricature of their political enemies, to be used to manipulate the unenlightened. They presented it, and it has been generally accepted, as a product of the objective methods of social science. They claimed, in effect, that an unbiased examination of all the relevant facts would convince any reasonable man of the fundamental validity of their main hypotheses.

Most of the critical literature since 1950 has quite properly focused on the empirical evidence for their hypotheses. Did the Berkeley group get the relevant facts right? This book has tried to throw some new light on that question. It has presented some new facts, and highlighted some old but neglected ones, in an effort to show that the relevant facts are fundamentally different from what they seemed to be in the wake of the California studies, and that they require a different interpretation from what the Berkeley group offered. Ethnocentrism now appears more complicated than it did initially. There is no general factor of ethnocentrism: people have different reactions to different ethnic and national groups. Ethnocentric attitudes are sometimes closely related to authoritarianism as measured by the F scale, but sometimes not. F-scale authoritarianism seems to have more to do with conventionalism and conformism than with "ego weakness" and psychopathology. It no longer seems necessary that conformists be insensitive to the real differences between different ethnic groups; indeed, a little reflection shows that they should be more sensitive than others to such differences. The preceding chapters thus suggest that we abandon the Berkeley group's broad concepts of ethnocentrism and authoritarianism; that we speak instead of particular prejudices or loyalties and related antipathies; that we regard the F scale as a measure of conservatism and conformism rather than conservatism and "ego weakness" or "acquiescence response set"; and that we expect some prejudices, but not all of them, to be linked to conformism. There appears to be no interesting general relationship between all ethnic prejudices and any fundamental "structure of personality." *The Authoritarian Personality*, it now seems, tried to solve a nonexistent problem (the problem of *the* relation between prejudice and personality) on the basis of bogus concepts (ethnocentrism and authoritarianism).

These banal conclusions would finish the discussion of *The Authoritarian Personality* were it simply a book about bigotry and were its methods (or approach) uncontroversial. It is not and they are not. It is a book about democracy as well as about bigotry, and it offers a new and apparently scientific analysis of the relations between reason and democracy, based on contemporary psychological theory and objective psychological research. On an important point it thus implicitly claims superiority to the long tradition of political philosophy. One more chapter is necessary, therefore, in which the Berkeley group's account of the antidemocratic type will be reviewed and certain limitations of their "scientific" approach to political questions will be considered.

11

Democracy and the Antidemocratic Type

> Had the orator to praise Athenians among Peloponnesians, or Pelo-
> ponnesians among Athenians, he must be a good rhetorician who could
> succeed and gain credit. But there is no difficulty in a man's winning
> applause when he is contending for fame among the persons who are
> being praised.
>
> Plato, *Menexenus*

The California studies were designed to throw light on the relation between ethnic prejudice and personality, but the Berkeley group did not wish to confine themselves to this narrow theme. Their ambition was to discuss, not just ethnic prejudice, but the antidemocratic personality. They hoped to delineate "the potentially fascist individual, one whose structure is such as to render him particularly susceptible to antidemocratic propaganda" (AP, 1). Their research revealed that the potential fascist, or anti-Semite, was a conservative who upheld conventional values and old-fashioned morality because he had a weak ego. The cause of ego weakness was inhibited and ego-alien sexuality, due to the severity of parental blocking of childhood sexuality and the resulting resolution of the Oedipus complex. Parents blocked their children's sexuality because they wanted to have nice children who would compete successfully in a society of greedy individualists. What emerged from the California studies, then, was a portrait of a "new 'anthropological' type," the antidemocratic, protofascist, or authoritarian personality. This new type was contrasted with the equalitarian or democratic type. The former, the Berkeley group maintained, provides the human basis for fascism; the latter, for progress and democracy.

Thus the Berkeley group began their concluding chapter by reiterating their working hypothesis:

The most crucial result of the present study, as it seems to the authors, is the demonstration of close correspondence in the type of approach and outlook a subject is likely to have in a great variety of areas, ranging from the most intimate features of family and sex adjustment through relationships to other people in general, to religion and to social and political philosophy. (AP, 971)

Then they summarized very briefly the two main types found in their research. First, the antidemocratic type:

Thus a basically hierarchical, authoritarian, exploitively dependent parent-child relationship is apt to carry over into a power-oriented, exploitively dependent attitude toward one's sex partner and one's God and may well culminate in a political philosophy and social outlook which has no room for anything but a desperate clinging to what appears to be strong and a disdainful rejection of whatever is relegated to the bottom. The inherent dramatization likewise extends from the parent-child dichotomy to the dichotomous conception of sex roles and of moral values, as well as to a dichotomous handling of social relations as manifested especially in the formation of stereotypes and of ingroup-outgroup cleavages. Conventionality, rigidity, repressive denial, and the ensuing breakthrough of one's weakness, fear and dependency are but other aspects of the same fundamental personality pattern, and they can be observed in personal life as well as in attitudes toward religion and social issues. (AP, 971)

The contrasting equalitarian or democratic type was more briefly described:

On the other hand there is a pattern characterized chiefly by affectionate, basically equalitarian, permissive interpersonal relationships. This pattern encompasses attitudes within the family and toward the opposite sex, as well as an internalization of religious and social values. Greater flexibility and the potentiality for more genuine satisfactions appear as results of this basic attitude. (AP, 971)

The authors warned that the homogeneity and distinctiveness of the two extremes should not be exaggerated; they must not be regarded as *absolutes*. "They emerge as a result of statistical analysis and thus have to be considered as syndromes of correlated and dynamically related factors," and they "leave plenty of room for variations of specific features" (AP, 971-72). These remarks and similar ones scattered through the 990 pages of the book recognized the limitations of survey methods and the difficulty of pressing all humanity into two pigeonholes.[1] Nonetheless it is no real distortion of the Berkeley group's work to reduce their complex and qualified generalizations to the following stark dichotomy:

Type A	*Type E*
fascistic	democratic
ethnocentric	humanitarian
conservative	liberal, radical
conformist	independent
punitive, moralistic	tolerant
weak ego	strong ego
sexually repressed	sexually liberated

How Much Simplification?

A number of questions can be raised about this simple dichotomy. Is it fundamentally sound, or is it a "dramatization" of differences better described in some other way? Is it an example of a "pervasive ingroup-outgroup distinction," and are those who employ it guilty of ethnocentrism? Is the distinction between fascistic and democratic the same as the distinction between ethnocentric and humanitarian? Is one of the characteristic features of democratic man really independence of mind, or does egalitarianism encourage conformism? Do fascists have a corner on moralism, or are democrats sometimes also moralistic (about ethnocentrism, for example)? What is the relation between unreason in politics and "ego weakness" in sexual morality? Eros and Logos may belong together, but do they both belong to democracy? In short, why a *dichotomy?* Why not three major types, or four, or five? Is there any good reason for supposing that the genus *homo politicus* divides naturally into only two species, *fascistic* and *democratic?* Or is this just a contemporary prejudice (due perhaps to intolerance of ambiguity)? Would some more complex typology be better suited to describing the naturally existing types (assuming there are such)? Would it perhaps be truer to the facts to think of a large number of *homo vulgaris* and a few more exotic types?

Many critics have disputed this or that detail of the Berkeley group's typology, but only Edward Shils seems to have questioned the usefulness of their broad contrast between democratic (left-wing) and antidemocratic (right-wing) types. He began his famous critique of *The Authoritarian Personality* with a brief explanation of the standard Right-Left dichotomy.[2] On the right is conservatism—belief in private property and the legitimacy of profits; hostility towards democracy and trade unions; repugnance for social welfare legislation; disapproval of state regulation of the economy; and generally, acceptance of inequality. On the left is radicalism—derogation of private property, the market economy, and pecuniary ambition; espousal of democracy, equality, collectivism, and humanitarianism; belief in progress; antagonism towards religious institutions and beliefs; and faith in science as the liberator and benefactor of mankind. As Shils explained, each of these main political positions can be treated as a coherent and indissoluble unity, but each also admits of variations in both directions. To the right of conservatism there is reaction; to the left of radicalism lie revolutionary socialism and anarchism; and between the two, "the center." Every political program or political outlook, according to those who defend the dichotomy, can be placed on this scale and fairly judged. "In the decades surrounding the turn of the century in Continental political life this simplification did have a certain descriptive truth," Shils conceded, but he questioned whether it was any longer useful, except for purely partisan purposes, and he suggested that the California studies were vitiated by the Berkeley group's failure to appreciate the limitations of the Right-Left dichotomy.[3]

Even during the nineteenth century, as Shils pointed out, Tory Radicalism in Great Britain and Bismarck's social legislation in Germany had strained the simple dichotomy of Right and Left. During the present century the radical features of fascism and the conservative backsliding of Soviet communism (the purges, the abortion laws, the introduction of school fees, the restriction of progressive education, the persistence and growth of pronounced inequalities in income and status, the reemergence of patriotism as an official policy) have caused the scheme to break down altogether. The old unities of Right and Left, and the notion of a gradual transition from one to the other, no longer have much relation to the real world, in which the diverse elements of conservative and radical ideology have been recombined in constellations that had not been imagined for many a year.

> Hostility towards private property [is] now seen to be capable of combination with anti-Semitism, inequality, the repression of civil liberties, etc. Welfare legislation [is] seen to enter into combination with political oligarchy, the elimination of civil liberties [combines] with an increase in equalitarianism. In short, what had once appeared to be a simple unidimensional scheme now [turns] out to be a complicated multidimensional pattern in which there [are] many different political positions. . . . [And] above all, the two poles of the continuum Right and Left which were once deemed incompatible and mutually antagonistic [are seen] to overlap in many very striking respects.[4]

Old prejudices die hard, however, and Shils lamented that many academics are still in the grip of the obsolete belief that all political philosophies can be described by their location on the Right-Left continuum.

> Even those of us who have seen the spurious nature of the polarity of "Right" and "Left" still find it hard to dispense with it. There has been no re-coalescence or regrouping of the constituent ideas of our political outlook which is at once sufficiently simple and convenient for our use. In general conversation we still use these terms although we know that they are at most a shorthand which will have to be replaced by particulars as soon as the discussion is joined.[5]

Having made these general points, Shils then tried to show that the Berkeley group were sensitive to the pathologies of the extreme Right, but blind to the same pathologies on the extreme Left. There is a left-wing authoritarianism, he contended, that is fundamentally the same as the right-wing authoritarianism analyzed by the Berkeley group. "The investigators . . . failed to observe that at the Left pole of their continuum, there is to be found an authoritarianism impressively like the authoritarianism of the Right."[6] A careful scrutiny of the data from the clinical interviews makes the basic similarities between the two authoritarianisms "vividly apparent," Shils claimed. Because the Berkeley group ignored these similarities, they blurred "the distinction between Leftists authoritarians and reasonable persons of humanitarian, equalitarian dispositions."[7] Distracted by the superficial differences between the extreme Right and the extreme Left, they unwittingly attributed the virtues of the best liberal democrats to fanatical communists. Or perhaps they deviously encouraged a prejudice, that the further left a person was, the healthier and more rational he must be. At any rate, according to Shils, both Left and Right extremists tend to be psychologically flawed and "authoritarian" (or "paranoid") by comparison with moderate democrats, liberal or conservative.

This standard criticism, which Shils expressed in a particularly clear and forceful way, has been accepted by many, and it has stimulated a great deal of empirical research,[8] but it is to some extent self-contradictory. Shils argued that the dichotomous classification of political positions is a gross simplification that "will have to be replaced by particulars as soon as the discussion is joined," but he also argued that the extreme Left is fundamentally the same as the extreme Right. The two arguments tended to work at cross-purposes, and Shils's attempt to put communists in the same category, psychologically, as fascists, in opposition to moderate democrats, unfortunately overshadowed his attempt to break out of a dichotomous view of the political world. The upshot of his criticisms was merely the replacement of one dubious dichotomy (Right vs. Left, or protofascists vs.

equalitarians) by another (left and right "authoritarians" vs. "open-minded" or "tender-minded" democrats).

Shils's argument about excessive simplification is more interesting than his argument about the authoritarianism of communists. What he plainly needed, as he himself seems to have recognized, was a richer simplification or typology of personalities and political outlooks than the outmoded Right-Left dichotomy provides. A crude dichotomy, it had served as long as politics "centered . . . around the ideals of the Liberal Enlightenment and the 'ideas of 1789',"⁹ but it was not comprehensive.

Where should we look for a more adequate typology? Shils did not say, and as a social scientist he does not seem to have felt any very pressing need to consider writers who antedated 1789, or more generally, the modern preoccupation with the conflict between democracy and oligarchy. But if the Berkeley group's basic problem was "narrowness of political imagination" and inability to let go of a "deforming intellectual tradition," then the remedy may lie in scholarly pursuits that will awaken a lively interest in much earlier and almost forgotten ways of seeing ourselves and our world. For this reason perhaps the oldest theories of politics and psychology and the most alien may have the most to teach us. There is no better way of seeing the basic problems of *The Authoritarian Personality*, I shall argue, than by returning to the very beginnings of systematic thought about politics and psychology, in the Platonic dialogues, and comparing the Berkeley group's dichotomy with Socrates' fivefold typology in the *Republic*. We shall find there some remarkable anticipations of recent discoveries and also a basic framework or "paradigm" that is radically different from that of *The Authoritarian Personality*.

A Platonic Perspective

As every undergraduate should know, Plato's Socrates distinguishes three parts in the soul, an appetitive part (suggested originally by the productive and reproductive activities of men and women in society), an honor-loving, angry, or "spirited" part (suggested by the need for "guardians" in an affluent city, and the ethnocentric and authoritarian qualities they must have), and finally, a reasoning or "calculating" part (suggested by the role of educators in forming the guardians and ordinary citizens). The first part corresponds roughly to the Freudian id; the second part is perhaps analogous to the Freudian superego; the third part is something like the Freudian ego. In books VIII and IX of the *Republic* Socrates outlines five regimes: the rule of the philosophers, never yet attained; conventional aristocracy, represented by the Spartan constitution; oligarchy, or the rule of the wealthy, perhaps the most common constitution; democracy, or popular rule; and tyranny, the lawless rule of one man in the name of the people. Five types of character correspond to these five regimes: the philosophical, timocratic, oligarchic, democratic, and tyrannical types.

Among Socrates' five types, one bears a striking resemblance, at least on the surface, to the contemporary conception of the authoritarian. This is the timocratic type, corresponding to the conventionally aristocratic or Spartan regime.

> "Who, then, is the man corresponding to this regime? How did he come into being and what sort of man is he?"
>
> "I suppose," said Adeimantus, "that as far as love of victory goes, he'd be somewhere near to Glaucon here."
>
> "Perhaps in that," I said, "but in these other respects his nature does not, in my opinion, correspond to Glaucon's."
>
> "Which respects?"
>
> "He must be more stubborn," I said, "and somewhat less apt at music although he loves it, and must be a lover of hearing although he's by no means skilled in rhetoric. With slaves such a man would be brutal, not merely despising slaves as the adequately educated man does. But with freemen he would be tame and to rulers most obedient. He is a lover of ruling and of honor, not basing his claim to rule on speaking or anything of the sort, but on warlike deeds and everything connected with war; he is a lover of gymnastic and the hunt."
>
> "Yes," he said, "that is the disposition belonging to this regime."
>
> "Wouldn't such a man," I said, "when he is young also despise money, but as he grows older take ever more delight in participating in the money-lover's nature and not be pure in his attachment to virtue, having been abandoned by the best guardian?"
>
> "What's that?" Adeimantus said.
>
> "Argument mixed with music," I said. "It alone, when it is present, dwells within the one possessing it as a savior of virtue throughout life."
>
> "What you say is fine," he said. (*Republic*, 548d–49b)[10]

There are at least four similarities here worth noting. First, there is the timocrat's obedience to rulers and brutality with slaves—"authoritarian submission" and "authoritarian aggression" in the current terminology. Second, there is his love of warlike deeds and manly activities—what we might today call "power and 'toughness'." Third, there is his stubbornness and lack of skill in music and rhetoric, which might be identified with some of the traits the Berkeley group discussed under "anti-intraception" and "superstition and stereotypy." Finally, there is the timocrat's secret love of money, which shows that his attachment to virtue is not pure; this is perhaps a simple way of describing what we would now diagnose scientifically as "conventionalism, an externalized superego, and rigid adherence to conventional, middle-class values."

The similarities between the contemporary authoritarian and the Platonic timocrat are more than just superficial; there are fundamental similarities, as well as fundamental differences, between the two types. These similarities and differences will be clearest if we first consider ego strength and ego weakness.

According to the Berkeley group's theory, derived from Reich and Fromm, all the surface traits of the authoritarian personality reflect underdevelopment of the ego, "that part of the personality which appreciates reality, integrates the other parts, and operates with the most conscious awareness" (AP, 11). A weak ego means an unregulated conflict between the appetitive part of the psyche, the id, and that part which incorporates society's restraints on natural egoism, the superego. Unable to acknowledge his own desires without overwhelming anxiety, and too weak, therefore, to challenge society's restraints on the satisfaction of those desires, the authoritarian simply conforms to the demands of others. He externalizes his conscience. He turns over the management of his psyche to the strongest external powers in his society, and he demands a similar slavish submission from others. He lives under a rule of excessive and irrational inhibitions, dominated by an unconscious and quite irrational fear of offending authority, a fear implanted during childhood by terrifying threats of abandonment or castration. His renunciations are not compensated by the satisfaction of any other desires, such as the desire for knowledge or the desire for public honor and glory. They are simply a loss, hence his secret envy and resentment and his dangerous inclination to attack all whom he suspects of "getting away with something" (AP, 232–34). In the behavior and attitudes of the authoritarian type we see the effects of a psychological mechanism that may be more or less rational from the standpoint of society—or at least "repressive bourgeois" society—but that generally causes unhappiness in individuals and conflict between groups. To escape from these crippling internal and external conflicts, the fully mature person must have a strong ego, one strong enough to appraise correctly the real risks he runs seeking the fullest possible satisfaction of his "primitive emotional needs" (AP, 5).

If we now turn to the timocratic type, we find that contentiousness, pride, irascibility, and ambition are his most striking traits, and that they reflect, according to the account in the *Republic*, an unresolved conflict between the demands of the rational or calculating part of the soul and the appetitive part, such that the spirited, aggressive, honor-loving part is able to determine his outlook and pursuits (Rep, 550a–b). Like the Berkeley group, then, Socrates points to a certain weakness in the rational part of the soul when he defines the timocratic-authoritarian type, but unlike them, Socrates does not imply that strengthening the timocrat's ego would necessarily change the timocrat into a democrat. In Socrates' typology "ego strength" seems to be characteristic, not of the democrat, but in different ways of the philosopher and the tyrant. What sets the timocrat apart from all the other types is his spiritedness: he represses all his bodily appetites for the sake of winning high office and being honored by his compatriots. The oligarch, by contrast, pursues wealth rather than glory, and he liberates the "necessary" appetites that are compatible with money-making.[11] The democrat, like the oligarch, favors the bodily appetites over the desire for honor, but he makes no distinction between necessary and unnecessary desires: he pursues whatever pleasures happen to attract him at the moment, and he believes in the equal right of everyone else to do the same. The last type, the tyrant, seeks the fullest possible satisfaction of all his appetites, and he recognizes that his satisfactions will increase to the degree that he is able to dominate and exploit others.

A related comparison has to do with the treatment of sexual liberation in the two typologies. According to the Berkeley group, the authoritarian represses and denies, while the equalitarian acknowledges and accepts "id impulses." In the Platonic typology, as just suggested, this difference corresponds to the key difference between the oligarchic and the democratic types. The oligarch tolerates only the "necessary" desires connected with money-making; he represses all the pleasures that are spendthrift and that do not conduce to money-making; he is "stingy and a toiler, satisfying only his necessary desires and not providing for other expenditures, but enslaving the other desires as vanities" (Rep, 554a). The democrat, by contrast, is said to treat all his pleasures equally. "To whichever one happens along, as though it were chosen by lot, he hands over the rule within himself until it is satisfied; and then again to another, dishonoring none but fostering them all on the basis of equality" (Rep, 561b). The idea that there are good and bad desires, and honorable and shameful pleasures, the democrat simply denies. "He shakes his head at all this and says that all are alike and must be honored on an equal basis" (Rep, 561c). He does not, like the timocrat, repress his unruly erotic desires for the sake of respectability, nor like the oligarch does he repress them for the sake of a stingy concentration on material accumulation. But he does not go so far in his devotion to Eros as the tyrant, who seems, in Socrates' description, to be characterized above all by his lawless pursuit of sexual pleasure (Rep, 573a–75b). The tyrant, Socrates says in a famous analogy, is like a composite creature governed by warring selves who "bite and fight and devour each other" (Rep, 589a), but to the extent that there is a definite direction in the chaos of his behavior, it is the direction favored by Eros, his inner tyrant, which leads him into every excess and the most shocking injustice. The democrat, on the other hand, is just *liberated*, "settled down exactly in the middle between the two ways; and enjoying each in measure, . . . he lives a life that is neither illiberal nor hostile to law, a man of the people come from an oligarchic man" (Rep, 572d).

A final comparison between the two typologies concerns independence of mind. The Berkeley group's contrast between authoritarian and equalitarian is, as we have seen, a contrast between conformism and independence. The equalitarian child-rearing they recommended was designed to produce strong egos and true individuals, and they were confident it would work. "It would not be difficult, on the basis of the clinical and genetic studies reported in this volume, to propose a program which, even in the present cultural pattern, could produce nonethnocentric personalities" (AP, 975). Conformism and ethnocentrism are also key themes in the *Republic*, but Plato offers no such clear contrast between two types, one conformist, the other independent, nor does he offer any assurances about his educational technology.

The discussion between Socrates and his companions in the *Republic* begins with questions about justice: What is justice, and who lives more naturally, the just man or the man who is successfully unjust? Socrates undertakes to defend justice against the charge that the just life is less desirable than tyrannical power, the embodiment of successful injustice. Thrasymachus, the main representative of tyrannical principles in the first stage of the dialogue, is defeated by Socrates, but for reasons that are left somewhat obscure. Do his difficulties spring from his aspirations to science or from his respect for merely conventional distinctions? We know only that he is unwilling to adopt the crudest and most vulgar but also perhaps most defensible version of his basic theory (Rep, 340a–41b). As the discussion proceeds, its character changes. Plato has Socrates examine politics in order to depict on a larger canvas the various possible disorders of the soul. It seems that the soul has several main forms of disorder; these correspond to the main forms of political disorder; the right order of the soul can be seen by analogy with the healthiest political order, which would be the rule of those few who are capable of attaining a comprehensive understanding of man and his place in the natural order and who are adequately motivated to act on this understanding, in short, the rule of philosophers. The other regimes—timocracy, oligarchy, democracy, and tyranny—all represent the rule of opinion, rather than knowledge, and an excessive concern for limited goods (the timocrats' honor, the oligarchs' wealth, the democrats' freedom, and the tyrants' pleasures). The right order of the soul, similarly, requires domination by the reasoning or "cognitive" faculty, the much greater development of which is what sets the philosopher apart from the other types. By comparison with the philosopher, all the other types are unreasonable, though in different ways and in different degrees, for all attach excessive importance to limited ends. The tyrannical type presents the greatest problem, for he reasons more clearly than the other types, being less bound by respect for convention than any type except the philosopher. But the effect of his rationality, given the fundamental disorder of his soul, is just to make him a greater danger to his friends, his family, and his country. The democratic type, by contrast, is less clearheaded but also less dangerous. He only flirts with tyranny, out of distaste for the stinginess of oligarchy, but in the end he is too timid to embrace it. He is at heart a harmless dilettante, dabbling in whatever catches his fancy—cookery, fitness, philosophy, politics, business, and so on (Rep, 561c–d).

Throughout the discussion Socrates emphasizes the power of convention and the difficulty of getting free of it. At one point he asks rhetorically whether it makes any sense to hold private educators, or sophists, responsible for the corruption of youth. The basic education of ordinary man is effected, he suggests, in the most important activities of everyday life, "when many gathered together sit down in assemblies, courts, theaters, army camps, or any other common meeting of a multitude, and, with a great deal of uproar, blame some of the things said or done, and praise others, both in excess, shouting and clapping" (Rep, 492b). Who can resist such authoritative opinions, Socrates asks, especially when they are backed by bribes and threats ("dishonor, fines, and death")? "What kind of private education will hold out for him and not be swept away by such blame and praise and go, borne by the flood, wherever it tends so that he'll say the same things are noble and base as they do, practice what they practice, and be such as they are?" (Rep, 492c). The sophists themselves will teach nothing but the conventional wisdom. "It is just like the case of a man who learns by heart the angers and desires of a great, strong beast he is rearing, how it should be approached and how taken hold of, when—and as a result of what—it becomes most difficult or most gentle, and, particularly, under what conditions it is accustomed to utter its several sounds, and, in turn, what sort of sounds uttered by another make it tame and angry. When he has learned all this from associating and spending time with the beast, he calls it wisdom and, organizing it as an art, turns to teaching" (Rep, 493a–b). The pretensions of such teachers are laughable, but is there any alternative to their kind of education? In the famous analogy of the cave, Socrates compares the liberation of the mind to a sudden, painful release from a lifetime of physical bondage. If someone were compelled to turn from the shadows of a cave to the source of light at its mouth, his eyes would hurt and he would want to turn back to the shadows. "And if someone dragged him away from there by force along the rough, steep, upward way and didn't let him go before he had dragged him out into the light of the sun, wouldn't he be distressed and annoyed at being so dragged? And when he came to the light, wouldn't he have his eyes full of its beam and be unable to see even one of the things now said to be true?" (Rep, 516a).

The *Republic* does not lend itself to condensation. It does not begin by asking how the ordinary man can be liberated from convention. It does not present independence of mind as an easy achievement for which there is a simple formula. It presents three distinct types, the timocrat, the oligarch, and the democrat, all of whom seem to be, in different ways, conformists, while two different sorts of independence are represented by the philosopher and the tyrant. The dialogue leads the reader to ask which of the last two is more truly free of convention. It warns the reader that an education designed to produce independence of mind can have more than one outcome: it may promise the philosopher but deliver the tyrant, no hero of the spirit, but a clever voluptuary, crawling about in the shadows.

The Berkeley group, too, present the road to enlightenment as a rocky one, but it is a descent into a cave rather than an ascent from one that they urge upon their readers. To free himself from the illusions of his people and his age, the would-be liberated individual has to plumb the depths of his own unconscious mind. He has to confront the monsters therein: he has to acknowledge his repressed id impulses and recollect those shadowy infantile "scenes" in which his repressions were formed. When exploring this cave the individual fortunately has a trusty compass that is fun to use: he must take his bearings from what is most obviously pleasurable rather than from what is conventionally proper.[12] The individual must expect some difficulties and disappointments on this road to enlightenment, but he should not fret about the possibility of an unending upward climb.

> We need not suppose that the tolerant have to wait and receive their rewards in heaven, as it were. Actually there is good reason to believe that the tolerant receive more gratification of basic needs. They are likely to pay for this satisfaction in conscious guilt feelings, since they frequently have to go against prevailing social standards, but the evidence is that they are, basically, happier than the prejudiced. Thus, we need not suppose that appeal to emotion belongs to those who strive in the direction of fascism, while democratic propaganda must limit itself to reason and restraint. If fear and destructiveness are the major emotional sources of fascism, *eros* belongs mainly to democracy. (AP, 976)

Two additional differences deserve brief mention. First, the Berkeley group say that the greatest variety of personalities will be found among democrats, but Plato's Socrates depicts a single democratic type and four nondemocratic types: the fundamental differences seem to be on the antidemocratic side of the line. Socrates points to the diversity of personality types to be found in the democratic city (Rep, 557b-d), and the variety of activities it tolerates (Rep, 561c-e), but he implies, nonetheless, that there is a particular constitution of the psyche, or structure of personality, that fits this type of city and that is cultivated by it. This democratic personality seems to consist essentially of a liberation of all desires, necessary and unnecessary, without a liberation from the restraints imposed by law and respect for others. We might describe this type as a strong id and ego combined with a strong superego, "that balance between superego, ego, and id which Freud deemed ideal" (AP, 771).

Second, the Berkeley group took their psychology from Freud, and Freud assumed, in effect, that the only active or "desiring" part of the psyche was the appetitive part, or id, the part that represents the bodily appetites. In Freud's system, if not for Freud himself, there were no other appetites. The Platonic typology, by contrast, rests on the assumption that each part of the soul has its own distinctive desires—the calculating part, or ego, for understanding; the spirited part, or superego, for honor; and the appetitive part, or id, for the pleasures associated with the satisfaction of various bodily needs and drives. For Freud, and thus for the Berkeley group, internal conflict was always fundamentally the conflict between desire (id) and society's restraints on desire (represented internally by the superego), while for Plato it could also arise from a conflict between fundamentally different desires—knowledge against appetite, appetite against honor, and so on. The main theme of the *Republic,* the contrast between the philosophical and tyrannical ways of life, is unintelligible without this assumption of diverse desires.

When the political psychology of *The Authoritarian Personality* is viewed from an adequate historical perspective, its most remarkable feature is not its psychologizing of politics, so much discussed in the critical literature of the past thirty years, but rather its remarkable simplicity. There are not five basic types, but only two. There are not three parts of the psyche with distinctive desires, but one desiring part and one fundamental desire. Liberation from convention is not a potential problem but simply the solution to a problem. The freeing of the "id impulses" has become the necessary and sufficient condition for the triumph of reason in the individual and in society.

Admittedly Plato has little standing today as a psychologist. He is generally thought to have been surpassed, and his analysis of the soul has been largely forgotten. For the sake of the argument, however, let us assume that Plato's typology of political personalities is fundamentally sound. We shall say that there are five basic types and that these are more or less as Plato's Socrates presents them—the knowledge-loving philosopher, the honor-loving timocrat, the money-loving oligarch, the equalitarian but law-abiding democrat, and the fully liberated tyrant. We shall not try to equate any of these types with the "fascist" and "communist" types of contemporary political controversy, but we shall assume that there are today, as there were in Plato's time, philosophers, timocrats, oligarchs, democrats, and tyrants—regardless of the regimes under which they live, the factions they favor, and the large or small role they play in public life.

How, then, did the Berkeley group deal with these different types? The short answer is that they put timocrats and oligarchs in one of their categories, philosophers and democrats in the other, and ignored the tyrants. Looking to their right, they saw first of all the "politico-economic conservative." He appeared dangerous and irrational—inclined to promote rule by the wealthy, openly or covertly opposed to democracy, sexually repressed, excessively conventional, and greedy. Looking past this "oligarch" or "genuine conservative," they dimly perceived the timocrat—the protofascist authoritarian who is even more conservative and irrational than the oligarch. This type is almost beyond the ken of democratic political psychology: the latest discoveries from clinical psychology must be deployed to throw light on this bizarre variant of oligarchic irrationality, this "pseudoconservative" who does not have the oligarch's economic stake in reactionary politics and who is not held quite so tightly in the grip of mindless respect for "middle class values." Turning to their left, the Berkeley group saw nothing of psychological interest. They gave no explicit attention to the tyrannical type, even though their fundamental psychology—their conception of the rational faculty and of "ego strength"—made the analysis of tyranny, in the Platonic sense, their main theme. They equated democratic radicalism—precisely the guise the tyrant would adopt in a democratic society—with reason and philosophy (AP, 10–11). Their disagreeable portrait of the radical democrat's enemy, the authoritarian, was compounded from features of the oligarchic and timocratic types plus general childishness and irrational envy. The democrat, by contrast, looked very good.

From this Platonic perspective, then, the correct charge about bias would be, not the orthodox charge, that they were soft on communism, but that they were soft on democracy. Indeed a Platonist might suspect that the Berkeley group were simply partisans, willing to conflate the more varied types noticed by thinkers not in the grip of contemporary evolutionary theories about man's basic nature.

It will perhaps come as no surprise that this Platonic criticism of the Berkeley group is outlined in the *Republic*. One of the most important features of the democratic city, according to Socrates, is the disrespect for law and convention that it encourages and against which, by itself, it has no adequate defense. The root of the problem, he suggests, is the democrats' love of freedom and their hatred of "authoritarianism." In the longest, most detailed, and most plausible analysis of the transition from one regime to another, Socrates explains how a democracy, holding the supreme good to be personal freedom, educates its citizens to be impatient of any restraint, including the restraint of the laws, and how growing disrespect for the laws paves the way for lawless rule. The democratic city, Socrates says, "spatters with mud those who are obedient, alleging that they are willing slaves of the rulers and nothings, while it praises and honors—both in private and in public—the rulers who are like the ruled and the ruled who are like the rulers" (Rep, 562d). Wishing to escape altogether from authority, the citizens of a democracy come to regard respect for law or convention as merely another form of slavishness. Unscrupulous politicians who pander to their envy cease to shock them. Increasing class conflict, and the threat of confiscation, drives the property owners to contemplate an oligarchic revolution to preserve their property, while the poor give their support to more and more daring spokesmen for their interests and their claims to respect. Unaware of the danger of tyranny, the democrats will concern themselves only with the threat of an oligarchic revolution, or "fascist takeover," as the Berkeley group did. "This is the beginning, so fair and heady, from which tyranny in my opinion naturally grows" (Rep, 563e).

The Berkeley group neglected this possible connection between democracy and tyranny. They glossed over the ambiguities of a "strong ego"; they encouraged the lifting of repressions by honoring those "willing to admit id tendencies and to take the consequences"; they found little to praise in habitual respect for law and convention and little to blame in those outspoken champions of the people who "cannot 'keep silent' if something wrong is being done"; they ignored the differences between philosophy, democracy, and tyranny; they entertained great hopes for the reasonableness and independence of the ordinary citizen. In short, they produced a rather rosy picture of the democratic equalitarian.

No more than Bach and the Beatles exhaust the possibilities in music, do Plato and the Berkeley group exhaust the possibilities in political psychology. As contemporary political psychologists like to point out, *all* the classical political theorists had theories about human nature. The Platonic typology has been outlined here, not in order to force a choice between ancient and contemporary psychology, but only to raise some obviously important questions. Are *authoritarian* and *equalitarian* the only important types? Can they be clearly defined without reference to other types? Is the philosopher a distinct type, and if so, do we know how to produce this type at will? Should we try to do so? What are the consequences of partial success? Is philosophy, in the Platonic sense, possible? Is it the most natural and most satisfying way of life? Or is our situation closer to that described by modern writers who stress the practical and "existential" character of all our thought? Is the real problem to understand the world or to change it? Assuming that fundamental change is possible, should we try to make life easier for the people or should we side with their rulers? Immensely difficult and unresolved—perhaps unresolvable—theoretical issues prevent any confident choice between these radically different alternatives. But unless we are inclined to dismiss Plato's thought as obviously outmoded by the achievements of the past few generations, and unless we are fully convinced, in other words, of the fundamental superiority of modern philosophy and political thought, we must regret that the Berkeley group did not address themselves more clearly, when formulating their theory about authoritarianism, to the many questions raised by the comparisons and contrasts just outlined.

If we peruse *The Authoritarian Personality* with these questions in mind, we must be struck by the abundance of careful methodology and the wealth of statistical detail, but the dearth—the virtual nonexistence—of coherent theoretical discussion. It is hard to avoid the impression that the Berkeley group labored under some strange preconceptions. They labored mightily, and their energy and attention to detail deserve praise, but was all this effort really necessary? Fifty or sixty pages surveying previous thought about ethnocentrism and personality, and clearly explaining its inadequacy, might have done more to convince a skeptical reader of the virtues of their theory than the 500 to 600 pages they devoted to analyzing extracts from the cogitations of their 10 psychiatric patients, 2 merchant marine officers, 12 San Quentin inmates, 2 veterans, 10 professional women, and 44 students. What was the rationale for such a strange distribution of effort?

Philosophy and/of/or Science

The Berkeley group's neglect of the philosophical tradition is typical of social science. It in no way distinguishes *The Authoritarian Personality* from thousands of recent books and articles that deal with politics and psychology. The great strength of all of them is methodology. Their authors discuss large questions without ever wandering very far from the new facts they have collected and digested statistically.

The poverty of philosophy characteristic of social science may, of course, be seen as a wealth of science—this is the line generally taken in "the philosophy of social science," which is a hornet's nest of controversy on complex issues like the nature of explanation, but which presents a united front on the broad question just raised. A defender of the Berkeley group schooled in this philosophy would have little difficulty putting together a persuasive defense of what they did.

He might begin by recalling Galileo and the Inquisition: scientists study the phenomena, he would say, and not what the authorities say about the phenomena. The greatest scientists have all recommended such an approach, for it produces new facts, and these new facts discredit many old theories. Modern developments in physiology, for example, and in the methods of experimental psychology (the correlation coefficient, attitude scaling, the Thematic Apperception Test, etc.) have put whole branches of psychology on entirely new factual foundations. We now know far more than our ancestors did about the physiology of the emotions, the statistical overlap of personality traits, and the quirks of perception. What excuse can there possibly be, he might ask, for wasting time on primitive theories like that of Plato, which located reason in the brain, courage in the heart, the appetites below the diaphragm, and which made the liver a sort of executive organ of the brain in the lower regions of the body?[13] Such notions are surely of interest only to antiquarians and not to scientists.

He might go on to point out that the past century has witnessed a profound transformation in our whole way of thinking about living things. Darwin's discoveries have revolutionized our understanding of human nature. Teleology and immutable forms, banished from natural science and biology, must be banished from the human sciences as well. Mental phenomena must be given a "functional" or "behavioral" interpretation. Freud has made by far the greatest and most interesting contribution to this task. His theories about human motivation may still rest on shaky foundations—the notoriously difficult practical arts of dream interpretation and the cure of hysterical disorders—and they may not yet enjoy the unquestioned acceptance given to Darwin's hypotheses, but the problem today is to advance in the direction indicated by Darwin and Freud, extending and testing their basic hypotheses by using the methods and overall approach of academic psychology. It is not the task of scientific psychology to keep alive earlier theories now of only historical interest.

He might complete his defense by repeating a familiar theory of scientific progress. In science as in life, he might say, there is a division of labor. Our task as scientists is to state and test empirical hypotheses, leaving to historians and philosophers the job of making whatever broad comparisons with earlier ideas they wish. Such comparisons are not a part of science since the large issues they raise cannot be settled "scientifically." The real issues for science are the *little* issues thrown up by a scientific theory or "paradigm." Uncritical acceptance of Freudian or Marxian ideas is not, from this standpoint, a burden or a limitation, but an example of the kind of "theoretical commitment" that makes fruitful scientific work possible. Scholars and philosophers remain free, of course, to offer whatever interpretations of scientific facts they can dream up. But the day has not yet come, he might conclude, when a man can be a scholar in the morning, a scientist in the afternoon, and a critical critic in the evening.

The great lesson taught by modern, post-Aristotelian natural science does indeed seem to be that specialization and respect for facts pay enormous dividends, not just in the advance of knowledge, but in the improvement of man's estate. The wonders of modern physics, the magic of modern chemistry, the enormous benefits of modern medicines, surgery, and pesticides—

all can be attributed to the willingness of scientists to engage in and to respect the results of careful, detailed, "experimental" research. Objectivity can be attained, it seems, by sticking close to the facts. Knowledge may begin with speculation, and new factual discoveries may stimulate fresh speculation, but speculation must always be disciplined by respect for the facts. The more numerous, the more detailed, and the more precise the facts an investigator can amass, the less likely is he to slip into merely subjective generalizations. For the individual scholar or scientist, objectivity consists precisely in a willingness to respect facts, that is to say, to adjust preconceived notions to fit the facts, and to abandon any conjectures that are disproved by the facts. An objectively valid theory or hypothesis is distinguished from mere subjective speculation by its consistency with, and by the reasonable explanation it provides for, the known facts about some subject.

This view of science is not hostile to theory, it must be insisted, but only to theory that is untestable or disproved. Theories are the lifeblood of science and the only danger is that they open the door to subjectivity, since there is necessarily more room to dispute the interpretation of facts than the facts themselves, and thus more room for purely subjective influences to determine the views that men hold. The goal of scientific research should be to develop theories that are closely linked to factual research—theories that are *testable*, or *verifiable*, or *falsifiable*. Heroic subjectivity—the creative scientific imagination of a Newton or an Einstein—may occasionally break the bank, but it is objectivity that pays regular dividends.

The contemporary philosophy of science is the result of long meditation on the successes of natural science by extraordinarily intelligent men. Most of this book was written in an effort to conform to its demands. My only purpose here is to suggest that the general acceptance of these demands goes a long way to explaining not only the strengths and weaknesses of *The Authoritarian Personality*, but also the deficiencies of the critical reaction to it.

If the Berkeley group's claim to objectivity is weak, it is not (pace Hyman and Sheatsley) mainly because of any easily corrigible flaws in their "research design" or "methodology." The problem lies rather in their unwillingness or incapacity to discuss their basic theory and to try to demonstrate, in a way designed to persuade a reasonable skeptic, why it should be preferred to alternative theories. They offered their main hypotheses dogmatically, with an evident impatience for the slow-moving reflections by which a reasonable man weighs all the diverse considerations that should bear on a difficult choice. Whatever exactly the source of this dogmatism and impatience, it is encouraged and excused by the prevailing philosophy of science. It will not be cured by insisting more loudly that scientists stick to their facts.

The imbalance between statistical and theoretical materials in *The Authoritarian Personality*, and between contemporary and ancient authorities, must strike any reader whose senses have not been numbed by too many courses in statistics and the philosophy of science. This imbalance is surely a fact, and it may be the most important fact about the whole research program the book reports. It must certainly have struck Max Horkheimer and Theodor Adorno, who were not narrow specialists. It is to them we now turn.

Critical Theory

Great sinners sometimes make great preachers. When Augustine inveighs against concupiscence, the effect is heightened by our knowledge that he has some experience of the fetters he condemns. St. Ignatius, too, seems to have gained some of his power over his followers by letting them know that his knowledge of sin was not purely theoretical. But the great preacher who has sinned must be a reformed sinner. Tartuffe is no Ignatius. Generally speaking, we want those who wag their fingers at us to be themselves beyond reproach.

Horkheimer and Adorno were moralists as well as scientists. Ethnocentrism was their specialty. They spent years ferreting out the remote causes and unsuspected effects of this vice. They postulated that ethnocentrism would be related to personality functioning and to support for democracy. They developed a simple dichotomy between two types of personality, an ethnocentric (dichotomizing), antidemocratic, and authoritarian personality, on the one hand, and a humanitarian, democratic, and equalitarian personality, on the other hand. They described the differences between these two types in terms of reasonableness (ego strength), sincerity (internalization of values), and happiness (satisfaction of primitive emotional needs). They helped to develop a test, the F scale, to measure the relevant differences in personality. They used this test to demonstrate that "authoritarianism" is in fact related to ethnic prejudice. They concluded with the remarkable claim, on the penultimate page of *The Authoritarian Personality*, that we now know how to produce "non-ethnocentric personalities."

If we compare their simple typology with the Platonic typology of regimes and types of personality, we are struck by some important similarities and some equally important differences. Having seen them, we must wonder why Horkheimer and Adorno did not make such a comparison part of *The Authoritarian Personality* itself. It seems odd that two German academics who intended to treat their subject fully and satisfactorily—as it should be treated in a 990-page book—did not even mention Socrates' conjectures. What were their reasons for preferring their own simple dichotomy to the more complex Platonic typology?

If Horkheimer and Adorno had been called to testify in their own defense, thirty years ago, they would presumably not have used the defense outline above. They were critics rather than practitioners of conventional social science. During the 1930s, when *The Authoritarian Personality* was just a gleam in his eye, Horkheimer was already making a name for himself as a vocal opponent of "positivism," "traditional theory," and "the worship of the fact." Adorno was far too sophisticated to commit himself wholeheartedly to Freudian theory: "In psycho-analysis nothing is true except the exaggerations."[14] They both had a far broader culture than the typical Ph.D. in psychology. They were not like the products of modern graduate education, which does not encourage students (or later, professors) to browse among writers whose assumptions are out of date and whose style of presentation is unfamiliar. Horkheimer and Adorno loved to browse; the books they published around the same time as *The Authoritarian Personality* are studded with erudite references to the classics. Sanford, Frenkel-Brunswik, and Levinson probably never dreamed that anything relevant to their research might be gleaned from ancient writers, but Horkheimer and Adorno knew that the whole problem of modern psychology could be understood only if you understood something about ancient thought. They rummaged in the dustbins, as it were, of European thought for clues to the psychology of politics. They studied contemporary philosophical writers, such as Husserl and Heidegger, and they knew from experience that the recent greats—Kant, Hegel, Schopenhauer, Marx, and Nietzsche—were worth the effort.

In short, if Horkheimer and Adorno were ethnocentric, they were not transparently so, like their artless collaborators. They would presumably have agreed that any truly scientific treatment of ethnocentrism would have to transcend the ethnocentrism of modern natural science and its social science imitations. Their whole "critical theory" was a protest against the forgetfulness of modern science and the imperialism of "dominating reason." But when writing *The Authoritarian Personality* they seem to have been no more sensitive than the other members of the Berkeley group to the unusual difficulties of their task. If they were to convince skeptical readers of their capacity to deal scientifically with ethnocentrism, broadly defined, they would first of all have to resist the temptation to stereotype their intellectual opponents. They would have to provide some clear and striking proofs that they had risen above the most important opinions of their own time about their subject. They would have to show that they could deal with those opinions objectively—clearly and dispassionately, in full consciousness of what they were. The needed demonstration might well have begun, I have suggested, with a detailed discussion of the main differences between their own theory and the one outlined in the *Republic*.

Horkheimer and Adorno had certainly read Plato. They were surely aware that ancient writers had had something to say about ethnocentrism and authoritarianism. But did they think it worth their time and ours to ponder the ancient view of their problems? Did they perhaps think that too much recollection of such a distant past would needlessly confuse their readers and interefere with the urgent task of forging intellectual weapons against prejudice? All we know is that they, like Sanford, Frenkel-Brunswik, and Levinson, kept silent about all opinions fundamentally different from their own. The five of them wrote a huge book crammed full of hard data and methodology.

In doing so Horkheimer and Adorno betrayed none of the vulgar prejudices of some Americans. Obviously, and for obvious reasons, they were not anti-Semites, did not hate blacks, and had no particular feelings about Oklahomans. But it is not so clear that they were above certain more important opinions that are typically modern and American—opinions having to do with the inferiority of ancient to modern science, and the superiority of democracy to all other forms of government.

Earlier we noted some difficulties facing anyone trying to summarize the thought of Horkheimer and Adorno. No one familiar with critical theory would lightheartedly undertake to plumb its depths and report the results in a page. Great claims, difficult to judge, are made on its behalf. According to one authority, Albrecht Wellmer, critical theory is to be understood "as a protest . . . against an apocalyptically self-obdurating system of alienation and reification, and as the spark whose preservation in a self-darkening world will keep alive the memory of something quite different."[15] The dominant opinions of our time, it seems, are dangerous as well as false; only critical theory can bring light into the contemporary darkness.

Critical theory draws its light from diverse sources. Horkheimer and his associates fused the ideas of thinkers with few obvious affinities—Freud and Marx, for example—in the fires of their dialectic. The resulting compound has been variously interpreted. All commentators seem agreed, however, that the critique of "instrumental reason" holds a central place in the thinking of the school. According to critical theory, a truncated concept of reason dominates modern science and technology. Reason today systematizes facts, expels values, and implicitly affirms the existing order. Its devotees develop the most amazing devices with scarcely a thought about how they will be used. But whatever reservations Horkheimer and his associates had about contemporary science, they were clearly not Luddites. They did not decry technology; they protested its distortion and misuse. They demanded that modern science fulfill its promise—of the liberation of mankind through the conquest of nature—and that the specter of technocratic tyranny be banished forever. They offered their criticisms of democracy in an equally forward-looking spirit. They had little respect for the conventions of parliamentary democracy; they were in the forefront of those attacking elite domination and false consciousness. But they were far from being antidemocratic. Democratic ideals and the democratic type were spared critical theory's usually unsparing criticism, as we have seen, and democratic practice was faulted only because it did not live up to its own high ideals. Their treatment of the Enlightenment and of the responsibilities of intellectuals showed similar discrimination. The school's thesis about the "dialectic of enlightenment" may be stated somewhat crudely as follows: reason, when it comes to fruition, destroys itself, and the fully rationalized society is manifestly irrational. "The fully enlightened earth radiates disaster triumphant."[16] All commentators are careful to point out, however, that Horkheimer and Adorno rejected, not the hopes of the Enlightenment, but its fruits in the twentieth century. The target of their criticism was not the philosophical ideal of a free and rational society, but the philistine complacency that views the events of this century as the realization of that ideal. Horkheimer and Adorno took the ideal far too seriously to be content with the usual apologetics. Indeed they seem to have seen themselves as latter-day *philosophes*, trying to save mankind from a new dark age. To do so they had to restore the negative or critical side of reason without reviving the mythologies of the past or challenging the fundamental Enlightenment goals of freedom and reason. They directed their critical fire at certain rather abstract myths, or ideological fetters, that they thought limited human freedom in the new context of secular, scientific society.

In all its major battles, critical theory pursues a common strategy. When constructing their doctrine (or method) of liberation, Horkheimer and his associates drew heavily upon modern German philosophy. In particular, Horkheimer and Adorno accepted the distinctively modern and German emphasis upon history: as they said, "the core of truth is historical, rather than an unchanging constant to be set against the movement of history."[17] They were aware, however, of the grave difficulties associated with radical relativism—at least equal to those of moral absolutism—so they practiced a method of "immanent criticism" that highlighted discrepancies between ideological claims and empirical realities, for example, between the ideal of equality and the reality of domination and class privilege. Criticism would achieve a relative objectivity, they thought, if it could show how objects generally failed to live up to the claims made on their behalf—how they stood in contradiction to their own norms. Rather than being judged by arbitrary standards imposed from outside, the objects criticized would reveal their own limitations and would point beyond themselves. Intellectual and artistic phenomena would be grasped, not by explaining their causes (as in the usual analysis of "ideology," which assigns particular cultural phenomena to particular interest groups), but rather by highlighting their contradictions. The discrepancy between the basic idea of a work and its pretension to correspond to reality, once revealed, would throw a new light on both the work itself and the society it reflected. "A successful work, according to immanent criticism, is not one which resolves objective contradictions in a spurious harmony, but one which expresses the idea of harmony negatively by embodying the contradictions, pure and uncomprehended, in its inner-most structure. Confronted with this kind of work, the verdict 'more ideology' loses its meaning."[18]

Whatever the merit of critical theory as a whole, one thing is clear: *The Authoritarian Personality* illustrates intellectual provincialism. The Berkeley group wrote almost a thousand pages about ethnocentrism and authoritarianism without ever hinting that anyone before the twentieth century might have had anything worthwhile to say on these themes. Their book contains no systematic discussion of any theories even slightly different from the one it favors. It nowhere suggests that knowledge of such theories might be of any value. Earlier theories are never discussed; the issues that any comparison would reveal are never clearly stated; the great choices are all made silently. Those who might favor alternative interpretations are not refuted; they are pigeonholed and advised to consult a psychoanalyst. Strong convictions take the place of strong arguments. In short, the Berkeley group behaved ethnocentrically.

In ordinary mortals, and perhaps even in scientists, ethnocentrism may not be a serious failing. It is certainly less of a problem, practically speaking, than brutality, or lechery, or greed. But for directors of conscience, or "straighteners," whose specialty is "rigid adherence to the culturally familiar," for experts in the secret sources and revealing signs of this vice, it is the fatal flaw. If they cannot overcome the evil in themselves, who but the credulous will believe that they can cure it in others?[19]

No good purpose would be served by speculating about the Berkeley group's reasons for thinking that ethnic prejudice has more to do with ego weakness than with differences between ethnic groups. Nothing would be achieved, except to illustrate how the unreasonable is sometimes historically comprehensible. Still less would come of trying to fathom their reasons for thinking that "ego weakness" is best measured by having people agree or disagree with a collection of statements about sex crimes, bad manners, astrology, the value of suffering, respect for parents, earthquakes, and plots among politicans.

Their book stands as an attempt, in the face of the terrible catastrophes of the twentieth century, to sustain faith in human nature, that is to say, belief in the possibility of general enlightenment. It argues that ethnocentrism is no more normal and need be no more common than tolerant cosmopolitanism and true individuality. Both are merely effects of particular circumstances and childhood experiences, which can be reformed and controlled. The fundamental cause of ethnocentrism, it suggests, is the fear and hostility of the ethnocentric person, not the variations in manners and morals that distinguish one nation from another, nor any ineradicable tendency of most human beings to accept uncritically the opinions of their associates and to become angry with those who challenge conventional views. Intolerance is a survival of the past, and an enlightened society, such as modern philosophy and child psychology are capable of producing, would be free of this evil.

Their theory seems to be disproved by the very dangers and disasters it tries to explain and control. The reasons for its popularity have more to do with politics than with science. The heart of the theory is a simple typology which contrasts an ethnocentric authoritarian verging on psychopathology with a tolerant, liberated, strong-minded, and freedom-loving democrat. This typology fosters the belief, always popular in a democracy, that the democratic type is the highest attainable ideal of personality. It expresses the good democrat's indignation against the enemies of enlightenment, bolsters his hopes for the future, vindicates his way of life, flatters his laziness and sensuality, and excuses him from any obligation to consider whether his superficial cosmopolitanism may not be the cause of the most pervasive and ultimately most destructive ethnocentrism. The Berkeley group made some methodological mistakes, their social science critics were quick to say, but "they have wisdom in their views." Theirs is the *critical* view of the modern world.

Appendix A

Study Design and Execution

The data used in Part II were collected in the spring of 1968 for a study of political socialization that was never completed. My interests shifted from "political socialization" to "political psychology," and the data I had collected for one purpose came to be used for another.

The resulting study conforms more or less to a "most similar nations design." It aims to test a theory developed with German and American nationalism in mind, by applying it to Canada's nationalisms. By far the greatest part of the literature on nationalism and personality is, of course, American, and any Canadian study will be at least implicitly comparative. The present study involves an explicit comparison, and the countries compared, Canada and the United States, are obviously "most similar nations."

Similarity is not identity, however, and the results of this study plainly require that we consider the differences between nationalism in Canada and nationalism in the United States. What conclusions we draw from the study depend upon how we describe these differences. They are discussed in Chapters 4, 8, and 10, where it is suggested that Canada is a smaller, weaker country than the United States, with a different colonial heritage, different internal divisions, a different role in international politics, and a less assured sense of what it stands for politically. Consequently nationalism has different connotations for Canadians than for Americans and finds expression in opinions about different issues. For the past twenty years the great issues for nationalism in Canada have been the preservation of "national unity" in the face of the growing conflict between the "internal" nationalisms of English and French Canadians, and the preservation of Canadian independence vis-à-vis the United States. Since World War II American nationalism, by contrast, has been intimately related to the Cold War. The

195

basic issue has been whether, and in what manner, the United States should use its military and economic strength to block the expansion of communist regimes in Western Europe and the Third World. For more than a generation "nationalism" among Americans has had strong connotations of belligerent anticommunism.

The study reported in Part II above used two questionnaires, one in English and the other in French. The French questionnaire was derived from the English questionnaire, but with some changes in the questions about nationalism in Quebec. The French questionnaire was drafted in English, then translated by a paid assistant, then revised and corrected with the help of two bilingual friends whose mother tongue was French and who had had university training in linguistics and translation.

All of the questionnaires were anonymous and consisted of two booklets, which were matched by means of repeated questions about sex and birthdate. The first booklet began with nonpolitical questions about school, careers, and family, and then moved on to straightforward questions about topical political issues and attitudes towards politics. The questions used to measure authoritarianism were in the first part of the first booklet of the questionnaires. The second booklets contained a series of concepts and rating scales, and then at the end, a series of questions to elicit information about language, national origin, social status, and religion. In order to reduce the cost of coding and to speed completion of the questionnaires by the students, almost all of the questions were answered by choosing from fixed lists of alternatives. Relatively few questions, however, were in the agree-disagree format. Little effort was made to disguise the point of the questions; it seemed more important to avoid boredom and irritation with the questionnaire because of confusion about its purposes and too much jumping from topic to topic.

Schools were selected to reflect some of the main differences from region to region within Canada. Oakville rather than Toronto was chosen to represent urban Ontario, mainly because it was easier to gain access to the schools there. In addition, it was easier to get a "representative" sample in Oakville than in Toronto. The smaller size of Oakville means that each school serves a relatively large cross-section of the city's population. The city has only four high schools, by comparison with about ninety in metropolitan Toronto. The high school that serves the wealthy eastern side of the city was not included in the sample, and the remaining three schools probably provide a better-balanced sample of urban Ontario students than would any three schools chosen from Toronto. Unfortunately, it was possible to secure the cooperation of only one high school in the French part of the Montreal Catholic school system. This school was in the east-central part of the city, and it seems to have provided a good sample of students from lower-middle and working-class families. It was the intention, at the outset, to collect more data from small towns and rural areas, but it was impossible to carry through this part of the plan because of the time it would have taken to make the necessary arrangements.

Table A1 shows the geographical distribution of the respondents to the questionnaires. The letters in the fourth column of the table identify which of four methods of administration were used:

A. In the students' classrooms without any interruption and with instructions from myself or another person associated with the study.

B. In a large hall without an interruption and with instructions from myself or another person associated with the study.

C. In the classrooms without an interruption, but with instructions given by the teacher or other school official.

D. In the classrooms with an interval between the completion of the first and second booklets and with instructions given by myself or another person associated with the study.

Generally speaking, no difficulties were encountered in the administration of the questionnaires. There was an extremely high rate of cooperation among the students; no more than a dozen questionnaires had to be discarded because of frivolous or insulting answers to the questions. The low rates of nonresponse to the questions at the end of the questionnaires show that virtually all of the students had enough time to answer all of the questions.

Table A2 shows some characteristics of the English and French samples. The modal age for both groups is about 18 years, but the French respondents are slightly younger, on the average, than the English group. Table A3 summarizes some information the students provided about their parents. From the figures in the table it is clear that the students were drawn disproportionately from the upper social strata. It is noteworthy that only 10 percent of the students in the English sample reported that a language other than English or French was spoken in their homes, and only 39 percent reported that one or both parents were born outside the country. Thus the sample is representative, I would guess, of older high school students in urban areas in the central regions of Canada where relatively few recent immigrants have settled.

Table A1 Sources of Data

City or Town	Schools	Grades	Methods	N =
English Study				
Quebec City	1	12	D	24
Montreal	5	11,12	B,C	179
Toronto	1	12	A	55
Oakville	3	12	B,C	348
Stayner	1	12	A	36
Milton	1	12	A	68
Winnipeg	7	12	A,B	371
Total				1081
French Study				
Quebec City	8	11,12	A,B,C	475
Montreal	1	12	B	269
Total				744

Table A2 Some Characteristics of the Respondents

Variables	English Students (N = 1,081)	French Students (N = 744)
1. Sex		
Male	57%	53%
Female	43	47
2. Year of Birth		
After 1951	1%	13%
1951	18	25
1950 (c. 18 years)	53	40
1949	18	18
Before 1949	9	4
3. Religion		
Protestant	55%	
Roman Catholic	22	96%
Jewish	4	
Other	5	
None	11	3
No response	2	1

Table A3 Some Characteristics of the Families of the Respondents

Variables	English Students	French Students
1. Language spoken at home:		
English only	87%	0.9%
French only	0.7	95
Other	10	3
Missing data (no response)	2	1
2. National origin of father:		
British Isles	49%	7%
France	4	42
Other European	30	6
Other and unclassifiable	4	7
Don't know	10	33
No response	3	5
3. National origin of mother:		
British Isles	48%	7%
France	4	35
Other European	30	4
Other and unclassifiable	5	8
Don't know	11	41
No response	3	6
4. Birthplace of parents:		
Both in Canada	60%	96%
Both outside Canada	23	1
Mixed	16	2
No response	2	1
5. Father's occupation:		
Professional	11%	12%
Business-Owners and Managers	21	17
Sales	6	7
Clerical	10	16
Skilled labor	30	30
Unskilled labor	10	10
Armed services	2	0.5
Farming	2	0.1
Unclassifiable	4	4
No response	4	3

Appendix B

The Measures of Attitudes and Personality

This appendix provides basic information about the ten scales used in Chapters 4 and 5 and some supplementary statistical detail for the other six scales introduced in Chapter 6. All the scales consist of simple, unweighted sums of responses to relatively small numbers of indicators (3 to 10 questions). Integer values have been assigned to particular responses in such a way that high scores always indicate more of the attitude, trait, or interest in question. The appendices of the doctoral dissertation from which this book was derived (University Microfilms No. DCJ76-30317) provide the original questionnaires and additional information about the methods of coding and the inter-item correlations for most of these scales.

Separatist Nationalism

The French questionnaire contained nine questions directly concerning the independence issue. The first three questions, about a third of the way through the questionnaire, were as follows:

45. On discute beaucoup depuis quelques années de la possibilité pour le Québec de se séparer du reste du Canada et de devenir un pays indépendant. Jusqu'à quel point êtes-vous intéressé par cette question du séparatisme?

    ____très intéressé (30%)
    ____intéressé (30%)
    ____peu intéressé (16%)
    ____pas intéressé du tout (24%)

46. Quelle est votre préférence pour l'avenir politique du pays?

    ____pas de changement (8%)
    ____Confédération renouvelée (30%)

_____statut particulier pour le Québec (21%)

_____états associés (17%)

_____indépendance du Québec (13%)

_____je ne sais pas (11%)

47. Quelle est votre opinion au sujet de l'indépendance pour le Québec?

    _____désirable et faisable immédiatement (2%)

    _____désirable, mais non faisable immédiatement (37%)

    _____désirable, mais pas faisable du tout (6%)

    _____non désirable (46%)

    _____indécis (7%)

    _____je ne sais pas (2%)

The numbers beside each response are the percentage of students who chose that response. These three questions were followed by a direct question about world government (see p. 208 below) and then by a series of agree-disagree items having to do with international organization as well as Quebec independence. Table B1 shows the items concerned with independence and their marginal frequencies. Finally, there was one additional direct question later in the questionnaire:

67. Si le Québec devenait indépendant, pensez-vous qu'il serait avantagé au point de vue économique, plus pauvre, ou qu'économiquement il demeurerait tel qu'il est maintenant?

    _____avantagé (15%)

    _____plus pauvre (68%)

    _____tel qu'il est maintenant (9%)

    _____je ne sais pas (8%)

All of these questions except the first, which defined the issue for the respondents and inquired about their interest in it, but which did not test their attitude for or against separation, were used to construct the Separatist Nationalism (SN) scale. Answers to the direct questions were classified as

Table B1 Items Used to Test Attitudes Towards Quebec Independence (French Respondents, N = 744)

Statements	% Agreement
1. Le Québec devrait montrer plus de vigueur pour influencer les autres gouvernements quand il croit avoir raison.	90
2. Le Québec doit avoir le contrôle absolu de ses destinées et être dégagé de toute influence extérieure.	50
3. Les Québécois devraient être prêts à faire plus de sacrifices pour obtenir leur indépendance nationale.	49
4. Dans la mesure du possible, le Québec devrait être à la fois économiquement et politiquement indépendant de tous les autres pays.	38
5. La meilleure façon de progresser pour les Québécois est de devenir une nation distincte et indépendante.	31

separatist, federalist, or intermediate. For Question 46, for example, "indépendance" was scored as separatist (score of 2); "Conféderation renouvelée," "états associés," "statut particulier," and "ne sait pas" were scored as intermediate (1); and "pas de changement" was scored as federalist (0). For Question 47, the first two responses were scored 2; the third and fifth, 1; the fourth, 0; and the last was treated as missing data. Responses to the statements of opinion were classified as either separatist (agree), with a score of 1, or federalist (disagree), with a score of 0. Each individual's score on the scale is simply the sum of his answers to these eight items.

National Unity

Five direct questions about separatism and national unity were included in the English questionnaire. The first question in the series was the following:

63. There has been quite a bit of talk recently about the possibility of the Province of Quebec separating from the rest of Canada and becoming an independent country. Would you be in favor of separation or opposed to it?

      ____Strongly in favor of separation (2%)

      ____Slightly in favor of separation (3%)

      ____Undecided (6%)

      ____Slightly opposed to separation (10%)

      ____Strongly opposed to separation (78%)

The important fact about these responses is that about nine out of ten of the students were either slightly or strongly opposed to separation. The real variation in attitudes among the English Canadians, therefore, is in how strongly they are opposed to separation. The following four questions in the series were, in effect, questions about the intensity of opposition to separatism:

66. Suppose a vote were taken and *most of the people* in Quebec voted *for* separation. What do you think the government in Ottawa should do then?

      ____Let Quebec become independent (22%)

      ____Try to keep Quebec in Canada (68%)

      ____I'm not sure (10%)

67. Do you think that the government in Ottawa should use military force, if necessary, to prevent Quebec from separating?

      ____Yes, use force if necessary (20%)

      ____No, force must never be used (70%)

      ____I'm not sure (10%)

68. If Quebec did separate from Canada, how serious do you think this would be for the future of the rest of Canada?

      ____Very serious (52%)

      ____Fairly serious (31%)

_____Not very serious (14%)

_____I don't know (3%)

70. How much do you, yourself, care whether Quebec stays in Canada or becomes independent?

_____Very much (69%)

_____Some (22%)

_____A little (4%)

_____Not at all (5%)

Integer values were assigned to the responses to these questions (e.g., the values 0, 1, 2, 3, and 4 respectively to the five possible responses to Question 63), and the National Unity (NU) scale is simply the sum of these values.

Separatism

About half way through the French questionnaire there were seven questions that can be used to define a dimension of Canadian vs. Québécois national identity. Three of these were direct questions about how the respondent would describe himself:

71. Combien de ces termes utilisez-vous pour vous décrire? (Marquez d'un crochet tous les mots qui s'appliquent à vous personnellement.)

_____Canadien (65%)	_____Belge (1%)
_____Canadien anglais (4%)	_____Britannique (1%)
_____Canadien français (78%)	_____Ecossais (2%)
_____Acadien (3%)	_____Français (15%)
_____Québécois (79%)	_____Irlandais (3%)
_____Américain (4%)	_____Italien (1%)
_____Anglais (1%)	_____Américain du Nord (30%)

This question was immediately followed by an open-ended question, "Comment vous considérez-vous—comme un Canadien français, ou Canadien anglais, ou Canadien allemand ou Canadien italien, comme simplement Canadien, ou comment?" The third question in the series forced a choice between three basic alternatives:

73. Des trois termes cités ci-dessous, lequel pourrait vous décrire le mieux?

_____Canadien (29%)

_____Canadien anglais (1%)

_____Canadien français (70%)

Responses to the open-ended question were first grouped in seven main categories:

Emphatically Canadian	10%
Simply Canadian	9%
Qualified Canadian	10%
Hyphenated Canadian	61%
Another Nationality	3%
Provincialist	5%
Internationalist	1%

Respondents were placed in the first category if they put a special emphasis, either in what they wrote (e.g., "Canadien tout court") or the way they wrote it (e.g., "CANADIEN!!!"), on the idea that they were simply Canadians and nothing else. They were put in the second category if they wrote down, in ordinary script, "Canadien." In the third category were put those who indicated that they were Canadians but with some qualification or elaboration, for example, "Canadien de langue française." Hyphenated Canadians are those who responded "Canadien français" or something equivalent. The Provincialist category contains those who said that they were "Québécois." The seventh category, Internationalist, contains those who said that they did not belong to any particular nationality, that they were human beings, that they did not believe in national distinctions, and so on. These eight categories were then reduced to three: Provincialist (score of 2), Emphatically Canadian (score of 0), and all the others (score of 1). Responses to the first question in the series were dichotomized: the 25% who checked "Québécois" but not "Canadien" were given a score of 1, and all the others, a score of 0. Responses to the forced-choice question were dichotomized: "Canadien" was scored 0, the others, 1. This method of scoring was used because it yields a simple Guttman scale (see H. D. Forbes, "Authoritarianism and Breadth of Identification," *Canadian Journal of Behavioural Science*, forthcoming) with the following categories and proportions in each:

Emphatic Canadian	9%
Canadian	19%
French Canadian	47%
Proto-Québécois	21%
Québécois	4%

These three direct questions were combined with four closely related questions, each of which raises from a slightly different angle the same fundamental issue, namely, the relative strength of the respondents' competing Canadian and Québécois loyalties.

61. Vous arrive-t-il de considérer les Canadiens anglais comme des étrangers?

    ____oui, toujours (11%)

    ____oui, quelquefois (56%)

    ____non, jamais (33%)

69. Que considérez-vous comme votre pays—le Canada tout entier ou seulement le Québec?

    ____le Canada tout entier (77%)

    ____seulement le Québec (20%)

    ____je ne suis pas sur (3%)

70. Croyez-vous que l'anglais et le français devraient être langues officielles au Québec, ou bien que le français devrait être la seule langue officielle au Québec?

_____l'anglas et le français devraient être langues officielles (61%)

_____le français devrait être la seule langue officielle (36%)

_____je ne suis pas sur (3%)

75. Des gens disent que ce serait bien mieux si tous les gens au Canada se disaient Canadiens tout simplement, au lieu de se dire Canadiens anglais ou encore Canadiens français. Etes-vous d'accord avec cette opinion ou pas d'accord?

_____d'accord (60%)

_____pas d'accord (31%)

_____je ne suis pas sur (9%)

Responses to each of these questions were scored 0, 1, or 2, and the sum of all the scores is a measure of federalist versus separatist feeling, but without any direct reference to constitutional options. The Separatism (SEP) scale is designed to measure separatist feeling in this sense.

Anti-French Feeling

The English questionnaire contained a series of seven questions that can be used to construct a scale of anti-French attitudes. The series began with the question:

53. Do you think of Canada right now as *equally French and English* or do you think of it as *basically an English country?*

_____Equally French and English (15%)

_____Basically an English country (82%)

_____I'm not sure (3%)

This was followed by an open-ended question: "What do you think Canada should be in the future?" The responses were coded in one of eight categories:

Equally French and English	24%
More French, but not equally	4%
Basically English	12%
Exclusively English	8%
Multicultural	4%
Just Canadian	3%
More independent	17%
Other	21%
No response	7%

These were reduced to four categories (the first two, the last five, the third, and the fourth) for the purposes of the scale. The next five questions in the series were:

55. Do you think that both French and English should be official languages in Canada, or do you think that English should be the only official language in Canada?

_____Both French and English should be official languages (67%)
_____English should be the only official language (29%)
_____I'm not sure (4%)

58. From what you have heard about French Canadians, or judging from your contacts with them, would you say that they treat other people as equals or that they act as if they were above others?
    _____Treat others as equals (54%)
    _____Act as if they were above others (24%)
    _____Neither, they feel inferior (9%)
    _____I don't know (12%)

59. Who would you say have *more in common*— (check one)
    _____French Canadians and French people from France (20%)
    _____French Canadians and English Canadians (66%)
    _____I'm not sure (14%)

60. Do you ever think of French Canadians as being like foreign people?
    _____Yes, always (4%)
    _____Yes, sometimes (35%)
    _____No, never (61%)

62. Over the next ten years, do you think that English-French relations in Canada will get better, get worse, or stay about the same as they are now?
    _____Get better (58%)
    _____Get worse (18%)
    _____Stay about the same as they are now (14%)
    _____I don't know (11%)

The six questions following the introductory question tapped some of the main anti-French opinions that circulated among English Canadians in 1968, and they can be used to construct an Anti-French (AF) scale, a high score on which indicates a respondent who believed that Canada should be an English country, that French Canadians make unreasonable demands, that their fundamental loyalties are not to Canada, but to some other country, and that their relations with English Canadians are probably going to be conflictful (bad) rather than cooperative (good). Such a respondent is anti-French in as much as he regards French Canadians as foreign and troublesome and believes that they should be treated simply as one among many minorities in Canada.

National Power

The English questionnaire also contained seven agree-disagree items designed to elicit general attitudes towards national power and solidarity in the face of external rivals. The first five of these items were taken from Kenneth W. Terhune, "Nationalism among Foreign and American Students: An Exploratory Study," *Journal of Conflict Resolution,* 8 (1964),

256–70; the sixth item was taken from Donald L. Sampson and Howard P. Smith, "A Scale to Measure World-Minded Attitudes," *Journal of Social Psychology*, 45 (1957), 99-106; the last item was adapted from M. B. Thiele and Louis L. Thurstone, *Scale for the Measurement of Attitude toward Patriotism* (Chicago: University of Chicago Press, 1931). Table B2 shows these seven items and their marginal frequencies. The National Power (NP) scale for the English respondents is simply the sum of these seven items, with agreement scored as 1 and disagreement as 0, except for the first item, where the distinction is between strong agreement and the other responses.

Table B2 Items Used to Test Attitudes Towards National Power (English Respondents, N = 1,081)

Statements	% Agreement
1. Canada should guard against nations which may try to push it around.	95
2. The best way for Canadians to progress is to maintain themselves as a distinct and independent nation.	81
3. To the degree possible, Canada should be both politically and economically independent of all other nations.	66
4. Canada must control its own destiny completely and be independent of all outside influences.	64
5. Canada should strive for power in the world.	58
5. We should be willing to fight for our country without questioning whether it is right or wrong.	35
7. There is no room in Canada for people who find fault with this country.	25

Independence/U.S.

Both the English and the French questionnaires included six questions about American influence in Canada and the maintenance of Canadian independence vis-à-vis the United States. The answers to these questions indicate the presence or absence of nationalist attitudes that have to do specifically with Canadian-American relations. The first of the questions asked respondents to say which of three problems they thought was the most important facing Canada:

34. Among the problems that Canada faces, which *one* of the following do you think is the most important?

 _____American control of Canadian industries

 _____The conflict between French Canadians and English Canadians

 _____The danger of war with the communist countries

 _____I don't know

The first response, "American control," indicates nationalist sentiment directed against American economic domination. It was chosen by 27 percent of the English respondents and 33 percent of the French respon-

Appendix B

dents. A few pages further on in the questionnaire there was a series of three questions dealing directly with American influence and the possibility of union with the United States. These questions and the distributions of responses to them are shown in Table B3. Finally, later in the questionnaire, students were asked to respond to a list of 10 possible advantages and 10 disadvantages of living in Canada by checking the advantages and disadvantages that they thought were most important. One of the advantages listed was that "Canada is protected by the power of the United States." It was checked by 20 percent of the English students and 23 percent of the French students. One of the disadvantages listed was: "Americans control too many things in Canada." It was checked by 67 percent of the English and 63 percent of the French students. The Independence/U.S. scale (or simply the US scale) was constructed by summing responses to these six questions.

Table B3 Questions Used to Test Attitudes Regarding American Influence

	Distributions	
Questions and Answers	English (N = 1,081)	French (N = 744)
1. Do you think that our way of life is, or is not, being influenced too much by the United States?		
Yes, too much	70%	64%
No, not too much	25	33
I'm not sure,	4	3
2. Do you think that Canada shows enough independence in its relations with the United States?		
Yes, enough independence	29%	29%
No, not enough independence	58	58
I'm not sure.	13	13
3. Are you in favour or not in favour of Canada and the United States joining together as one country?		
In favour	9%	29%
Not in favour	84	58
I'm not sure.	7	13

Independence/U.K.

For the reasons discussed in Chapter 4, it is difficult to find questions that will elicit whatever "anti-British" nationalist sentiment still exists among Canadians. In the early 1960s such sentiment would probably have been revealed by questions about what kind of flag Canada should have. But by 1968, when these surveys were done, questions about the flag had lost their former significance, especially among young people. The only symbol of British influence that continued to be discussed was the monarchy itself. Both the English and the French questionnaires included a broad direct question about the respondent's attitude towards British influence in Canada in the past, and then a more specific question about the monarchy.

43. Check the statement which best expresses your feelings about British influence in Canada in the past.

_____It has been a *great help* to Canada

_____It has *helped* Canada to some extent

_____It has *not made much difference* one way or the other

_____It has *probably hurt* Canada

_____It has *definitely hurt* Canada

44. Do you think that Canada should continue to pay allegiance to the Queen, or do you think that we should become a republic with an elected President?

_____Should continue to pay allegiance to the Queen

_____Should become a republic with an elected President

_____I'm not sure

_____I couldn't care less

Table B4 shows the distributions of responses to these two questions. In addition, the lists of advantages and disadvantages mentioned above included two relevant items that were used. One of the advantages the respondents could choose was: "Being part of the British Commonwealth under the Queen." This was chosen by 12 percent of the English students and 3 percent of the French students. One of the disadvantages was: "We still seem to be a colony of Great Britain." It was checked by 22 percent of the English students and 27 percent of the French students. The Indepen-

Table B4 Questions Used to Test Attitudes Regarding British Influence

	Distributions	
Questions and Answers	English (N = 1,081)	French (N = 744)
1. Check the statement which best expresses your feelings about British influence in Canada in the past.		
Great help to Canada	28%	11%
Helped to some extent	54	64
Not made much difference	9	4
Probably hurt Canada	7	16
Definitely hurt Canada	2	6
2. Do you think that Canada should continue to pay allegiance to the Queen, or do you think that we should become a republic with an elected President?		
Continue to pay allegiance	42%	16%
Become a republic	36	62
I'm not sure	15	10
I couldn't care less.	7	12

dence/U.K. (or simply UK) scale consists of the sum of the responses to the four items just described.

Internationalism

Both the English and the French questionnaires contained five opinion statements about the United Nations and the ideal of world government. These statements can be used to measure the attitude often considered the opposite of nationalism, namely, internationalism. The first of these statements raised the question of world government:

39. Some people say that there should be a world government able to control the laws made by each country. Do you agree with this opinion or disagree?

      _____Agree

      _____Disagree

      _____I'm not sure

Twenty-five percent of the English respondents and 37 percent of the French respondents agreed that there should be a world government. In both questionnaires this question immediately preceded eleven agree-disagree items, seven of which concerned national power and the remaining four of which concerned international organization. The items on international organization were taken from the scales developed by Sampson and Smith, "A Scale to Measure World-Minded Attitudes" (cited above) and Daniel R. Lutzker, "Internationalism as a Predictor of Cooperative Behavior," *Journal of Conflict Resolution*, 4 (1960), 426–30. These four statements and their marginal frequencies are shown in table B5. For three of the statements the proportions agreeing are almost exactly the same among the

Table B5   Items Used to Test Attitudes Towards International Organization

	% Agree	
Statements	English (N = 1,081)	French (N = 744)
1. The United Nations should have more power so that it could make countries obey its decisions.	76	50
2. An international police force should be in the only group in the world allowed to have weapons like tanks and missiles.	66	66
3. We must be willing to give up Canada's independence if, at some time, it becomes possible to set up a democratic world government.	50	52
4. It would be better to be a citizen of the world than of any particular country.	42	42

English and the French respondents. There is a large discrepancy only for the first item, about the United Nations, and it is not clear how this is to be explained, but it was probably due to a slip in translation: "the United Nations" was translated as "les Nations unies" rather than "l'Organisation des Nations Unies (ONU)." Despite this mistake, however, the inter-item correlations show that this item still belongs as part of the cluster of items dealing with international organization. The Internationalism (IN) scale is the sum of the responses to these five items.

Authoritarianism

Authoritarianism was measured in the customary manner, by means of opinion statements with which the respondents agreed or disagreed. The statements were selected on the assumption that authoritarianism results from the excessive repression, and consequently the projection and displacement, of morally problematic impulses, particularly sexual and aggressive impulses, and that what had to be measured, therefore was (a) uncritical acceptance of conventional ideas about good and bad behavior, (b) submissiveness towards ingroup authorities, particularly parents, and denial of rebellious impulses, (c) a tendency to attribute defects of character to low-status people, and (d) extreme hostility towards those who deviate from conventional standards of right conduct.

Table B6 shows the ten statements used and the proportions of each sample that agreed with each statement. The first six of the ten statements are simplified versions of statements used in the original F scale. Items 1 to 4 in the table were taken from a short F scale developed by means of latent structure analysis and found in Leo Srole, "Social Integration and Certain Corollaries: An Exploratory Study," *American Sociological Review*, 21 (1956), 709–16. Items 7 and 8 were taken from one of the most carefully reasoned attempts to create "reversed" F-scale items, Arthur Couch and Kenneth Keniston, "Yeasayers and Naysayers: Agreeing Response Set as a Personality Variable," *Journal of Abnormal and Social Psychology*, 60 (1960), 151–74. The last two items represent my own attempts to write new statements to tap authoritarianism that would be suitable for use with teenage respondents. The measure of authoritarianism used in this study is simply the sum of the responses to these ten items. For statements 1 to 6, 9, and 10, the scoring was as follows: 0 for strongly disagree, 1 for slightly disagree, 3 for slightly agree, and 4 for strongly agree. For statements 7 and 8, the scoring was the reverse.

Thus only two of the statements are worded in such a way that authoritarianism is indicated by disagreement with the statement. Many scholars have emphasized the importance of creating a balanced measure of authoritarianism—a scale in which there would be an equal number of positively

Table B6   Items Used to Test for Authoritarianism

	% Agree	
Statements	English (N = 1,081)	French (N = 744)
1. Any good leader should be strict with people under him in order to gain their respect.	50	52
2. There are two kinds of people in the world: the weak and the strong.	35	48
3. The most important thing to teach children is absolute obedience to their parents.	23	30
4. Prison is too good for sex criminals. They should be publicly whipped or worse.	20	31
5. Most people who don't get ahead just don't have enough willpower.	61	62
6. No normal person could ever think of hurting a close friend or relative.	52	71
7. It may well be that children who talk back to their parents actually respect them more in the long run.	36	50
8. People tend to place too much emphasis on respect for authority.	62	44
9. Young people these days do not have enough respect for their parents.	57	54
10. The main reason for the increase in crime is that punishment is too mild.	38	54

and negatively worded statements (for a recent discussion of this issue and a guide to the literature see J. J. Ray, "Reviving the Problem of Acquiescent Response Bias," *Journal of Social Psychology*, 121 [1983], 81–96). The problem, however, is to find suitable statements that will measure authoritarianism by expressing its opposite. There is little agreement about the meaning of authoritarianism; there is even less about its opposite. Given the ambiguity of authoritarianism, most balanced scales have been constructed by simply reversing some of the statements in the original F scale (e.g., "Familiarity does not breed contempt"). There is no reason to believe that the addition of such reversed statements to a questionnaire contributes to the validity of the F scale. Balanced scales based upon *political* or *cultural* (rather than *logical*) reversals of the original items make more sense—for example, the scale described in R. E. Lee and P. B. Warr, "The Development and Standardization of a Balanced F-Scale," *Journal of General Psychology*, 81 (1969), 109–29. Such scales bring out very clearly the conservative ideological content of the original F scale (cf. J. J. Ray, "Alternatives to the F Scale in the Measurement of Authoritarianism: A Catalog," *Journal of Social Psychology*, 122 [1984], 105–19).

The coefficients of reliability for the English and French versions of the F scale are .47 and .48 respectively (see tables B7 and B8). These figures are low, but it is important to compare them with the results from other studies. The Berkeley group estimated reliability by the split-half technique, and they reported a coefficient of .90 for their final 30-item F scale (Forms 45 and 40) (AP, 257). This result implies that a 10-item scale should have a coefficient of reliability of about .75 (Jum C. Nunnally, *Psychometric Theory* [New York: McGraw-Hill, 1967], pp. 223-25). In fact, however, 10-item measures of authoritarianism seem to have quite a bit lower reliability. One study analyzed responses to a 10-item positively-worded F scale by seven samples of undergraduates, graduate students, medical students, and schoolteachers, and reported reliabilities ranging from .34 to .78, with a mean value of .62 (Richard Christie, Joan Havel, and Bernard Seidenberg, "Is the F Scale Irreversible?" *Journal of Abnormal and Social Psychology*, 56 [1958], p. 155). Hilde T. Himmelweit and Betty Swift (in "Adolescent and Adult Authoritarianism Reexamined: Its Organization and Stability Over Time," *European Journal of Social Psychology*, 1 [1971], p. 379) report a coefficient of reliability (alpha) of .59 for a 10-term *empirically-derived* scale measuring the "Authoritarian View of Society." Their respondents were English adolescents, thirteen to fourteen years of age. The items in the scale were selected from a larger pool of items to maximize the homogeneity of the scale and hence its reliability. In light of these results, it seems reasonable to conclude that coefficients of .47 and .48, though low, are not much lower than should be expected.

Political Involvement

Both questionnaires contained the following four questions about interest in politics and attention to political affairs in the media.

32. Would you say that you have a great deal of interest in politics, a mild interest, or no real interest at all?
    ____A great deal of interest
    ____A mild interest
    ____No real interest at all

92. Some people seem to think about what's going on in government all the time, whether there's an election going on or not. Others aren't that interested. How often do you follow what's going on in government?
    ____Most of the time
    ____Some of the time
    ____Only now and then
    ____Hardly at all

93. How often do you read about politics in the newspaper?
    ____Nearly every day
    ____About once a week
    ____From time to time
    ____Almost never

94. How often do you talk about politics with other people?

_____Nearly every day

_____About once a week

_____From time to time

_____Almost never

The Index of Political Involvement used in Chapter 5 is simply an unweighted sum of the responses to these four questions.

Tables B7 and B8 provide some basic statistics, including estimates of the reliability of each scale. Reliability, inasmuch as it is distinct from the stability of the respondents' attitudes, is simply a function of the homogeneity of the attitude domain and the length of the attitude test (i.e., the number of opinion statements or questions in the scale), and it is thus easily measured. Cronbach's coefficient "alpha," which is used here, estimates the reliability of a psychological test on the assumption that the items composing it are a random sample of all the items in the domain of the test. It is equivalent to the Kuder-Richardson formula 20.

Table B7 Means and Standard Deviations of the Main Variables in the English Study

Variables	α	Males $\bar{X}$	s	N	Females $\bar{X}$	s	N
National Power	.52	3.94	1.64	582	3.84	1.64	432
National Unity	.65	9.55	2.86	589	9.52	2.28	424
Anti-French Feeling	.64	4.15	3.02	553	3.50	2.68	422
Independence/US	.59	6.26	2.26	596	6.20	2.15	444
Independence/UK	.52	5.28	2.92	596	4.87	2.82	440
Internationalism	.61	3.18	1.85	577	2.62	1.64	428
Authoritarianism	.47	12.96	4.31	597	13.58	4.21	445
Political Involvement	.85	6.52	3.01	597	5.17	2.75	447
CANADA	.74	4.58	.72	607	4.69	.72	453
ENGLISH CANADIANS	.78	3.91	.92	606	4.10	.87	448
FRENCH CANADIANS	.84	3.74	1.13	604	3.85	1.00	448
AMERICANS	.66	3.77	1.03	608	3.85	.95	453
BRITISH PEOPLE	.72	4.22	1.08	604	4.32	1.14	451

Table B8 Means and Standard Deviations of the Main Variables in the French Study

Variables	α	Males X̄	s	N	Females X̄	s	N
Separatist Nationalism	.78	4.52	3.00	370	4.61	2.98	330
Separatism	.72	5.35	3.04	368	5.82	2.81	335
Independence/US	.58	5.48	2.49	385	5.80	2.37	343
Independence/UK	.43	7.'5	2.50	387	6.48	2.48	345
Internationalism	.56	3.35	1.85	379	2.50	1.70	332
Authoritarianism	.48	15.57	4.17	378	14.94	4.26	335
Political Involvement	.84	6.42	2.88	384	6.24	2.82	340
CANADA	.73	4.72	.79	375	4.75	.73	336
ENGLISH CANADIANS	.80	3.51	1.13	379	3.56	1.09	339
FRENCH CANADIANS	.70	4.24	.97	378	4.34	.92	342
AMERICANS	.56	4.01	.98	376	4.06	1.08	339
FRENCHMEN	.75	3.85	1.51	378	3.83	1.30	344

Appendix C

Correlation Matrices

This appendix contains eight correlation matrices, four from the English data and four from the French data. All the variables have been numbered, and correlations are identified by the pairs of numbers in the left-most columns of the tables. The differences analyzed in Chapter 7 are the differences between the last two columns.

English Data

1. National Unity
2. Anti-French Feeling
3. National Power
4. Independence/U.S.
5. Independence/U.K.
6. Internationalism

7. CANADA
8. ENGLISH CANADIANS
9. FRENCH CANADIANS
10. AMERICANS
11. BRITISH PEOPLE

Variables	Basic Correlation	Corrected for Attenuation	Low F	High F
1–2	− .181	− .280	− .095	− .185
3	.037	.063	.024	.083
4	.100	.161	.169	.004
5	− .077	− .140	− .097	− .042
6	.018	.029	.022	.082
7	.058	.083	− .041	.031
8	− .026	− .037	− .001	− .095
9	.087	.118	− .073	.058

Variables	Basic Correlation	Corrected for Attenuation	Low F	High F
10	−.082	−.126	−.090	−.022
11	−.004	−.006	.026	−.056
2–3	.085	.117	.119	−.040
4	−.108	−.182	−.122	−.077
5	.032	.053	.083	−.004
6	.002	.019	.045	.025
7	−.070	−.089	−.026	−.028
8	.077	.104	.097	.122
9	−.543	−.751	−.510	−.548
10	.098	.166	.174	.129
11	.068	.102	.044	.108
3–4	.219	.396	.283	.294
5	.009	.046	.014	.003
6	−.019	−.034	.064	.116
7	.113	.182	.215	.177
8	.072	.114	.081	.089
9	−.060	−.090	−.011	.080
10	−.056	−.096	−.046	−.120
11	.037	.061	.124	.069
4–5	−.001	−.020	.046	−.036
6	.031	.052	.085	−.022
7	.006	.009	.084	−.020
8	−.094	−.139	−.146	−.098
9	.059	.084	.112	−.047
10	−.365	−.584	−.430	−.377
11	−.020	−.030	.063	−.055
5–6	.078	.114	.054	.031
7	−.139	−.251	−.256	−.048
8	−.117	−.198	−.208	−.010
9	.030	.041	−.080	.078
10	−.026	−.035	−.085	.054
11	−.234	−.439	−.305	−.185
6–7	−.042	−.062	.075	−.022
8	−.048	−.069	−.049	.145
9	.038	.054	.065	−.028
10	−.045	−.071	−.052	.039
11	.004	.006	.064	.035
7–8	.490	.645	.461	.537

Variables	Basic Correlation	Corrected for Attenuation	Low F	High F
9	.229	.290	.221	.117
10	.141	.202	.088	.106
11	.328	.450	.418	.327
8–9	.079	.098	.080	−.035
10	.263	.367	.325	.313
11	.415	.554	.496	.442
9–10	.094	.127	.048	.096
11	.088	.113	.114	.029
10–11	.218	.316	.190	.263

French Data

1. Separatist Nationalism
2. Separatism
3. Independence/U.S.
4. Independence/U.K.
5. Internationalism

6. CANADA
7. ENGLISH CANADIANS
8. FRENCH CANADIANS
9. AMERICANS
10. FRENCHMEN FROM FRANCE

Variables	Basic Correlation	Corrected for Attenuation	Low F	High F
1–2	.595	.807	.615	.539
3	.186	.277	.248	.141
4	.279	.481	.422	.169
5	−.058	−.088	−.070	−.060
6	−.115	−.153	−.131	.096
7	−.281	−.356	−.341	−.182
8	.137	.186	.170	.232
9	−.190	−.287	−.234	−.099
10	.121	.158	.024	.230
2–3	.240	.388	.299	.226
4	.226	.424	.362	.094
5	−.097	−.162	−.193	−.070
6	−.182	−.257	−.240	−.081
7	−.414	−.556	−.360	−.332
8	.124	.193	.100	.213
9	−.233	−.357	−.330	−.142
10	.100	.136	−.063	.158

Variables	Basic Correlation	Corrected for Attenuation	Low F	High F
3–4	.118	.236	.114	.093
5	−.065	−.114	.026	−.028
6	−.054	−.084	−.104	−.116
7	−.160	−.235	−.179	−.146
8	−.056	−.087	−.091	−.122
9	−.314	−.551	−.500	−.271
10	.006	.010	−.077	−.014
4–5	−.091	−.186	−.062	−.174
6	−.033	−.059	−.038	.114
7	−.262	−.447	−.337	−.188
8	.054	.098	.064	.052
9	−.098	−.200	−.179	.037
10	.081	.143	−.036	.115
5–6	.030	.048	.101	.028
7	.021	.032	.066	−.080
8	−.034	−.055	.028	−.134
9	−.037	−.066	.004	−.164
10	.038	.058	.013	.004
6–7	.372	.487	.387	.367
8	.435	.609	.569	.525
9	.314	.491	.376	.301
10	.063	.085	.215	.138
7–8	.117	.156	.217	.246
9	.367	.549	.377	.399
10	.073	.094	.119	.117
8–9	.194	.310	.230	.253
10	.283	.390	.366	.241
9–10	.064	.099	.160	.023

Notes

Introduction

1. T. W. Adorno, Else Frenkel-Brunswick, Daniel J. Levinson, and R. Nevitt Sanford, *The Authoritarian Personality*, Studies in Prejudice, ed. Max Horkheimer and Samuel H. Flowerman (New York: Harper & Row, 1950). Henceforth this volume will be cited by means of the abbreviation AP followed by page numbers. Important statements of closely related theories are Wilhelm Reich, *The Mass Psychology of Fascism*, trans. Vincent R. Carfagno (New York: Farrar, Straus & Giroux, 1970), the first edition of which was published in 1933; Erich Fromm, *Escape from Freedom* (New York: Rinehart, 1941); and Jean-Paul Sartre, *Anti-Semite and Jew*, trans. George J. Becker (New York: Schocken Books, 1948).

2. There are useful reviews of the literature by Richard Christie and Peggy Cook, "A Guide to the Published Literature Relating to the Authoritarian Personality through 1956," *Journal of Psychology*, 45 (1958), 171–99; John P. Kirscht and Ronald C. Dillehay, *Dimensions of Authoritarianism: A Review of Research and Theory* (Lexington: University of Kentucky Press, 1967); Nevitt Sanford, "Authoritarian Personality in Contemporary Perspective," in *Handbook of Political Psychology*, ed. Jeanne N. Knutson (San Francisco: Jossey-Bass, 1973), pp. 139–70; Frances Cherry and Donn Byrne, "Authoritarianism," in *Personality Variables in Social Behavior*, ed. Thomas Blass (Hillsdale, N.J.: Lawrence Erlbaum Associates, 1977), pp. 109–33; Bob Altemeyer, *Right-Wing Authoritarianism* (Winnipeg: University of Manitoba Press, 1981), chap. 1; and J. J. Ray, "Alternatives to the F Scale in the Measurement of Authoritarianism," *Journal of Social Psychology*, 122 (1984), 105–19.

3. Edward A. Shils, "Authoritarianism: 'Right' and 'Left'," in *Studies in the Scope and Method of "The Authoritarian Personality,"* ed. Richard Christie and Marie Jahoda (Glencoe, Ill.: The Free Press, 1954), p. 44.

4. Ibid., pp. 27–28, 37.

5. An excellent review of the controversy up to 1965 concluded that "it has not been demonstrated that fascists and communists resemble one another in authoritarianism or in any other dimension of ideology. No one thus far has shown that there is

an authoritarian of the left." Roger Brown, *Social Psychology* (New York: The Free Press, 1965), p. 542. Cf. William P. Kreml, *The Anti-Authoritarian Personality* (Oxford: Pergamon Press, 1977); Kreml, *Relativism and the Natural Left* (New York: New York University Press, 1983); W. F. Stone, "The Myth of Left-Wing Authoritarianism," *Political Psychology*, 2(3–4) (1980), 3–19; and Stanley Rothman and S. Robert Lichter, *Roots of Radicalism: Jews, Christians, and the New Left* (New York: Oxford University Press, 1982).

6. Shils, "Authoritarianism: 'Right' and 'Left'," pp. 42–43.

7. Herbert H. Hyman and Paul B. Sheatsley, "'The Authoritarian Personality'—A Methodological Critique," in *Studies in the Scope and Method of "The Authoritarian Personality,"* p. 122.

8. M. Brewster Smith, Foreword, in Kirscht and Dillehay, *Dimensions of Authoritarianism*, pp. vii–ix.

9. Gertrude J. Selznick and Stephen Steinberg, *The Tenacity of Prejudice: Anti-Semitism in Contemporary America* (New York: Harper & Row, 1969), p. 168.

10. Glenn D. Wilson, "The Concept of Conservatism," in *The Psychology of Conservatism*, ed. Glenn D. Wilson (London: Academic Press, 1973), pp. 3–15.

11. Michael Billig, *Ideology and Social Psychology: Extremism, Moderation and Contradiction* (Oxford: Basil Blackwell, 1982), p. 182.

12. Ibid., p. 87.

13. Michael Billig, *Fascists: A Social Psychological View of the National Front* (London: Academic Press, 1978), p. 36.

14. J. J. Ray, "The Authoritarian as Measured by a Personality Scale: Solid Citizen or Misfit?" *Journal of Clinical Psychology*, 35 (1979), p. 746.

15. John Madge, *The Origins of Scientific Sociology* (New York: The Free Press, 1962), pp. 377, 382, 423.

16. Martin Jay, *The Dialectical Imagination: A History of the Frankfurt School and the Institute of Social Research, 1923–1950* (Boston: Little, Brown, 1973), p. 250.

17. David Held, *Introduction to Critical Theory: Horkheimer to Habermas* (Berkeley: University of California Press, 1980), pp. 140, 144, 146.

18. Rothman and Lichter, *Roots of Radicalism*, p. 146. "Our model has been the pioneering work in this field, *The Authoritarian Personality*. Critical as we are of that work, it still stands head and shoulders above most of the studies that have followed it" (p. xiii).

19. Ibid., pp. 388–89.

20. The recent literature on "critical theory" includes the following major studies: Jay, *The Dialectical Imagination;* Held, *Introduction to Critical Theory;* Susan Buck-Morss, *The Origin of Negative Dialectics: Theodor W. Adorno, Walter Benjamin, and the Frankfurt Institute* (New York: The Free Press, 1977); Phil Slater, *Origins and Significance of the Frankfurt School: A Marxist Perspective* (London: Routledge & Kegan Paul, 1977); Gillian Rose, *The Melancholy Science: An Introduction to the Thought of Theodor W. Adorno* (London: Macmillan, 1978); Garbis Kortian, *Metacritique: The Philosophical Argument of Jürgen Habermas*, trans. John Raffan (Cambridge: Cambridge University Press, 1980); Morton Schoolman, *The Imaginary Witness: The Critical Theory of Herbert Marcuse* (New York: The Free Press, 1980); Raymond Geuss, *The Idea of a Critical Theory: Habermas and the Frankfurt School* (Cambridge: Cambridge University Press, 1981); George Friedman, *The Political Philosophy of the Frankfurt School* (Ithaca: Cornell University

Press, 1981); and Thomas McCarthy, *The Critical Theory of Jürgen Habermas* (Cambridge: MIT Press, 1982).

21. Albrecht Wellmer, *Critical Theory of Society,* trans. John Cumming (New York: Herder and Herder, 1971), p. 52.

22. Russell Jacoby, *Social Amnesia: A Critique of Contemporary Psychology from Adler to Laing* (Boston: Beacon Press, 1975), p. 1.

23. Ibid., pp. 3–4

24. Theophrastus, *The Characters,* with Menander, *Plays and Fragments,* trans. Philip Vallacott, 2d ed. (Harmondsworth: Penguin, 1973), pp. 55–56. Theophrastus was born about 372 B.C. and died about 287. "He studied at Athens under Aristotle, and when Aristotle was forced to retire in 323 he became the head of the Lyceum, the academy in Athens founded by Aristotle. Under Theophrastus the enrollment of pupils and auditors reached its highest point. . . . His notable *Charakteres* (many English translations) consist of 30 brief and vigorous character sketches delineating moral types derived from studies that Aristotle had made for ethical and rhetorical purposes." *Encyclopedia Britannica,* 15th ed., vol. 9, p. 940.

25. "An Appeal from the New to the Old Whigs," in *Works of the Right Honorable Edmund Burke,* 4th ed., 12 vols. (Boston: Little, Brown, 1871), vol. 4, pp. 212–13.

Chapter One

1. The history of the project is discussed in Nevitt Sanford, "The Approach of 'The Authoritarian Personality', " in *A Source Book for the Study of Personality and Politics,* ed. Fred I. Greenstein and Michael Lerner (Chicago: Markham, 1971), pp. 308–11; Nevitt Sanford, "Authoritarian Personality in Contemporary Perspective," in *Handbook of Political Psychology,* ed. Jeanne N. Knutson (San Francisco: Jossey-Bass, 1973), pp. 139–43; T. W. Adorno, "Scientific Experiences of a European Scholar in America," in *The Intellectual Migration: Europe and America, 1930–1960,* ed. Donald Fleming and Bernard Bailyn (Cambridge: Harvard University Press, 1969); Martin Jay, *The Dialectical Imagination: A History of the Frankfurt School and the Institute of Social Research, 1923-1950* (Boston: Little, Brown, 1973), chap. 7; Susanne Petra Schad, *Empirical Social Research in Weimar-Germany,* Publications of the International Social Science Council No. 15 (Paris: Mouton, 1972), pp. 82–96; and Richard I. Evans, *The Making of Social Psychology: Discussions with Creative Contributors* (New York: Gardner Press, 1980), pp. 52–62.

2. Daniel J. Levinson and R. Nevitt Sanford, "A Scale for Measuring Anti-Semitism," *Journal of Psychology,* 17 (1944), 339–70.

3. The Berkeley group adopted this striking locution as a reminder that those who scored low on the A-S scale were not necessarily pro-Semitic (i.e., they did not necessarily harbour any irrational bias in favor of Jews); they simply rejected the irrationally anti-Semitic opinions that were tapped by the scale. Cf. Norman M. Prentice, "The Comparability of Positive and Negative Items in Scales of Ethnic Prejudice," *Journal of Abnormal and Social Psychology,* 52 (1956), 420–21; Norman M. Prentice, "The Influence of Ethnic Attitudes on Reasoning about Groups," *Journal of Abnormal and Social Psychology,* 55 (1957), 270–72; Howard Schuman

and John Harding, "Prejudice and the Norm of Rationality," *Sociometry*, 27 (1964), 353–71.

4. "One of the facts of which we are most certain is that people who reject one out-group will tend to reject other out-groups. If a person is anti-Jewish, he is likely to be anti-Catholic, anti-Negro, anti any out-group." Gordon W. Allport, *The Nature of Prejudice* (Reading, Mass.: Addison-Wesley, 1954), p. 68. Allport cities four studies published during the thirties and forties in support of this statement (p. 80, nn. 1, 4). The most interesting of these is Gardner Murphy and Rensis Likert, *Public Opinion and the Individual: A Psychological Study of Student Attitudes on Public Questions* (New York: Harper & Bros., 1938), which is remarkably similar to *The Authoritarian Personality* in its objectives, design, methods, and findings, and which first drew attention to the connection between prejudice and nationalism.

5. Differences in prejudice are no doubt partly the result of different experiences with members of minority groups. Members of a dominant or majority group may encounter relatively few members of any particular minority, and different individuals may thus encounter quite different *samples* of that minority. If people generalized about minorities from the small samples of their members they had known personally, then sampling variability might explain individual differences in prejudice. Small samples could differ considerably, on the average, in their objective pleasantness, honesty, friendliness, intelligence, and so on. This reasoning sounds sensible, and it probably has something to do with explaining individual differences in prejudice. But it cannot explain strong correlations between different hostile attitudes, for it is not reasonable to suppose that those who happen to have encountered bad samples of Jews, for example, will also happen to have had bad luck with Negroes and Oklahomans.

6. It belongs to the family of neologisms based upon *ethnos* that was created by nineteenth-century anthropology—ethnography, ethnology, ethnopsychology, ethnogeny, and so on. Its closest relative is "ethnomaniac," defined by the *Oxford English Dictionary* as "one who is crazy about racial autonomy."

7. William Graham Sumner, *Folkways* (New York: Ginn, 1906), pp. 12–13.

8. Cf. Robert A. LeVine and Donald T. Campbell, *Ethnocentrism: Theories of Conflict, Ethnic Attitudes, and Group Behavior* (New York: Wiley, 1972), pp. 1–21.

9. Levinson writes "concentric circles around a bull's-eye" (AP, 148), but his point is really that they are not *concentric:* the center shifts depending upon the topic being discussed.

Chapter Two

1. Max Horkheimer and Theodor W. Adorno, *Dialectic of Enlightenment*, trans. John Cumming (New York: Herder and Herder, 1972), pp. 170–72, 187–200. From the standpoint of Horkheimer and Adorno the California studies were the continuation of empirical work done by the Institut für Sozialforschung at the University of Frankfurt, just before Hitler's rise to power. See Max Horkheimer, ed., *Studien über Autorität und Familie* (Paris: Felix Alcan, 1936); Horkheimer's essay on "Authority and the Family," in *Critical Theory: Selected Essays*, trans. John Cumming (New York: Herder and Herder, 1972), pp. 47–131; and Herbert Marcuse, "A Study on

Authority," in *Studies in Critical Philosophy*, trans. Joris De Bres (Boston: Beacon Press, 1973), pp. 49–155.

2. R. Nevitt Sanford and Herbert S. Conrad, "Some Personality Correlates of Morale," *Journal of Abnormal and Social Psychology*, 38 (1943), 3–20, and R. Nevitt Sanford and Herbert S. Conrad, "High and Low Morale as Exemplified in Two Cases," *Character and Personality*, 12 (1944), 207–27. The scale is described in John Harding, "A Scale for Measuring Civilian Morale," *Journal of Psychology*, 12 (1941), 101–10.

3. R. Nevitt Sanford, Herbert S. Conrad, and Kate Franck, "Psychological Determinants of Optimism Regarding Consequences of the War," *Journal of Psychology*, 22 (1946), 207–35.

4. Horkheimer and Adorno apparently decided to collaborate with the Berkeley group on the studies eventually published as *The Authoritarian Personality* partly because they recognized the similarity between these early results and their own conception of authoritarianism. See Martin Jay, *The Dialectical Imagination: A History of the Frankfurt School and the Institute of Social Research, 1923–1950* (Boston: Little, Brown, 1973), p. 239.

5. Sanford and Conrad, "Some Personality Correlates of Morale," pp. 16 and 19.

6. Sanford and Conrad, "High and Low Morale as Exemplified in Two Cases," p. 225.

7. Sanford, Conrad, and Franck, "Psychological Determinants of Optimism," p. 232.

8. Else Frenkel-Brunswik and R. Nevitt Sanford, "Some Personality Factors in Anti-Semitism," *Journal of Psychology*, 20 (1945), 271–91.

9. Ibid., pp. 275–76.

10. The Thematic Apperception Test, or TAT, is a projective test of personality developed by Henry Murray. It involves the presentation of a standard series of ambiguous but emotionally provocative pictures to the subjects being tested. The subjects tell stories about the pictures, and then the psychologists tell, by examining the themes and imagery of the subjects' stories, what kinds of personalities they have. The Berkeley group used nine of Murray's pictures and four of their own, especially chosen to bring out attitudes towards ingroups and outgroups. The following material summarizes pp. 277–84 of the article cited in note 8.

11. Ibid., pp. 285-86.

12. Not, as some have supposed, those high and low on authoritarianism as measured by the F scale. Cf. Rupert Wilkinson, *The Broken Rebel: A Study in Culture, Politics and Authoritarian Character* (New York: Harper & Row, 1972), pp. 54, 328 (n. 6), 329 (n. 11), and 331 (n. 9).

13. Any correlation between ideology and personality implies of course a distinction between them, and the Berkeley group made such a distinction, not in terms of organization or structure, but in terms of psychological depth. Thus they defined *ideology* as "an organization of opinions, attitudes, and values—a way of thinking about man and society" (AP, 2). To study ideology was to investigate "consistent patterns" or "organized totalities," but since opinions, attitudes, and values are expressed more or less openly in words, they are psychologically "on the surface" (AP, 3). A person's ideology existed in what he said and thought; it could be

described by summarizing his opinions. Personality, by contrast, was deep and mute, "a more or less enduring organization of forces within the individual" (AP, 5). These forces were *needs,* and personality was essentially an organization of needs. "The forces of personality are primarily *needs* (drives, wishes, emotional impulses) which vary from one individual to another in their quality, their intensity, their mode of gratification, and the objects of their attachment, and which interact with other needs in harmonious or conflicting patterns. There are primitive emotional needs, there are needs to avoid punishment and to keep the good will of the social group, there are needs to maintain harmony and integration within the self" (AP, 5). As these distinctions suggest, and as the Berkeley group acknowledged, they leaned upon Freud "for theory as to the structure of personality" (AP, 5).

14. The Berkeley group recognized that the psychological approach they employed with anti-Semitism would be less relevant for some ideologies than it was for others. They conceded that there were some ideologies that were best understood, not in relation to personality defects, but in relation to the evidence for their validity. These ideologies were such as "a reasonable man, with some understanding of the role of such [psychological] determinants as those discussed above, and with complete access to the necessary facts [would] organize for himself" (AP, 10–11). Such "rational systems" were still related to personality, since they had to be motivated, but the kind of personality organization from which they sprang was the "mature personality" in which the ego, "that part of the personality which appreciates reality, integrates the other parts, and operates with the most conscious awareness," was strong and effective and in which, consequently, it could "take responsibility for nonrational forces operating within the personality" (AP, 11). To understand such ideologies we would have to understand the arguments in their favor; we would have to enter sympathetically into their proponents' view of the world, a world "complex and difficult to know"; and we would have to consider their "real interests [as they conflicted] with the real interests of other men" (AP, 11). Only by holding open the possibility of such an approach to ideology, they argued, can we avoid "the destructive view . . . that since all ideologies, all philosophies, derive from non-rational sources, there is no basis for saying that one has more merit than another" (AP, 11).

15. The Berkeley group wanted to develop a method for identifying and estimating the number of those "whose outlook was such as to indicate that they would readily accept fascism if it should become a strong or acceptable social movement" (AP, 1). They equated this "inner readiness" with a particular kind of "personality" defined by a structure of needs rather than by a set of opinions, and the evidence of the relevant needs, in the American context, was acceptance of ethnocentric ideology. The ground-breaking work along these lines was done by Erich Fromm, and his discussions of some of the methodological (or conceptual) problems are illuminating. See the Appendix to *Escape from Freedom* (New York: Rinehart, 1941); the articles from the *Zeitschrift für Sozialforschung* reprinted in *The Crises of Psychoanalysis: Essays on Freud, Marx, and Social Psychology* (New York: Holt, Rinehart and Winston, 1970), chaps. 8 and 9; and the article on "The Revolutionary Character" in *The Dogma of Christ, and Other Essays on Religion, Psychology and Culture* (New York: Holt, Rinehart and Winston, 1963). pp. 145–66.

16. Cf. Konrad Lorenz, *On Aggression,* trans. Marjorie Latzke (London:

Methuen, 1966), especially pp. 223–35. From a classification of possible forms of social behavior and possible forms of society, and from data about the correlation between personal bonding and aggression across species, Lorenz argues that human beings, like many other species, have an aggressive instinct that would serve, under natural conditions, to ensure the survival of the individual and the species, but that has become destructive in civilization. Lorenz calls the most important manifestation of this instinct in man "militant enthusiasm," and he means by this something very close to what the Berkeley group meant by ethnocentrism.

17. Cf. Jean-Paul Sartre, *Anti-Semite and Jew*, trans. George J. Becker (New York: Schocken Books, 1948), pp. 7–54. This essay was originally published in 1946, and an excerpt, under the title "Portrait of the Anti-Semite," appeared in the *Partisan Review* that year. The Berkeley group noted the striking resemblance between Sartre's "phenomenological 'portrait'" and "the syndrome which slowly emerged from [their own] empirical observations and quantitative analysis," and they found these similarities "remarkable" (AP, 971).

18. Cf. A. H. Maslow, "The Authoritarian Character Structure," *Journal of Social Psychology*, 18 (1943), 401–41, which presents a fundamentally different interpretation of many of the same traits.

19. "Our high extremes are *over*-conformist; they adhere *rigidly* to middle class values and are made anxious by the appearance, in themselves or in others, of tendencies of an opposite character. This points to insecurity as the condition with which these subjects are struggling. . . . Thus it is not so much middle class values themselves that we would call into question, but rather the rigidity with which they are adhered to." Frenkel-Brunswik and Sanford, "Some Personality Factors," p. 289. In a later paper Frenkel-Brunswik distinguished between "genuine and constructive conformity," on the one hand, and "rigid and compulsive conformity," on the other hand. See "Environmental Controls and the Impoverishment of Thought," in *Totalitarianism*, ed. Carl J. Friedrich (Cambridge: Harvard University Press, 1954), p. 178. The relation between conformity and authoritarianism will be examined in Chapter 10 below.

20. There is no criterion measure of ego strength: "Research findings usually point out serious problems in the validation of ego strength measures. First of all . . . it has proved to be particularly difficult to demonstrate a positive relationship between different measures of ego strength." Uriel Last, "Ego Strength," in *Encyclopedia of Clinical Assessment*, ed. Robert Henley Woody, 2 vols. (San Francisco: Jossey-Bass, 1980), vol. 1, p. 345. Evidently the term means different things in different contexts. What it means in the present context must be inferred from a closer examination of the correlates of ethnocentrism and authoritarianism. The problem will be taken up again in Chapters 5 and 10 below.

21. Ross Stagner, "Fascist Attitudes: An Exploratory Study," *Journal of Social Psychology*, 7 (1936), 309–19; Ross Stagner, "Studies of Aggressive Social Attitudes: I. Measurement and Interrelation of Selected Attitudes," *Journal of Social Psychology*, 20 (1944), 109–20; and Allen L. Edwards, "Unlabelled Fascist Attitudes," *Journal of Abnormal and Social Psychology*, 36 (1941), 575–82.

22. Cf. Alan Hughes, *Psychology and the Political Experience* (Cambridge: Cambridge University Press, 1975), pp. 44–48, and R. A. Altemeyer, *Right-Wing Authoritarianism* (Winnipeg: University of Manitoba Press, 1981), p. 25.

23. See Franz Samelson, "From 'Race Psychology' to 'Studies in Prejudice': Some Observations on the Thematic Reversal in Social Psychology," *Journal of the History of the Behavioral Sciences*, 14 (1978), 265–78.

24. Indirectly the theory may also owe something to Nietzsche's well-known writings about *ressentiment* as a source of egalitarian values, but three main differences separate Nietzsche's speculations from those of the Berkeley group. First, regarding causes, Nietzsche's theory is more "materialist": it highlights biological factors (innate constitutional weakness, lack of vitality) and contemporary circumstances (membership in a subordinate nation, an exploited class, etc.), rather than psychological factors (a particular resolution of the Oedipus complex that leads to a weak ego). Second, regarding motivation, the older theory emphasizes frustrations having to do with power, status, and control over others (the will to power), while the newer theory emphasizes sexual frustrations (id and libido) that lead to reactive aggression. Finally, regarding consequences, the older theory shows how resentment can create new, revolutionary values (the "transvaluation of values" by which the slaves' way of life becomes good, the masters' evil), while the newer theory presents resentment as a factor in stabilizing the power and privileges of the masters ("conventionalism" and "authoritarian submission"). See Friedrich Nietzsche, *The Genealogy of Morals* and *Beyond Good and Evil*, parts V and IX. Cf. Max Scheler, *Ressentiment*, trans. W. H. Holdheim (New York: Schocken Books, 1961), and Helmut Schoeck, *Envy: A Theory of Social Behaviour*, trans. Michael Glenny and Betty Ross (New York: Harcourt, Brace & World, 1970).

25. In obsessional neurosis, libido that is subject to repression is transformed into anxiety that is then bound to an external danger. Provided the individual can maintain the illusion of being threatened from outside, and provided he can carry out whatever obsessive rituals ward off this danger for him, he can avoid any conscious awareness of his repressed libido, and he can minimize the troublesome and inexplicable anxiety derived from it. The ethnocentrist's attitude towards outgroups can thus be seen as an obsessional neurosis—as a by-product of the projection outwards of repressed libido. See Sigmund Freud, *Introductory Lectures on Psycho-Analysis*, in *The Standard Edition of the Complete Psychological Works of Sigmund Freud*, ed. James Strachey et al., 24 vols. (London: Hogarth Press, 1953–66), vol. 16, Lectures 17 and 25. Cf. "Notes upon a Case of Obsessional Neurosis," in *Standard Edition*, vol. 10, pp. 232–33 and 245–48.

26. Freud, "Libidinal Types," *Standard Edition*, vol. 21, p. 218.

27. Ibid., p. 219.

28. Ibid.

29. Ibid.

30. Wilhelm Reich, *The Mass Psychology of Fascism*, trans. Vincent R. Carfagno (New York: Farrar, Straus & Giroux, 1970), p. 27. There are good brief accounts of Reich's theories in Philip Rieff, *The Triumph of the Therapeutic: Uses of Faith after Freud* (New York: Harper & Row, 1966), chap. 6; Paul Edwards, "Wilhelm Reich," in *The Encyclopedia of Philosophy*, ed. Paul Edwards, 8 vols. (New York: Macmillan, 1967), vol. 7, pp. 104–15; Paul A. Robinson, *The Freudian Left: Wilhelm Reich, Geza Roheim, Herbert Marcuse* (New York: Harper & Row, 1969), pp. 9–73; and Bertell Ollman, *Social and Sexual Revolution: Essays on Marx and Reich* (Montreal: Black Rose Books, 1978), chaps. 6 and 7.

31. Reich, *The Mass Psychology of Fascism*, p. 30.

32. This vague formula is given a much clearer meaning by Reich's practical proposals. See Wilhelm Reich, *The Sexual Revolution* (New York: Noonday Press, 1962), pp. 75–79, 112, 191, 258, and 263. As one commentator observes, his attention to "administrative detail—his disregard for the niceties of academic discourse and its concern with maintaining the proper level of abstraction—has a refreshing quality about it." Robinson, *The Freudian Left*, p. 55.

33. Here too there is an annoying vagueness, and others have been much clearer. Sartre, for example, declared that "anti-Semitism would have no existence in a society without classes and founded on collective ownership of the instruments of labour, one in which man, freed of his hallucinations inherited from an older world, would at long last throw himself wholeheartedly into *his* enterprise—which is to create the kingdom of man. Anti-Semitism would then be cut at its roots." Sartre, *Anti-Semite and Jew*, p. 150.

Chapter Three

1. Leonard Doob, *Patriotism and Nationalism: Their Psychological Foundations* (New Haven: Yale University Press, 1964). This book, the most recent major psychological study of nationalism, after carefully equating patriotism and national-ism, almost casually separates patriotism from ethnic prejudice and xenophobia: "Whatever relation does in fact exist between [patriotism and personality] is prob-ably different from that between prejudice and personality. For there is no reason to suppose that the personality traits associated with love of country are the same as those connected with hostility toward foreign countries or foreigners" (p. 128). It does not distinguish types of nationalism and does not deal with individual differ-ences and the problem of susceptibility. It stresses the *ordinariness* of nationalism, its basically unproblematic psychological character. Its main point is that if you under-stand learning (you understand learning if you understand the simple principles animal trainers use), then you have understood all that psychologists have to teach about the psychology of patriotism and nationalism.

2. M. Brewster Smith, Jerome S. Bruner, and Robert W. White, *Opinions and Personality* (New York: John Wiley & Sons, 1956). This classic statement of the "functional approach," although not presented as a study of nationalism, is actually concerned with American attitudes towards the Soviet Union. It comes closest to providing a thorough discussion of the Berkeley group's theory from the standpoint of nationalism, but for reasons that will be explained in Chapters 7 and 10 below, its treatment must be considered unsatisfactory.

3. Howard P. Smith and Ellen W. Rosen, "Some Psychological Correlates of Worldmindedness and Authoritarianism," *Journal of Personality*, 26 (1958), 170–83. The concept of "worldmindedness" was introduced and a scale described in Donald L. Sampson and Howard P. Smith, "A Scale to Measure World-Minded Attitudes," *Journal of Social Psychology*, 45 (1957), 99–106. "The concept *world-mindedness* . . . designates purely a value orientation, or frame of reference, apart from knowledge about, or interest in, international relations. We identify as highly worldminded the individual who favors a world-view of the problems of humanity,

whose primary reference group is mankind, rather than Americans, English, Chinese, etc. . . . Worldmindedness [is] at one end of the continuum and national-mindedness at the other end" (pp. 99–100).

4. Smith and Rosen, "Some Psychological Correlates of Worldmindedness," pp. 179–82.

5. Daniel J. Levinson, "Authoritarian Personality and Foreign Policy," *Journal of Conflict Resolution*, 1 (1957), 37–47. On the background to the study and the sample, see Daniel J. Levinson, "The Intergroup Relations Workshop: Its Psychological Aims and Effect," *Journal of Psychology*, 38 (1954), 103–26.

6. Levinson, "Authoritarian Personality and Foreign Policy," pp. 38–39.

7. Ibid., p. 44.

8. Nancy C. Morse and Floyd H. Allport, "The Causation of Anti-Semitism: An Investigation of Seven Hypotheses," *Journal of Psychology*, 34 (1952), 197–233. The data for this study must have been collected in 1945 or 1946, around the same time as the data for the California studies. The National Involvement scale, which showed the strongest relations with anti-Semitism, is reproduced in Harold Guetzkow, *Multiple Loyalties: Theoretical Approach to a Problem in International Organization*, Publication No. 4 of the Center for Research on World Political Institutions (Princeton, N.J.: Princeton University Press, 1955), p. 14.

9. Morse and Allport, "The Causation of Anti-Semitism," p. 219. Cf. Frederick D. Herzon, John Kincaid, and Verne Dalton, "Personality and Public Opinion: The Case of Authoritarianism, Prejudice, and Support for the Korean and Vietnam Wars," *Polity*, 11 (1978), 92–113.

10. Paul V. Gump, "Anti-Democratic Trends and Student Reaction to President Truman's Dismissal of General MacArthur," *Journal of Social Psychology*, 38 (1953), 131–35; Morris Janowitz and Dwaine Marvick, "Authoritarianism and Political Behavior," *Public Opinion Quarterly*, 17 (1953), 185–201; Robert E. Lane, "Political Personality and Electoral Choice," *American Political Science Review*, 49 (1955), 173–90; Howard P. Smith, "Do Intercultural Experiences Affect Attitudes?" *Journal of Abnormal and Social Psychology*, 51 (1955), 469–77; Elizabeth G. French and Raymond R. Ernest, "The Relation between Authoritarianism and Acceptance of Military Ideology," *Journal of Personality*, 24 (1956), 181–91; Sampson and Smith, "A Scale to Measure World-Minded Attitudes"; William J. MacKinnon and Richard Centers, "Authoritarianism and Internationalism," *Public Opinion Quarterly*, 20 (1957), 621–30; and "Socio-Psychological Factors in Public Orientation toward an Out-Group," *American Journal of Sociology*, 63 (1958), 415–19; Bernard Fensterwald, "The Anatomy of American 'Isolationism' and Expansionism, II," *Journal of Conflict Resolution*, 2 (1958), 280–309; James G. Martin and Frank R. Westie, "The Tolerant Personality," *American Sociological Review*, 24 (1959), 521–28; Charles D. Farris, "Selected Attitudes on Foreign Affairs as Correlates of Authoritarianism and Anomie," *Journal of Politics*, 22 (1960), 50–67; Carl D. Williams, "Authoritarianism and Student Reaction to Airplane Hijacking," *Journal of Social Psychology*, 60 (1963), 289–91; James G. Martin, *The Tolerant Personality* (Detroit: Wayne State University Press, 1964); and Milton J. Rosenberg, "Images in Relation to the Policy Process: American Public Opinion on Cold-War Issues," in *International Behavior: A Socio-Psychological Analysis*, ed. Herbert C. Kelman (New York: Holt, Rinehart and Winston, 1965), p. 326.

11. Richard R. Izzett, "Authoritarianism and Attitudes toward the Vietnam War as Reflected in Behavioral and Self-Report Measures," *Journal of Personality and Social Psychology*, 17 (1971), 145–48; Joan Aldous and Irving Tallman, "Immediacy of Situation and Conventionality as Influences on Attitudes toward War," *Sociology and Social Research*, 56 (1972), 356–67; Donald Granberg and Gail Corrigan, "Authoritarianism, Dogmatism, and Orientations toward the Vietnam War," *Sociometry*, 35 (1972), 468–76; and David Mark Mantell, *True Americanism: Green Berets and War Resisters, A Study of Commitment* (New York: Teacher's College Press, 1974), p. 215. See also Thomas L. Brewer, "Military Officers and Arms Control: Personality Correlates of Attitudes," *Journal of Political and Military Sociology*, 3 (1975), 15–25.

12. Kenneth W. Terhune, "Nationalism among Foreign and American Students: An Exploratory Study," *Journal of Conflict Resolution*, 8 (1964), 256–70.

13. Mark Chesler and Richard Schmuck, "Student Reactions to the Cuban Crisis and Public Dissent," *Public Opinion Quarterly*, 28 (1964), 467–82, and Mark Chesler and Richard Schmuck, "Social Psychological Characteristics of Super-Patriots," in *The American Right Wing: Readings in Political Behavior*, ed. Robert A. Schoenberger (New York: Holt, Rinehart and Winston, 1969), p. 185.

14. Stuart A. Karabenick and R. Ward Wilson, "Dogmatism among War Hawks and Peace Doves," *Psychological Reports*, 25 (1969), 419–22; Daniel W. Bailes and Irving B. Guller, "Dogmatism and Attitudes toward the Vietnam War," *Sociometry*, 33 (1970), 140–46; Granberg and Corrigan, "Authoritarianism, Dogmatism, and Orientations toward the Vietnam War." Cf. Mantell, *True Americanism*, p. 215.

15. Martin F. Rosenman, "Dogmatism and the Movie 'Dr. Strangelove'," *Psychological Reports*, 20 (1967), 942.

16. Herbert McClosky, "Personality and Attitude Correlates of Foreign Policy Orientations," in *Domestic Sources of Foreign Policy*, ed. J. N. Rosenau (New York: The Free Press, 1967).

17. Ibid., p. 123.

18. Paul M. Sniderman and Jack Citrin, "Psychological Sources of Political Beliefs: Self-Esteem and Isolationist Attitudes," *American Political Science Review*, 65 (1971), 401–17.

19. Morris Rosenberg, "Misanthropy and Attitudes toward International Affairs," *Journal of Conflict Resolution*, 1 (1957), 340–45.

20. Kenneth W. Terhune, "Nationalism among Foreign and American Students." Cf. Walter C. Kaufman, "Status, Authoritarianism, and Anti-Semitism," *American Journal of Sociology*, 62 (1957), 379–82.

21. Knud S. Larsen and Henry L. Minton, "Attributed Social Power: A Scale and Some Validity," *Journal of Social Psychology*, 85 (1971), 37–39.

22. Daniel R. Lutzker, "Internationalism as a Predictor of Cooperative Behavior," *Journal of Conflict Resolution*, 4 (1960), 426–30, and Charles G. McClintock et al., "Internationalism-Isolationism, Strategy of the Other Player, and Two-Person Game Behaviour," *Journal of Abnormal and Social Psychology*, 67 (1963), 631–36. Cf. Marc Pilisuk et al., "War Hawks and Peace Doves: Alternate Resolutions of Experimental Conflicts," *Journal of Conflict Resolution*, 9 (1965), 491–508.

23. Maurice L. Farber, "The Anal Character and Political Aggression," *Journal of Abnormal and Social Psychology*, 51 (1955), 486–89.

24. Kurt Danziger, "Value Differences among South African Students," *Journal of Abnormal and Social Psychology*, 57 (1958), 339–46, and Christopher Orpen, "The Effect of Cultural Factors on the Relationship between Prejudice and Personality," *Journal of Psychology*, 78 (1971), 73–79. Cf. Patrick C. L. Heaven, "Afrikaner Patriotism Today: The Role of Attitudes and Personality," *Canadian Review of Studies in Nationalism*, 11 (1984), 133–39.

25. Alan Hughes, *Psychology and the Political Experience* (London: Cambridge University Press, 1975), p. 133 ("Defence Leftism" could be called internationalism), and John J. Ray, "The New Australian Nationalism," *Quadrant*, 25 (Jan.–Feb., 1981), 60–62.

26. W. Doise, "Autoritarisme, dogmatisme et mode d'approche des relations internationales," *Journal de psychologie normale et pathologique*, 66 (1969), 35–53.

27. Kevin Marjoribanks and Nina Josefowitz, "Kerlinger's Theory of Social Attitudes: An Analysis," *Psychological Reports*, 37 (1975), 819–23; Richard H. Willis, "Political and Child-Rearing Attitudes in Sweden," *Journal of Abnormal and Social Psychology*, 53 (1956), 74–77; E. Terry Prothro and Jack D. Keehn, "The Structure of Social Attitudes in Lebanon," *Journal of Abnormal and Social Psychology*, 53 (1956), 157–60; and David R. Thomas, "Authoritarianism, Child-Rearing Practices and Ethnocentrism in Seven Pacific Island Groups," *International Journal of Psychology*, 10 (1975), 235–46.

28. William Eckhardt and Alan Newcombe, "Militarism, Personality, and Other Social Attitudes," *Journal of Conflict Resolution*, 13 (1969), 210–19; William Eckhardt, "The Factor of Militarism," *Journal of Peace Research*, 6 (1969), 123–32; and William Eckhardt and Norman Z. Alcock, "Ideology and Personality in War/Peace Attitudes," *Journal of Social Psychology*, 81 (1970), 105–16. Cf. Thomas N. Trenton, "Canadian Nationalism, Dogmatism and Internationalism: A Case of Independence?" *Canadian Review of Studies in Nationalism*, 5 (1978), 104–13, which will be discussed in Chapter 5 below.

29. Cf. Lawrence A. Dombrose and Daniel J. Levinson, "Ideological 'Militancy' and 'Pacifism' in Democratic Individuals," *Journal of Social Psychology*, 32 (1950), 101–13. This rather complicated study clarified the distinction between democratic militancy and ethnocentrism. It examined the interrelations among three variables—acceptance of democratic ideology (as measured by the E scale), authoritarianism (as measured by the F scale), and a new variable, militancy vs. pacifism, which had to do with methods of attaining democratic goals. "A 'militant democratic' ideology is one which rejects or makes secondary pacifistic methods (education is secondary to more direct methods), which proposes the use of law and force to achieve democratic values [of racial integration and tolerance] immediately, or within a relatively short period of time, whether or not there be universal acceptance of these values, and which would attempt to change the existing socioeconomic framework wherever present institutions hinder democratic achievement" (p. 102). The empirical research of Dombrose and Levinson brought to light a curious fact: while there was the usual *positive* correlation between authoritarianism (the F scale) and hostility against outgroups (the E scale), there was a *negative* correlation between authoritarianism and militancy—forceful opposition to the bigots and reactionaries who stand in the way of the immediate implementation of democratic values. The authoritarians were less likely than the equalitarians to oppose the enemies of democracy. In short, authoritarians are generally too aggressive and rejecting of nonconformists, but sometimes they are too timid and accept-

ing. The authors came to the broad conclusion that "the greater the intensity of support for democratic ideology, the greater the tendency to prefer militant forms of social action" (p. 107).

30. Joseph B. Adelson, "A Study of Minority Group Authoritarianism," *Journal of Abnormal and Social Psychology*, 48 (1953), p. 480. Similar differences have been reported by Jerome Himelhoch, "Tolerance and Personality Needs: A Study of the Liberalization of Ethnic Attitudes among Minority Group College Students," *American Sociological Review*, 15 (1950), 79–88; Irving Sarnoff, "Identification with the Aggressor: Some Personality Correlates of Anti-Semitism among Jews," *Journal of Personality*, 20 (1951), 199–218; Marian Radke-Yarrow and Bernard Lande, "Personality Correlates of Differential Reactions to Minority Group-Belonging," *Journal of Social Psychology*, 38 (1953), 253–72; Alvin Scodel, "Some Correlates of Different Degrees of Jewish Identification in Jewish College Students," *Journal of Social Psychology*, 49 (1959), 87–94; and Moshe Anisfeld, Stanley R. Munoz, and Wallace C. Lambert, "The Structure and Dynamics of the Ethnic Attitudes of Jewish Adolescents," *Journal of Abnormal and Social Psychology*, 66 (1963), 31–36.

31. Gary T. Marx, *Protest and Prejudice: A Study of Belief in the Black Community* (New York: Harper & Row, 1967), p. 81. See also George A. Steckler, "Authoritarian Ideology in Negro College Students," *Journal of Abnormal and Social Psychology*, 54 (1957), 396–99; Donald L. Noel, "Group Identification among Negroes: An Empirical Analysis," *Journal of Social Issues*, 20(2) (1964), 71–84; and James S. House and Robert D. Fischer, "Authoritarianism, Age, and Black Militancy," *Sociometry*, 34 (1971), 174–97.

32. Charles C. Moskos, *The Sociology of Political Independence: A Study of Nationalist Attitudes among West Indian Leaders* (Cambridge, Mass.: Schenkman, 1967), p. 55. Unfortunately Moskos did not use an objective measure of authoritarianism, such as the F scale or the D scale, to penetrate the veil of ideology and make contact with underlying structures of personality. Moskos' study cannot be ignored, however, for his results coincide with the results of the studies of minority-group authoritarianism just cited, and these studies did employ F scales as measures of authoritarianism. Cf. A. James Gregor, *The Ideology of Fascism: The Rationale of Totalitarianism* (New York: The Free Press, 1969), chap. 8.

33. Marx, *Protest and Prejudice*, pp. 122, 193. See also Martin M. Grossack, "Group Belongingness among Negroes," *Journal of Social Psychology*, 43 (1956), 167–80; Steckler, "Authoritarian Ideology in Negro College Students"; Donald L. Noel and Alphonso Pinkney, "Correlates of Prejudice: Some Racial Similarities and Differences," *American Journal of Sociology*, 69 (1964), 609–22; House and Fischer, "Authoritarianism, Age and Black Militancy"; and Edward C. Chang and Edward H. Ritter, "Ethnocentrism in Black College Students," *Journal of Social Psychology*, 100 (1976), 89-98.

34. "Although nationalists glorify America as a symbol, they are inclined to regard most of the American population as an alien out-group. They are activated, it would seem, less by love of Americans and their heritage than by a sense of hostility and anxiety regarding other nations and 'outsiders' generally. Internationalists, being under less compulsion either to glorify their own nation or to condemn others, show a more genuine attachment to their cultural traditions." Levinson, "Authoritarian Personality and Foreign Policy," p. 42.

35. Cf. Carlton J. H. Hayes, *Nationalism: A Religion* (New York: Macmillan, 1960), p. vii: "Particularly in France a curious distinction is drawn between *le*

patriotisme national and *le nationalisme:* the one, as held by progressive 'Leftists,' is good; the other, confined to reactionary 'Rightists,' is bad."

36. This is the distinction that seems to have dominated—insofar as any one distinction has—the older English-language literature on nationalism written by historians and political scientists, e.g., A. D. Lindsay, *The Modern Democratic State* (New York: Oxford University Press, 1943), chap. 6; Hans Kohn, *The Idea of Nationalism: A Study of Its Origins and Background* (New York: Macmillan, 1944), p. 574; Louis L. Snyder, *The Meaning of Nationalism* (New Brunswick, N.J.: Rutgers University Press, 1954), pp. 117–22; Ramsay Cook, *The Maple Leaf Forever: Essays on Nationalism and Politics in Canada* (Toronto: Macmillan, 1971), pp. 5–6; and John Plamenatz, "Two Types of Nationalism," in *Nationalism: The Nature and Evolution of an Idea,* ed. Eugene Kamenka (Canberra: Australian National University Press, 1973), pp. 22–36. It is also found in the more recent sociological literature, for example, Joshua A. Fishman, *Language and Nationalism: Two Integrative Essays* (Rowley, Mass.: Newbury House Publishers, 1972).

37. The problem of defining fair treatment obviously raises delicate questions respecting the rights of majorities and minorities. Generally speaking, the touchstone of genuineness for the patriotism of a member of a dominant group is that it avoid any ethnocentric demands for the assimilation or exclusion of ethnic minorities or other outgroups. Among minorities the test of genuiness is almost the same: every ethnic group should have the right to establish organizations, and even states, devoted to the cultivation of its own distinctive culture, provided only that membership is open to all individuals who meet the requirements of the group. Cf. *The Authoritarian Personality,* pp. 99–100.

38. There is no consensus, for example, about whether contemporary nationalism in English Canada is a rational and public-spirited protest against American economic exploitation and domination, or merely an irrational mixture of envy, ambition, pride, special pleading, and xenophobia in the false colors of patriotism. Similarly, there is no consensus whether separatist nationalism in Quebec is genuinely a *nationalisme de libération,* or whether it is merely an attempt, appealing to *ressentiment* and xenophobia, to advance the narrow economic interests of the French "new middle class" and to make life uncomfortable for the local English minority. It is surely unnecessary to cite evidence of this lack of consensus, which is well known to anyone at all familiar with Canadian politics. The evidence would consist of long lists of books and articles pro and con the various positions, and no purpose would be served by such lists at this point.

39. Nevitt Sanford, "The Approach of 'The Authoritarian Personality'," in *A Source Book for the Study of Personality and Politics,* ed. Fred I. Greenstein and Michael Lerner (Chicago: Markham, 1971), p. 330.

Chapter Four

1. See Peter Russell, ed., *Nationalism in Canada* (Toronto: McGraw-Hill, 1966), Ramsay Cook, ed., *French-Canadian Nationalism: An Anthology* (Toronto: Macmillan, 1969), and H. D. Forbes, ed., *Canadian Political Thought* (Toronto: Oxford University Press, 1985).

2. See Carl Berger, *The Sense of Power: Studies in the Ideas of Canadian Imperialism, 1867–1914* (Toronto: University of Toronto Press, 1970), Frank H. Underhill, *The Image of Confederation*, The Massey Lectures, 1963 (Toronto: Canadian Broadcasting Corporation, 1964), chaps. 3 and 4, and Casey Murrow, *Henri Bourassa and French-Canadian Nationalism: Opposition to Empire* (Montreal: Harvest House, 1968).

3. Cf. James M. Minifie, *Peacemaker or Powder-Monkey: Canada's Role in a Revolutionary World* (Toronto: McClelland and Stewart, 1960).

4. Thomas N. Trenton, "Canadian Nationalism, Dogmatism, and Internationalism: A Case of Independence?" *Canadian Review of Studies in Nationalism*, 5 (1978), 104–13.

5. Jean-Paul Sartre, *Anti-Semite and Jew*, trans. George J. Becker (New York: Schocken Books, 1948), p. 47.

6. Trenton, "Canadian Nationalism, Dogmatism, and Internationalism," p. 110.

Chapter Five

1. There have been very few studies of the relation between authoritarianism and political or ethnic attitudes among high school students, and unfortunately their results seem contradictory. The most relevant studies are: Harrison G. Gough, "Studies of Social Intolerance: I. Some Psychological and Sociological Correlates of Anti-Semitism," *Journal of Social Psychology*, 33 (1951), 237–46; David J. Bordua, "Authoritarianism and Intolerance of Nonconformists," *Sociometry*, 24 (1961), 198–216; F. Knopfelmacher and D. Armstrong, "Authoritarianism, Ethnocentrism, and Religious Denomination," *American Catholic Sociological Review*, 24 (1963), 99–144; Cigdem Kagitcibasi, "Social Norms and Authoritarianism: A Turkish-American Comparison," *Journal of Personality and Social Psychology*, 16 (1970), 444–51; and Charles Y. Glock et al., *Adolescent Prejudice* (New York: Harper & Row, 1975).

2. Elaine S. Brand, René A. Ruiz, and Amando M. Padilla, "Ethnic Identification and Preference: A Review," *Psychological Bulletin*, 81 (1974), p. 880. Cf. Frances E. Aboud and Shelagh A. Skerry, "The Development of Ethnic Attitudes: A Critical Review," *Journal of Cross-Cultural Psychology*, 15 (1984), 3–34.

3. Else Frenkel-Brunswik, "A Study of Prejudice in Children," *Human Relations*, 1 (1948), 295–306. See also Shelley Phillips, "Prejudice in Middle Childhood," *Journal of Psychology*, 110 (1982), 91–99.

4. Hilde T. Himmelweit and Betty Swift, "Adolescent and Adult Authoritarianism Re-Examined: Its Organization and Stability over Time," *European Journal of Social Psychology*, 1 (1971), 357–83.

5. See especially Gustav Jahoda, "The Development of Scottish Children's Ideas and Attitudes about Other Countries," *Journal of Social Psychology*, 58 (1962), 91–108; Gustav Jahoda, "Children's Concepts of Nationality: A Critical Study of Piaget's Stages," *Child Development*, 35 (1964), 1081–92; and Joseph Adelson and Robert P. O'Neill, "Growth of Political Ideas in Adolescence: The Sense of Community," *Journal of Personality and Social Psychology*, 4 (1966), 295–306. The pioneering study in this field was Jean Piaget and Anne-Marie Weil, "The Develop-

ment in Children of the Idea of the Homeland and of Relations with Other Countries," *International Social Science Bulletin*, 3 (1951), 561–78.

6. An unusually careful study has shown that the overall amount of negative thinking, or prejudice, among grade school children was strongly (inversely) related to the development of moral judgment, and that it declined with increasing age. Among the younger and morally less mature children, prejudice seemed to be largely the result of a general inability to respect others and to take the role of the other. See Florence H. Davidson, "Ability to Respect Persons Compared to Ethnic Prejudice in Childhood," *Journal of Personality and Social Psychology*, 34 (1976), 1256–67.

7. M. Kent Jennings and Richard G. Neimi, *The Political Character of Adolescence: The Influence of Families and Schools* (Princeton: Princeton University Press, 1974), especially pp. 94, 112, 140–44, 256, 267, and 272.

8. M. Kent Jennings and Richard G. Niemi, *Generations and Politics: A Panel Study of Young Adults and Their Parents* (Princeton: Princeton University Press, 1981), chap. 3. See also Benjamin S. Bloom, *Stability and Change in Human Characteristics* (New York: John Wiley & Sons, 1964), chap. 5, and the studies cited there. Cf. Bernard Kutner and Norman B. Gordon, "Cognitive Functioning and Prejudice: A Nine-Year Follow-Up Study," *Sociometry*, 27 (1964), p. 71.

9. Jennings and Niemi, *The Political Character of Adolescence*, chaps. 2, 3, and 8, and Jennings and Niemi, *Generations and Politics*, chap. 4.

10. E.g. Charles Bird, Elio D. Monachesi, and Harvey Burdick, "Infiltration and the Attitudes of White and Negro Parents and Children," *Journal of Abnormal and Social Psychology*, 47 (1952), 688–99; Kenneth Helfant, "Parents' Attitudes vs. Adolescent Hostility in the Determination of Adolescent Sociopolitical Attitudes," *Psychological Monographs*, 66 (1952), whole no. 345; Donald L. Mosher and Alvin Scodel, "Relationships between Ethnocentrism in Children and the Ethnocentrism and Authoritarian Rearing Practices of Their Mothers," *Child Development*, 31 (1960), 369–76; and David F. Bush et al., "Patterns of Authoritarianism between Generations," *Journal of Social Psychology*, 116 (1982), 91–97.

11. Several different methods of estimating reliability are in use. Cronbach's method, which is used here, derives estimates from the intercorrelations among the items making up a scale, and it is comparable to the method of "split-half reliability." The coefficient indicates how much of the variation in a set of scores may be attributed to real differences in the variable (or variables) the test is measuring; the remaining variation is the random error. Thus a coefficient of .90 implies 10 percent random error and a value of .50 implies 50 percent error. See Jum C. Nunnally, *Psychometric Theory*, 2d ed. (New York: McGraw-Hill, 1978), chaps. 6 and 7, or any similar textbook.

12. Ibid., pp. 219–20.

13. The reasoning here is explained more fully and some examples are discussed in Morris Rosenberg, "The Logical Status of Suppressor Variables," *Public Opinion Quarterly*, 37 (1973), 359–72. See also Morris Rosenberg, *The Logic of Survey Analysis* (New York: Basic Books, 1968), chap. 4.

14. Aids to the imagination include Albert Breton, "The Economics of Nationalism," *Journal of Political Economy*, 72 (1964), 376–86, and Seymour Martin Lipset, *Political Man: The Social Bases of Politics* (New York: Doubleday, 1960), chap. 4. Some relevant evidence is presented in Carl J. Cuneo and James E. Curtis,

"Quebec Separatism: An Analysis of Determinants within Social-Class Levels," *Canadian Review of Sociology and Anthropology*, 11 (1974), 1–29; Richard Hamilton and Maurice Pinard, "The Bases of Parti Québécois Support in Recent Quebec Elections," *Canadian Journal of Political Science*, 9 (1976), 3–26; and Maurice Pinard and Richard Hamilton, "The Parti Québécois Comes to Power: An Analysis of the 1976 Quebec Election," *Canadian Journal of Political Science*, 11 (1978), 739–75; and Richard F. Hamilton, *Class and Politics in the United States* (New York: John Wiley & Sons, 1972), chap. 11, and the literature cited there.

15. W. Lloyd Warner, Marcia Meeker, and Kenneth Eells, *Social Class in America: A Manual of Procedure for the Measurement of Social Status* (Chicago: Science Research Associates, 1949).

16. Only if these basic correlations are large can the partial correlations between nationalism and authoritarianism, controlling for parental SES, be substantially larger than the zero-order correlations. See William L. Hays, *Statistics for the Social Sciences*, 2d ed. (New York: Holt, Rinehart and Winston, 1973), pp. 710–12, or any similar textbook.

17. Cf. Ted G. Harvey, Susan K. Hunter-Harvey, and W. George Vance, "Nationalist Sentiment among Canadian Adolescents: The Prevalence and Social Correlates of Nationalistic Feelings," in *Socialization and Values in Canadian Society*, ed. Elia Zureik and Robert M. Pike, vol. I: *Political Socialization* (Toronto: McClelland and Stewart, 1975), p. 250.

18. See Nunnally, *Psychometric Theory*, pp. 658–72, for a brief review. Cf. Frederick D. Herzon, "A Review of Acquiescence Response Set in the California F Scale," *Social Science Quarterly*, 53 (1972), 66–78, and John J. Ray, "Reviving the Problem of Acquiescent Response Bias," *Journal of Social Psychology*, 121 (1983), 81–96.

19. The basic principle is that the correlation between any two variables is equal to the sum of the products of their common factor loadings. The relevant equation can be written: $r_{12} = r_{1A}r_{2A} + r_{1B}r_{2B} + \ldots + r_{1K}r_{2K}$. See Stanley A. Mulaik, *The Foundations of Factor Analysis* (New York: McGraw-Hill, 1972), p. 100, or any similar textbook.

20. E.g., Bernard M. Bass, "Authoritarianism or Acquiescence?" *Journal of Abnormal and Social Psychology*, 51 (1955), 616–23.

21. Leonard G. Rorer, "The Great Response-Style Myth," *Psychological Bulletin*, 63 (1965), 129–56.

22. Franz Samelson, "Agreement Set and Anti-Content Attitudes in the F Scale: A Reinterpretation," *Journal of Abnormal and Social Psychology*, 68 (1964), 338–42, and Franz Samelson and Jacques F. Yates, "Acquiescence and the F Scale: Old Assumptions and New Data," *Psychological Bulletin*, 68 (1967), 91–103.

23. Jack Block, "The Shifting Definitions of Acquiescence," *Psychological Bulletin*, 78 (1972), p. 11.

24. Samelson and Yates, "Acquiescence and the F Scale," p. 101. Cf. Ray, "Reviving the Problem of Acquiescent Response Bias." The relation between authoritarianism, as measured by the F scale, and acquiescence, understood as *conformism* rather than as a response set, will be discussed in detail in Chapter 10 below.

25. The Berkeley group reported such correlations but in their discussion emphasized that they were weaker than expected (AP, 185–207, 280–88). Cf.

Richard Christie, "Authoritarianism Re-examined," in *Studies in the Scope and Method of "The Authoritarian Personality,"* ed. Richard Christie and Marie Jahoda (Glencoe, Ill.: The Free Press, 1954), pp. 167–82; Thomas S. Cohn, "The Relation of the F Scale to Intelligence," *Journal of Social Psychology*, 46 (1957), 207–17; and Frank N. Jacobson and Salomon Rettig, "Authoritarianism and Intelligence," *Journal of Social Psychology*, 50 (1959), 213–19.

26. Thomas S. Cohn, "Is the F Scale Indirect?" *Journal of Abnormal and Social Psychology*, 47 (1952), 732, and Bernard A. Stotsky, "The Authoritarian Personality as a Stereotype," *Journal of Psychology*, 39 (1955), 325–28.

27. Richard Christie and Peggy Cook, "A Guide to the Published Literature Relating to the Authoritarian Personality through 1956," *Journal of Psychology*, 45 (1958), p. 188. Cf. Paul Hartmann, "A Perspective on the Study of Social Attitudes," *European Journal of Social Psychology*, 7 (1977), p. 91.

28. Gertrude J. Selznick and Stephen Steinberg, *The Tenacity of Prejudice: Anti-Semitism in Contemporary America* (New York: Harper & Row, 1969), chap. 8.

29. Ibid., p. 157.

30. Ibid.; see also pp. 141–42.

31. Ibid., p. 136.

32. Ibid., p. 140.

33. Ibid., pp. 142–43.

34. Ibid., p. 158.

35. Ibid., p. 169.

36. Ibid., p. 156.

37. Daniel J. Levinson, "Authoritarian Personality and Foreign Policy," *Journal of Conflict Resolution*, 1 (1957), p. 41.

38. "One can be politically conservative, just as one can be patriotic (in the sense of firm attachment to American culture and tradition), without being ethnocentric. We should like to use the term '*genuine conservative*' to refer to the individual with this broad pattern of thought. He is 'genuine' because, whatever the merits of his political views, he is seriously concerned with fostering what is most vital in the American democratic tradition." AP, 181–82.

39. Nevitt Sanford pointed out in a later article that the two subjects presented in detail in the book, Mack and Larry, had been chosen to illustrate this distinction. "In order to accent the complexity to the conservatism-ethnocentrism relationship, and to dramatise the differences among conservatives—and, I must confess, to counteract the then widespread tendency to regard all conservatives as 'bad'—we chose a highly conservative young man as the subject of a case study that would exemplify the low extremes on ethnocentrism and potential fascism and contrast with the case of another conservative young man who was at the opposite extreme on these dimensions." Nevitt Sanford, "Recent Developments in Connection with the Investigation of the Authoritarian Personality," *Sociological Review*, n.s. 2 (1954), pp. 26–27.

40. Edward Shils, "Authoritarianism: 'Right' and 'Left'," in *Studies in the Scope and Method of "The Authoritarian Personality,"* ed. Richard Christie and Marie Jahoda (Glencoe, Ill.: The Free Press, 1954), pp. 29, 37. See also Christie, "Authoritarianism Re-examined," pp. 126–33.

41. J. J. Ray, "Authoritarianism in California 30 years Later—With Some Cross-Cultural Comparisons," *Journal of Social Psychology*, 111 (1980), p. 16. See

also Stanley Rothman and S. Robert Lichter, *Roots of Radicalism: Jews, Christians, and the New Left* (New York: Oxford University Press, 1982), pp. 56–57, 59–61, 158, 236.

42. Jack M. Hicks and John H. Wright, "Convergent-Discriminant Validation and Factor Analysis of Five Scales of Liberalism-Conservatism," *Journal of Personality and Social Psychology*, 14 (1970), 114–20; Glenn D. Wilson, "Development and Evaluation of the C-Scale," in *The Psychology of Conservatism*, ed. Glenn D. Wilson (London: Academic Press, 1973), p. 68; and Victor C. Joe, "Personality Correlates of Conservatism," *Journal of Social Psychology*, 93 (1974), 309–10. Cf. Irwin Mahler, "Attitudes toward Socialized Medicine," *Journal of Social Psychology*, 38 (1953), 273–82, and Dean Peabody, "Attitude Content and Agreement Set in Scales of Authoritarianism, Dogmatism, Anti-Semitism, and Economic Conservatism," *Journal of Abnormal and Social Psychology*, 63 (1961), p. 7.

43. Herbert McClosky, "Conservatism and Personality," *American Political Science Review*, 52 (1958), 27–45; Robert C. Thompson and Jerry B. Michel, "Measuring Authoritarianism: A Comparison of the F and D Scales," *Journal of Personality*, 40 (1972), 180–90; John J. Ray, "Dogmatism in Relation to Some Sub-Types of Conservatism: Some Australian Data," *European Journal of Social Psychology*, 3 (1973), 221–32; and William D. Brant, Knud S. Larsen, and Don Langenberg, "Authoritarian Traits as Predictors of Candidate Preference in 1976 United States Presidential Election," *Psychological Reports*, 43 (1978), 313–14, and the studies cited there.

44. W. Edgar Gregory, "The Orthodoxy of the Authoritarian Personality," *Journal of Social Psychology*, 45 (1957), 217–32; L. B. Brown, "A Study of Religious Belief," *British Journal of Psychology*, 53 (1962), 259–72; John D. Photiadis and Jeanne Biggar, "Religiosity, Education, and Ethnic Distance," *American Journal of Sociology*, 67 (1962), 666–72; J. Weima, "Authoritarianism, Religious Conservatism, and Sociocentric Attitudes in Roman Catholic Groups," *Human Relations*, 18 (1965), 231–39; Leonard Weller et al., "Religiosity and Authoritarianism," *Journal of Social Psychology*, 95 (1975), 11–18; and Lawrence A. Fehr and Mark E. Heintzelman, "Personality and Attitude Correlates of Religiosity: A Source of Controversy," *Journal of Psychology*, 95 (1977), 63–66.

45. Daniel J. Levinson and Phyllis E. Huffman, "Traditional Family Ideology and Its Relation to Personality," *Journal of Personality*, 23 (1955), 251–73, and Ray, "Some Sub-Types of Conservatism."

46. N. T. Feather, "Protestant Ethic, Conservatism, and Values," *Journal of Personality and Social Psychology*, 46 (1984), 1132–41, and the literature cited there.

47. Doris C. Gilbert and Daniel J. Levinson, "Ideology, Personality, and Institutional Policy in the Mental Hospital," *Journal of Abnormal and Social Psychology*, 53 (1956), 263–71, and William E. Alberts, "Personality and Attitudes toward Juvenile Delinquency: A Study of Protestant Ministers," *Journal of Social Psychology*, 60 (1963), 71–83.

48. Ronald J. Knapp, "Authoritarianism, Alienation, and Related Variables: A Correlational and Factor-Analytic Study," *Psychological Bulletin*, 83 (1976), 194–212, and the studies cited there. See also Herbert McClosky and John H. Schaar, "Psychological Dimensions of Anomie," *American Sociological Review*, 30 (1965), 14–40.

49. Selznick and Steinberg, *The Tenacity of Prejudice*, p. 158.

50. Ibid., p. 159. "What is at issue is not the face meaning of F beliefs but the reasons they are accepted. Does acceptance of F beliefs have psychological sources and intellectual consequences, as the original study claimed? Or does acceptance of F beliefs have intellectual sources and psychological consequences, as their relation to education strongly suggests?" (p. 141).

51. Ibid., pp. 148 and 157. "The significance of lack of education is that it is a form of social isolation from the ideal culture" (p. 158).

52. Ibid., p. 191.

53. Ibid., pp. 168–69; cf. p. 138.

54. Ibid., pp. 159–60. At this point in the book Selznick and Steinberg are describing the "orthodox Freudian view" and they do not clearly identify themselves with this view. But both earlier (p. 138) and later (pp. 190-91) they do so, even going a step beyond the orthodox view with a reference to "the primitive psychic satisfactions to be gained by . . . obedience to the id-inspired dictates of the superego" (p. 191).

55. Ibid., p. 160, n. 28.

56. Ibid., p. 168.

57. Ibid., p. 168; cf. pp. 159, 190.

Chapter Six

1. "One of the most durable relationships in social psychology is the positive correlation between the California F scale and racist attitudes. . . . No matter what one controls for, the relationship always seems to emerge." John J. Ray, "Half of All Racists are Left Wing," *Political Psychology*, 5 (1984), 227. The study which Ray describes in this article found a correlation of .48 between a balanced F scale and an "Australian ethnocentrism scale" that measured support for a white Australia. Cf. Richard A. Apostle et al., *The Anatomy of Racial Attitudes* (Berkeley: University of California Press, 1983), pp. 172–76.

2. Charles E. Osgood, G. J. Suci, and P. H. Tannenbaum, *The Measurement of Meaning* (Urbana, Ill.: University of Illinois Press, 1957). Rating scales of this type were first used in a study of nationalist attitudes by Ross Stagner and Charles E. Osgood, "An Experimental Analysis of a Nationalistic Frame of Reference," *Journal of Social Psychology*, 14 (1941), 389–401.

3. It should be noted here, however, that several earlier studies have reported very weak correlations between ethnic prejudice and authoritarianism, leading one authority to observe that "the major conclusion of *The Authoritarian Personality*— that authoritarianism is highly related to prejudice—is still unconfirmed, long after it has been assimilated into our culture." R. A. Altemeyer, *Right-Wing Authoritarianism* (Winnipeg: University of Manitoba Press, 1981), p. 33. Altemeyer cites four studies reporting correlations of less than .30 (see his table 2). Nine others are: Edward B. Klein, "Stylistic Components of Response as Related to Attitude Change," *Journal of Personality*, 31 (1963), p. 47; Susan Hesselbart and Howard Schuman, "Racial Attitudes, Educational Level, and a Personality Measure," *Public Opinion Quarterly*, 40 (1976), 108–14; Charles Y. Glock et al., *Adolescent Prejudice* (New York: Harper & Row, 1975), pp. 69, 145; Christopher Orpen and Georgia Tsapogas, "Racial Prejudice and Authoritarianism: A Test in White South

Africa," *Psychological Reports*, 30 (1972), 441–42; Christopher Orpen and Lesley van der Schyff, "Prejudice and Personality in White South Africa: A 'Differential Learning' Alternative to the Authoritarian Personality," *Journal of Social Psychology*, 87 (1972), 313–14; and Christopher Orpen, "Authoritarianism Revisited: A Critical Examination of 'Expressive' Theories of Prejudice," in *Contemporary South Africa: Social Psychological Perspectives*, ed. Stanley J. Morse and Christopher Orpen (Cape Town: Juta & Company, 1975), pp. 103–11; E. T. Prothro and L. H. Melikian, "Generalized Ethnic Attitudes in the Arab Near East," *Sociology and Social Research*, 37 (1952), 375–79; Yoel Yinon, "Authoritarianism and Prejudice among Married Couples with Similar or Different Ethnic Origin in Israel," *Journal of Marriage and the Family*, 37 (1975), p. 218; and Aaron Wolfe Siegman, "A Cross-Cultural Investigation of the Relationship between Ethnic Prejudice, Authoritarian Ideology, and Personality," *Journal of Abnormal and Social Psychology*, 63 (1961), 654–55. The findings of these studies have not, however, been regarded as typical. Thus Glock and his collaborators, for example, do not question the conventional generalization that ethnocentrism goes with authoritarianism; rather they question the validity of their measure of authoritarianism, Christie's balanced F scale (p. 68).

4. Subjective national identity was measured by means of the first three items of the Separatism scale (see Appendix B). It is worth noting, incidentally, that the same ambiguity about ingroups and outgroups exists when, for example, the attitudes of white Christian Americans towards Jewish Americans or black Americans are being studied, but it never seems to have been necessary, in order to find correlations between prejudice and personality among Americans, to distinguish respondents who identified with America as a whole from those who identified with white Christian Americans.

5. Robert C. Gardner and Wallace E. Lambert, *Attitudes and Motivation in Second-Language Learning* (Rowley, Mass.: Newbury House Publishers, 1972).

6. It may be better to think of different correlations in different populations. The variation among the figures in table 6.5 is greater than can be attributed to sampling fluctuation. William L. Hays, *Statistics for the Social Sciences*, 2d ed. (New York: Holt, Rinehart and Winston, 1973), p. 664, provides a test for the consistency of correlations, that is to say, for the null hypothesis H_o: $\rho_1 = \rho_2 = \ldots = \rho_{\mathcal{J}}$. The test statistic is distributed as chi square with $\mathcal{J} - 1$ degrees of freedom when the null hypothesis is true. In this case the statistic has the value 10.70 with 4 degrees of freedom, which justifies rejection of the null hypothesis at the .05 level of significance. It is worth noting that the samples in the Gardner-Lambert studies were all selected because of their interest and skill (or lack of it) in learning French. The English sample in this study is probably more representative of the population of English-speaking North American high school students than are any of the samples used by Gardner and Lambert.

7. Gardner and Lambert, *Attitudes and Motivation*, pp. 206, 167, 170, and 173.

Chapter Seven

1. Cf. Kenneth N. Waltz, *Man, the State and War* (New York: Columbia University Press, 1954), chaps. 2 and 3, and Jessie Bernard, "Parties and Issues in Conflict," *Journal of Conflict Resolution*, 1 (1957), 111–21.

2. M. Brewster Smith, Jerome S. Bruner, and Robert W. White, *Opinions and Personality* (New York: Wiley, 1956), p. 241.

3. Ibid., p. 278.

4. Ibid., p. 275.

5. Ibid.

6. Cf. Daniel Katz, Herbert Kelman, and Richard Flacks, "The National Role: Some Hypotheses about the Relation of Individuals to Nation in America Today," Peace Research Society (International), *Papers*, 1 (1964), p. 115, and subsequent contributions by "the Michigan group," especially Herbert C. Kelman and Alfred H. Bloom, "Assumptive Frameworks in International Politics," in *Handbook of Political Psychology*, ed. Jeanne N. Knutson (San Francisco: Jossey-Bass, 1973), pp. 261–95.

7. Cf. Daniel Katz, Charles McClintock, and Irving Sarnoff, "The Measurement of Ego Defence as Related to Attitude Change," *Journal of Personality*, 25 (1957), 465–74.

8. Cf. Paul M. Sniderman and Jack Citrin, "Psychological Sources of Political Belief: Self-Esteem and Isolationist Attitudes," *American Political Science Review*, 65 (1971), 401–17.

9. See W. L. Hays, *Statistics for the Social Sciences*, 2d ed. (New York: Holt, Rinehart and Winston, 1973), pp. 663–64, or any similar textbook.

10. The close correspondence of the empirical distribution to the normal form is clear if the differences are plotted on normal probability paper. This was done for both the English and the French distributions, but the results are not shown since graphs are expensive to print and the method is not widely known.

Chapter Eight

1. See especially Donald T. Campbell and Boyd R. McCandless, "Ethnocentrism, Xenophobia, and Personality," *Human Relations*, 4 (1951), 185–91, and Nancy C. Morse and Floyd H. Allport, "The Causation of Anti-Semitism: An Investigation of Seven Hypotheses," *Journal of Psychology*, 34 (1952), 197–233. There is a useful review of the basic literature in Richard Christie, "Authoritarianism Re-examined," in *Studies in the Scope and Method of "The Authoritarian Personality,"* ed. Richard Christie and Marie Jahoda (Glencoe, Ill.: The Free Press, 1954), pp. 149–54. The most important recent evidence is reported in Gertrude J. Selznick and Stephen Steinberg, *The Tenacity of Prejudice: Anti-Semitism in Contemporary America* (New York: Harper & Row, 1969), pp. 152–56 and 180–82, and Gregory Martire and Ruth Clark, *Anti-Semitism in the United States: A Study of Prejudice in the 1980s* (New York: Praeger, 1982), chap. 6. See also John W. Berry, Rudolph Kalin, and Donald M. Taylor, *Multiculturalism and Ethnic Attitudes in Canada* (Ottawa: Supply and Services Canada, 1977), pp. 181–90. Cf. Peter R. Hofstaetter, "A Factorial Study of Prejudice," *Journal of Personality*, 21 (1952), 228–39.

2. John Harding et al., "Prejudice and Ethnic Relations," in *The Handbook of Social Psychology*, 2d ed., ed. Gardner Lindzey and Elliot Aronson (Reading, Mass.: Addison-Wesley, 1968–69), vol. 5, p. 17. Cf. Christie, "Authoritarianism Re-examined," p. 154.

3. D. N. Lawley and A. E. Maxwell, *Factor Analysis as a Statistical Method*, (London: Butterworths, 1963), and S. A. Mulaik, *The Foundations of Factor Analysis* (New York: McGraw-Hill, 1972), provide good explanations of the method. Before calculating principal components, the variables were standardized by correcting all the basic correlations for attenuation so that the true components of the scores would receive equal weight in the analysis (Mulaik, *Foundations*, pp. 179–81). Without this correction or some equivalent adjustment, the random errors of measurement associated with each variable would have counted as evidence against the hypothesis of a single underlying dimension of variation. Random errors attenuate correlations, and this effect is indistinguishable from, and normally confounded with, the effects of multiple underlying dimensions. The matrices of intercorrelations are given in Appendix C. The calculations were done using the Statistical Package for the Social Sciences (SPSS).

4. It is customary to say that there exist as many "real" underlying dimensions or factors as there are principal components with eigenvalues greater than one. By this standard there are four independent dimensions of variation in the English data and three in the French data.

5. Guy Michelat and Jean-Pierre H. Thomas, *Dimensions du nationalisme: enquête par questionnaire (1962)*, Cahiers de la Fondation Nationale des Sciences Politiques, No. 143 (Paris: Armand Colin, 1966).

6. In classical factor analysis, by contrast with principal components analysis, each variable is weighted by its "communality," which is chosen either to minimize the number of factors needed to account for the observed correlations or to minimize the differences between the observed and the reproduced correlations (the correlations implied by a set of factor loadings) for any given number of factors. It is thus "covariance oriented," while principal components analysis is "variance oriented" (Lawley and Maxwell, *Factor Analysis*, p. 3). The results to be reported are the principal components solutions for the matrices of correlations corrected for attenuation (Appendix C) with the communalities estimated by iteration, using the Statistical Package for the Social Sciences (SPSS).

7. Patrick L. Sullivan and Joseph Adelson, "Ethnocentrism and Misanthropy," *Journal of Abnormal and Social Psychology*, 49 (1954), 246–50; Bernard Spilka and E. L. Struening, "A Questionnaire Study of Personality and Ethnocentrism," *Journal of Social Psychology*, 44 (1956), 65–71; Mark A Chesler, "Ethnocentrism and Attitudes toward the Physically Disabled," *Journal of Personality and Social Psychology*, 2 (1965), 877–82; and Paul M. Sniderman, *Personality and Democratic Politics* (Berkeley: University of California Press, 1975), pp. 194 and 215.

8. Cf. Leonard W. Doob, *Patriotism and Nationalism: Their Psychological Foundations* (New Haven: Yale University Press, 1964), p. 128. A distinction can obviously be made between support for national independence and hostile attitudes towards outgroups. Even among our respondents, many could be found to illustrate this distinction, for the correlations between the relevant variables are far from unity. Nonetheless the distinction does not seem to be an important one in the following sense: it is not one that must be used to account parsimoniously for the correlations between measures of nationalist attitudes. To insist upon the distinction would be a bit like insisting upon the distinction between length of the right leg and length of the left leg, to the neglect of the distinction between those who are tall and those who are short. The distinction can be made, but why make it? A tailor

outfitting a king would measure both his legs and take into account any difference there might be, but a manufacturer producing pants for the mass market need have only a few standard patterns, all of which make both legs the same length. An intellectual historian discussing, say, Hegel and Hitler would have to make some distinctions that the survey researcher can afford to neglect. The latter is interested in having a good supply of a few standard outfits to get the bulk of his respondents dressed up in such a way as to identify their roles in the popular political drama. The distinction between loving one's own nation and hating foreign nations, like the distinction between a rangy right leg and a stumpy left one, has to do with unusual, and sometimes rather subtle, differences between people, and not with the common and obvious differences. It may be an important distinction to make in some circumstances, but it is not important, it seems, when drawing a first crude sketch of nationalist attitudes.

9. Daniel J. Levinson, "Authoritarian Personality and Foreign Policy," *Journal of Conflict Resolution,* 1 (1957), 37–47.

Chapter Nine

1. T. B. Macaulay, "Bentham's Defence of Mill—Utilitarian System of Philosophy," in *Utilitarian Logic and Politics,* ed. Jack Lively and John Rees (Oxford: Oxford University Press, 1978), p. 155.

2. K. J. Gergen, "Towards Intellectual Audacity in Social Psychology," in *The Development of Social Psychology,* ed. Robin Gilmour and Steve Duck (London: Academic Press, 1980), pp. 247, 252–53, 261. Emphasis in the original. Elsewhere this audacious theorist has called for a social psychology "liberated both from the press of immediate fact and the necessity for verification": "The responsible scholar need not hesitate to develop and disseminate his or her ideas for lack of empirical test; the massive hours absorbed in the process of executing such tests may be reinvested in significant intellectual work." K. J. Gergen, "Toward Generative Theory," *Journal of Personality and Social Psychology,* 36 (1978), pp. 1344, 1352–53.

3. Max Horkheimer, "Traditional and Critical Theory," in *Critical Theory: Selected Essays,* trans. M. J. O'Connell et al. (New York: Herder and Herder, 1972), pp. 227–28. "We never regarded the theory [of *The Authoritarian Personality*] simply as a set of hypotheses but as in some sense standing on its own feet, and therefore did not intend to prove or disprove the theory through our findings but only to derive from it concrete questions for investigation, which must then be judged on their own merit, and demonstrate certain prevalent socio-psychological structures." Theodor W. Adorno, "Scientific Experiences of a European Scholar in America," in *The Intellectual Migration: Europe and America, 1930–1960,* ed. Donald Fleming and Bernard Bailyn (Cambridge: Harvard University Press, 1969), p. 363.

4. Horkheimer, "Traditional and Critical Theory," p. 199.

5. David Held, *Introduction to Critical Theory: Horkheimer to Habermas* (Berkeley: University of California Press, 1980), p. 382.

6. Ibid., p. 386.

7. Horkheimer, "Notes on Science and the Crisis," in *Critical Theory,* pp. 7-8.

8. Ibid., p. 8.

Chapter Ten

1. Montaigne, *Essays*, II, 12; Plutarch, *Table-Talk*, I, 10.
2. J. J. Ray, "Do Authoritarians Hold Authoritarian Attitudes?" *Human Relations*, 29 (1976), pp. 322–23.
3. J. J. Ray and W. Kiefl, "Authoritarianism and Achievement Motivation in Contemporary West Germany," *Journal of Social Psychology*, 122 (1984), p. 7, and the studies cited there.
4. E. P. Hollander, "Authoritarianism and Leadership Choice in a Military Setting," *Journal of Abnormal and Social Psychology*, 49 (1954), 365–70; H. E. Titus, "F Scale Validity Considered Against Peer Nomination Criteria," *Psychological Record*, 18 (1968), 395–403; A. Perry and W. H. Cunningham, "A Behavioral Test of Three F Scales," *Journal of Social Psychology*, 96 (1975), 271–75. Cf. A. C. Elms and S. Milgram, "Personality Characteristics Associated with Obedience and Defiance toward Authoritative Command," *Journal of Experimental Research on Personality*, 1 (1966), 282–89.
5. Rupert Wilkinson, *The Broken Rebel: A Study in Culture, Politics and Authoritarian Character* (New York: Harper & Row, 1972), p. 57.
6. Cf. Henry V. Dicks, "Personality Traits and National Socialist Ideology," *Human Relations*, 3 (1950), p. 143, and Max Horkheimer and Theodor W. Adorno, *Dialectic of Enlightenment*, trans. John Cumming (New York: Herder and Herder, 1972), pp. 192-93.
7. Larry D. Spence, *The Politics of Social Knowledge* (University Park, Pa.: Pennsylvania State University Press, 1978), p. 110.
8. Joseph M. Masling, "How Neurotic Is the Authoritarian?" *Journal of Abnormal and Social Psychology*, 49 (1954), 316–18; Anthony Davids, "Some Personality and Intellectual Correlates of Intolerance of Ambiguity," *Journal of Abnormal and Social Psychology*, 51 (1955), 415–20; Bernard A. Stotsky, "The Authoritarian Personality as a Stereotype," *Journal of Psychology*, 39 (1955), 325-28; Mervin Freedman, Harold Webster, and Nevitt Sanford, "A Study of Authoritarianism and Psychopathology," *Journal of Psychology*, 41 (1956), 315–22; Anthony Davids and Charles W. Eriksen, "Some Social and Cultural Factors Determining Relations between Authoritarianism and Measures of Neuroticism," *Journal of Consulting Psychology*, 21 (1957), 155–59; John J. Ray, "Militarism, Authoritarianism, Neuroticism, and Antisocial Behaviour," *Journal of Conflict Resolution*, 16 (1972), 319–40; J. J. Ray, "Do Authoritarian Attitudes or Authoritarian Personalities Reflect Mental Illness?" *South African Journal of Psychology*, 11 (1981), 153–57; and Ray and Kiefl, "Authoritarianism and Achievement Orientation in Contemporary West Germany." Cf. Paul Kline and Colin Cooper, "A Factorial Analysis of the Authoritarian Personality," *British Journal of Psychology*, 75 (1984), 171–76.
9. Freedman, Webster, and Sanford, "A Study of Authoritarianism and Psychopathology," p. 322.
10. Ray and Kiefl, "Authoritarianism and Achievement Motivation," p. 6
11. To show that authoritarianism, as measured by the F scale, is unrelated to psychopathology is not, it should be noted, to disprove anything that the Berkeley group said about authoritarianism. In the first published report of their research,

Frenkel-Brunswik and Sanford observed that it would be a mistake to assume "that our low extremes [the tolerant equalitarians] are closer to the 'normal' [than the highs] or that the lower a person stands on our anti-Semitism scale the better off he is from the point of view of mental health." Else Frenkel-Brunswik and R. Nevitt Sanford, "Some Personality Factors in Anti-Semitism," *Journal of Psychology*, 20 (1945), p. 287. In the chapter of *The Authoritarian Personality* on "Psychological Ill Health in Relation to Potential Fascism," Maria Levinson showed that a sample of psychiatric patients did not have higher-than-average scores on the E scale. In explicit opposition to two common hypotheses about the relation between ethnocentrism and mental illness, that there is a positive correlation and that there is a negative correlation, Levinson concluded that "one is likely to find people with more or less severe psychological disturbances in the high, low, and middle quartile [of the E scale] although we cannot say in what proportions" (AP, 968). This is the closest approach to a discussion of the relations between authoritarianism and mental health that one finds in the book, but the principal authors seem to have silently respected Maria Levinson's conclusions when discussing their own special topics. Adorno remarks at one point that "the ultimate theoretical explanation of an entirely irrational symptom which nevertheless does not appear to affect the 'normality' of those who show the symptom is beyond the scope of the present research" (AP, 618). It was not, however, beyond the powers of the philosophical school of which Adorno was a member. The explanation they proposed was fundamentally very simple: a mad society—a society that uses violence to uphold scarcity and domination when liberation and abundance for all are possible—requires madness among its members as a condition for "normality." As Adorno said, "today's world, which offers such a reality basis for everybody's sense of being persecuted, calls for paranoic characters." Theodor W. Adorno, "The Stars Down to Earth: The *Los Angeles Times* Astrology Column: A Study in Secondary Superstition," in *Gesammelte Schriften*, ed. Susan Buck-Morss and Rolf Tiedemann, vol. 9, part 2 (Frankfurt am Main: Suhrkamp Verlag, 1975), p. 119. See also the lugubrious "aphorism" in his *Minima Moralia*, trans. E. F. N. Jephcott (London: New Left Books, 1974), pp. 58-59.

12. Gordon W. Allport, "Prejudice: A Problem in Psychological and Social Causation," in *Toward a General Theory of Action*, ed. Talcott Parsons and Edward Shils (Cambridge, Mass.: Harvard University Press, 1951), p. 377. This insight is one of the foundations of the "functional approach," and it also underlies the analysis of anti-Semitism in Gertrude J. Selznick and Stephen Steinberg, *The Tenacity of Prejudice* (New York: Harper and Row, 1969).

13. If we are to understand why some opinions are "normative" while others are odd and reprehensible, surely we must understand the basic reasons (or motives) for holding those different opinions—reasons or motives more basic than the desire to conform to others. If men had no other motives in choosing and expressing opinions than the desire to please others by echoing their opinions, then there would be no basis whatever for explaining the "norms" upon which groups converged. They would be completely indeterminate. We could predict that all the members of an isolated group would hold the same opinions, but we could say nothing about what these opinions might be. To ask why one group had different opinions than another would be like asking why some experimental groups in Sherif's famous studies of the autokinetic effect decided that the stationary spot of light was moving to the

right, while other groups decided that it was moving to the left. (See Muzafer Sherif, *The Psychology of Social Norms* [New York: Harper, 1936].) As models of the real world, these experiments leave the reader musing about naked emperors and professional investors. "Professional investment may be likened to those newspaper competitions in which the competitors have to pick out the six prettiest faces from a hundred photographs, the prize being awarded to the competitor whose choice most nearly corresponds to the average preferences of the competitors as a whole; so that each competitor has to pick, not those faces which he himself finds prettiest, but those which he thinks likeliest to catch the fancy of the other competitors. It is not a case of choosing those which, to the best of one's judgement, are really the prettiest, nor even those which average opinion genuinely thinks the prettiest. We have reached the third degree where we devote our intelligences to anticipating what average opinion expects the average opinion to be. And there are some, I believe, who practise the fourth, fifth, and higher degrees." John Maynard Keynes, *The General Theory of Employment, Interest, and Money* (London: Macmillan, 1936), p. 156.

14. Thomas F. Pettigrew, "Personality and Sociocultural Factors in Intergroup Attitudes: A Cross-National Comparison," *Journal of Conflict Resolution*, 2 (1958), 29–42.

15. J. M. Nieuwoudt and Elizabeth M. Nel, "The Relationship between Ethnic Prejudice, Authoritarianism, and Conformity among South African Students," in *Contemporary South Africa: Social Psychological Perspectives*, ed. Stanley J. Morse and Christopher Orpen (Cape Town: Juta, 1975), p. 97.

16. Christopher Orpen, "Prejudice and Adjustment to Cultural Norms among English-Speaking South Africans," *Journal of Psychology*, 77 (1971), 217–18.

17. P. C. L. Heaven, "Individual vs. Intergroup Explanations of Prejudice among Afrikaners," *Journal of Social Psychology*, 121 (1983), 201–10, and J. J. Ray and P. C. L. Heaven, "Conservatism and Authoritarianism among Urban Afrikaners," *Journal of Social Psychology*, 122 (1984), 163–70.

18. Milton Malof and Albert J. Lott, "Ethnocentrism and the Acceptance of Negro Support in a Group Pressure Situation," *Journal of Abnormal and Social Psychology*, 65 (1962), 254–58. See also Jeanne Block and Jack Block, "An Interpersonal Experiment on Reactions to Authority," *Human Relations*, 5 (1952), 91–98. For an explanation of the "Asch paradigm," see Solomon E. Asch, *Social Psychology* (New York: Prentice-Hall, 1952), chap. 14.

19. Edwin D. Lawson and Ross Stagner, "Group Pressure, Attitude Change, and Autonomic Involvement," *Journal of Social Psychology*, 45 (1957), 299–312.

20. Eugene B. Nadler, "Yielding, Authoritarianism, and Authoritarian Ideology Regarding Groups," *Journal of Abnormal and Social Psychology*, 58 (1959), 408–10.

21. See, for example, the reasoning in Thomas F. Pettigrew, "Regional Differences in Anti-Negro Prejudice," *Journal of Abnormal and Social Psychology*, 59 (1959), p. 34; Pettigrew, "Personality and Sociocultural Factors in Intergroup Attitudes," pp. 34–35, 38, and 40; and Orpen, "Prejudice and Adjustment to Cultural Norms among English-Speaking South Africans," p. 218.

22. Proof of this point would require precise assumptions about sampling and measurement, but no more than the standard assumptions of interval levels of measurement and random errors (or disturbances) that are involved in *any* rigorous

interpretation of correlation and regression statistics. It is easy to imagine these conditions not being fulfilled in the studies cited, but if they are not, then the studies really show nothing at all, not even the obvious validity of the simplest model of conformity.

23. The most important studies are: Richard S. Crutchfield, "Conformity and Character," *American Psychologist*, 19 (1955), 191–98; William D. Wells, Guy Weinert, and Marilyn Rubel, "Conformity Pressure and Authoritarian Personality," *Journal of Psychology*, 42 (1956), 133–36; Nadler, "Yielding, Authoritarianism, and Authoritarian Ideology Regarding Groups"; and Graham M. Vaughan and Kenneth D. White, "Conformity and Authoritarianism Reexamined," *Journal of Personality and Social Psychology*, 3 (1966), 363–66. Additional support for the hypothesis is provided by: Halla Beloff, "Two Forms of Social Conformity: Acquiescence and Conventionality," *Journal of Abnormal and Social Psychology*, 56 (1958), 99–104; Thomas F. Pettigrew, "Social Distance Attitudes of South African Students," *Social Forces*, 38 (1960), 246–53 (note 9); Richard Centers and Miriam Horowitz, "Social Character and Conformity," *Journal of Social Psychology*, 60 (1963), 343–49; Homer H. Johnson, James M. Torcivia, and Mary Ann Poprick, "Effects of Source Credibility on the Relationship between Authoritarianism and Attitude Change," *Journal of Personality and Social Psychology*, 9 (1968), 179–83; Graham M. Vaughan, "Authoritarian Scales as Criteria of Conformity," *Perceptual and Motor Skills*, 28 (1969), 776–78; Richard Centers, Robert William Shomer, and Aroldo Rodrigues, "A Field Experiment in Interpersonal Persuasion Using Authoritarian Influence," *Journal of Personality*, 38 (1970), 393–403; James C. Moore and Edward Krupat, "Relationships between Source Status, Authoritarianism, and Conformity in a Social Influence Setting," *Sociometry*, 34 (1971), 122–34; Orpen, "Prejudice and Adjustment to Cultural Norms"; Nieuwoudt and Nel, "The Relationship between Ethnic Prejudice, Authoritarianism, and Conformity among South African Students"; and Ray and Heaven, "Conservatism and Authoritarianism among Urban Afrikaners." See also: Frank Barron, "Some Personality Correlates of Independence of Judgement," *Journal of Personality*, 21 (1953), 287–97; Morton Wagman, "Attitude Change and Authoritarian Personality," *Journal of Psychology*, 40 (1955), 3–24; Ray R. Canning and James M. Baker, "Effects of the Group on Authoritarian and Non-Authoritarian Persons," *American Journal of Sociology*, 64 (1959), 579–81; Harriet Linton and Elaine Graham, "Some Personality Correlates of Persuasibility," in *Personality and Persuasibility*, ed. Carl I. Hovland and Irving L. Janis (New Haven: Yale University Press, 1959), pp. 69–101; O. J. Harvey and George D. Beverly, "Some Personality Correlates of Concept Change through Role Playing," *Journal of Abnormal and Social Psychology*, 63 (1961), 125–30; and Jack M. Wright and O. J. Harvey, "Attitude Change as a Function of Authoritarianism and Punitiveness," *Journal of Personality and Social Psychology*, 1 (1965), 177–81.

24. John P. Kirscht and Ronald C. Dillehay, *Dimensions of Authoritarianism* (Lexington: University of Kentucky Press, 1967), pp. 108–12, and R. A. Altemeyer, *Right-Wing Authoritarianism* (Winnipeg: University of Manitoba Press, 1981), pp. 53–56.

25. The studies most frequently cited are: Leonard Berkowitz and Richard M. Lundy, "Personality Characteristics Related to Susceptibility to Influence by Peers or Authority Figures," *Journal of Personality*, 25 (1957), 306–16; Kenneth R.

Hardy, "Determinants of Conformity and Attitude Change," *Journal of Abnormal and Social Psychology*, 54 (1957), 289–94; Martin L. Hoffman, "Conformity as a Defense Mechanism and as a Form of Resistance to Genuine Group Influence," *Journal of Personality*, 25 (1957), 412–24; Norman S. Endler, "Conformity Analysed and Related to Personality," *Journal of Social Psychology*, 53 (1961), 271–83; Harold Weiner and Elliott McGinnies, "Authoritarianism, Conformity, and Confidence in a Perceptual Judgement Situation," *Journal of Social Psychology*, 55 (1961), 77–84; J. J. Lasky, "Effects of Prestige Suggestion and Peer Standards on California F Scale Scores," *Psychological Reports*, 11 (1962), 187–91; Ivan D. Steiner and Joseph S. Vannoy, "Personality Correlates of Two Types of Conformity Behavior," *Journal of Personality and Social Psychology*, 4 (1966), 307–15; and Homer H. Johnson and Ivan D. Steiner, "Some Effects of Discrepancy Level on Relationships between Authoritarianism and Conformity," *Journal of Social Psychology*, 73 (1967), 199–204. The crucial difference between these studies and the ones cited earlier seems to be the amount of conflict between private beliefs and social norms used in defining conformism operationally. In the study by Weiner and McGinnies, for example, subjects were asked to classify tachistoscopically presented faces (exposure of .01 second) as either "smiling" or "frowning." Some of the faces were neither smiling nor frowning. The two instructed confederates of the experimenter sometimes gave misleading reports of their perceptions of these faces (i.e., they both classified them as "smiling" or "frowning"). It is hardly surprising that when the confederates agreed on these judgments, the experimental subjects, regardless of whether they stood high or low on the F scale, tended to go along with their judgments, and hence that there was no correlation between authoritarianism and conformism or conformity. The same basic criticism applies to the other seven studies. Only one study flatly contradicts the best studies cited above, namely, David Gorfein, "Conformity Behavior and the 'Authoritarian Personality'," *Journal of Social Psychology*, 53 (1961), 121–25, which reports an insignificant negative correlation between F-scale authoritarianism and yielding in an Asch-type situation. The experiment involved twenty-four subjects, each of whom made 12 judgments, on 7 of which there was social pressure contrary to individual opinion.

26. David Riesman with Reuel Denney and Nathan Glazer, *The Lonely Crowd: A Study of the Changing American Character* (New Haven: Yale University Press, 1950), especially pp. 22, 26, 32, 69–77, 144–47, 160–69.

27. Cf. Beloff, "Two Forms of Social Conformity," and Guiseppe Di Palma and Herbert McClosky, "Personality and Conformity: The Learning of Political Attitudes," *American Political Science Review*, 64 (1970), 1054–73.

28. Ivan D. Steiner and Homer H. Johnson, "Authoritarianism and Conformity," *Sociometry*, 26 (1963), 21–34. They concluded their discussion of their findings by remarking that "it seems inappropriate to regard the authoritarian as a person with a 'conformist personality,' for like the non-authoritarian, he conforms in some situations but not in others. Moreover, given certain situations he may conform to some people but not to others" (p. 34).

29. The technical virtuosity of contemporary psychology is shown by the way anxiety was measured: "The experimenter obtained 'palmar sweat' data from the middle finger of each participant's left hand. . . . A fingerprint was produced on a piece of Dietzgen paper which had been saturated in a five percent solution of tannic acid. The density of the print is known to reflect the amount of perspiration on the

fingertip, and thus serves as measure of anxiety. After the experimental session had been completed the density of the naive subject's print was determined through the use of a densitometer which measured the amount of light which passed through the print and struck a photoelectric cell. A dark print, such as would be obtained if the subject had perspiration on his fingertip, permits little light to strike the photoelectric cell, and this fact is registered on a microammeter." Ibid., pp. 25–26.

30. Cf. DiPalma and McClosky, "Personality and Conformity," and Herbert McClosky, "Conservatism and Personality," *American Political Science Review*, 52 (1958), 27–45.

31. Harold J. Leavitt, Herbert Hax, and James H. Roche, "'Authoritarianism' and Agreement with Things Authoritative," *Journal of Psychology*, 40 (1955), p. 216.

32. N. L. Gage, George S. Leavitt, and Goerge C. Stone, "The Psychological Meaning of Acquiescence Set for Authoritarianism," *Journal of Abnormal and Social Psychology*, 55 (1957), pp. 100, 103.

33. Leavitt, Hax, and Roche, "'Authoritarianism' and Agreement with Things Authoritative," report correlations of about .40 between the F scale and agreement with 42 diverse maxims. Gloria L. Carey, Arnold A. Rogow, and Calista Farrell, "The Relationship between the F Scale and Aphorism Usage and Agreement," *Journal of Psychology*, 43 (1957), 163–67, report correlations of about the same magnitude with scales of both "positive" (conventionally optimistic and trusting) and "negative" (conventionally cynical) aphorisms. Bernard M. Bass, "Development and Evaluation of a Scale for Measuring Social Acquiescence," *Journal of Abnormal and Social Psychology*, 53 (1956), 296–99, reports similar correlations between F and agreement with 56 "famous sayings," which constituted a scale designed to measure "social acquiescence."

34. Cf. J. J. Ray, "Reviving the Problem of Acquiescent Response Bias," *Journal of Social Psychology*, 121 (1983), 81–96. There are some relevant data in P. C. L. Heaven, "Authoritarianism or Acquiescence? South African Findings," *Journal of Social Psychology*, 119 (1983), 11–15.

Chapter Eleven

1. The most interesting of these remarks are found at the beginning of chapter 19 on "Types and Syndromes" where Adorno discusses the philosophical foundations of pigeonholing. He recognized that students of prejudice have to be particularly cautious in dealing with this question. "To express it pointedly, the rigidity of constructing types is itself indicative of the 'stereopathic' mentality which belongs to the basic constituents of the potentially fascist character" (AP, 746). He conceded that typologies, especially dichotomies, may often be less useful in psychological research and less "humane" than continuous variables—that it may make more sense, for example, to speak of a dimension of intelligence, with most people clustered around "average intelligence," than to speak of two distinct types, the smart and the dumb. Nonetheless Adorno advocated the typological approach—not because he believed that human traits are really "static, quasi-biological characteristics," but because of his consciousness of the impact of historical and social factors

on individual humans. "The fact that human society has been up to now divided into classes affects more than the external relations of men. The marks of social repression are left within the individual soul. . . . People form psychological 'classes,' inasmuch as they are stamped by variegated social processes. This in all probability holds good for our own standardized mass culture to even higher a degree than for previous periods. The relative rigidity of our high scorers, and of some of our low scorers, reflects psychologically the increasing rigidity according to which our society falls into two more or less crude opposing camps. . . . [T]he critique of typology should not neglect the fact that large numbers of people are no longer, or rather never were, 'individuals' in the sense of traditional nineteenth-century philosophy. . . . There is reason to look for psychological types because the world in which we live is typed and 'produces' different 'types' of persons." (AP, 747). Those who denied that individuals conformed to types, Adorno contended, were obscuring one of the most pernicious effects of modern society; they were drawing an "ideological veil" across its "intrinsic tendency towards the 'subsumption' of everything"; their scientific scruples served to disguise oppression by the dominant capitalist class. Moreover a practical need—"the necessity that science provide weapons against the potential threat of the fascist mentality"—also pointed in the same direction: "There is no psychological defense against prejudice which is not oriented toward certain psychological 'types'"(AP, 748). What was required, then, was a "*critical* typology," one that comprehended "the typification of man itself as a social function" (AP, 749). Such an approach would distinguish between genuine types (e.g., the pseudopatriot or the pseudoconservative) and those "who can be called types only in a formal-logical sense and who often may be characterized just by the *absence* of standard qualities" (e.g., the genuine liberal) (AP, 749).

As these remarks suggest, Adorno viewed social stereotyping from the perspective of a possible classless society: it is only "up to now" that society has been divided into classes. In a classless society individuals would be able to be individuals—in the full sense of traditional nineteenth-century philosophy. In such a society all would be able to enjoy what earlier centuries might have called philosophy, sainthood, freedom of the will, or the state of grace. All would be spontaneous and creative, the authors of their own being, true individuals. All would have personality. None would simply play roles written for them by others. This was the human meaning of socialism, and it was this consummation of human history that the capitalist class and their ideological lackeys opposed.

2. Edward Shils, "Authoritarianism: 'Right' and 'Left'," in *Studies in the Scope and Method of "The Authoritarian Personality*," ed. Richard Christie and Marie Jahoda (Glencoe, Ill.: The Free Press, 1954). This essay should be read together with Shils, "The End of Ideology?" *Encounter*, 5, no. 5 (1955), 52–58.

3. Shils, "Authoritarianism," p. 25.

4. Ibid., p. 27.

5. Ibid., p. 28.

6. Ibid., p. 38.

7. Ibid., p. 37.

8. See especially H. J. Eysenck, *The Psychology of Politics* (London: Routledge & Kegan Paul, 1954); Milton Rokeach, *The Open and Closed Mind: Investigations into the Nature of Belief Systems and Personality Systems* (New York: Basic Books,

1960); William P. Kreml, *The Anti-Authoritarian Personality* (Oxford: Pergamon Press, 1977); and Stanley Rothman and S. Robert Lichter, *Roots of Radicalism: Jews, Christians, and the New Left* (New York: Oxford University Press, 1982).

9. Shils, "Authoritarianism," p. 25.

10. The translation quoted is that of Allan Bloom, *The Republic of Plato* (New York: Basic Books, 1968).

11. According to Socrates, the oligarch, because of his love for money, "thrusts love of honor and spiritedness headlong out of the throne of his soul" and puts the "desiring and money-loving part" in its place. "He makes the calculating and spirited parts sit by it on the ground on either side and be slaves, letting the one neither calculate about nor consider anything but where more money will come from less; and letting the other admire and honor nothing but wealth and the wealthy, while loving the enjoyment of no other honor than that resulting from the possession of money and anything that happens to contribute to getting it" (Rep, 553b–d).

12. One of the things Horkheimer and Adorno valued most highly in Freud was his uncovering of the conflict between the individual's desire for sexual gratification and the constraints of civilization. An appreciation of the depth of this conflict was the key to liberation, they thought, for it would save the individual from false optimism and conformism, and motivate him to resist the demands of reality. As Martin Jay has noted, "the libido, which implied a stratum of human existence stubbornly out of reach of total social control, was an indispensable concept." *The Dialectical Imagination: A History of the Frankfurt School and the Institute for Social Research, 1923–1950* (Boston: Little, Brown, 1973), p. 103. Their reservations had to do with Freud's "bourgeois contempt of instinct. . . . As a late opponent of hypocrisy, he stands ambivalently between desire for the open emancipation of the oppressed, and apology for open oppression." T. W. Adorno, *Minima Moralia: Reflections from Damaged Life,* trans. E. F. N. Jephcott (London: New Left Books, 1974), pp. 60–61.

13. Cf. George Sidney Brett, *A History of Psychology: Ancient and Patristic* (London: George Allen, 1912), chaps. 7–9, and especially pp. 67–70. Even if Plato's imaginary physiology did not lead him astray, his obsession with the Ideas surely did. "Since Plato's chief interest is in ultimates, we must not expect to find in him a rich yield of psychological details." Gardner Murphy, *Historical Introduction to Modern Psychology,* 5th ed. (London: Routledge & Kegan Paul, 1949), p. 8.

14. Adorno, *Minima Moralia,* p. 49. Horkheimer was interested enough at one point, however, to spend a year in analysis. Jay, *The Dialectical Imagination,* pp. 87–88.

15. Albrecht Wellmer, *Critical Theory of Society,* trans. John Cumming (New York: Herder and Herder, 1971), p. 52.

16. Max Horkheimer and Theodor W. Adorno, *Dialectic of Enlightenment,* trans. John Cumming (New York: Herder and Herder, 1972), p. 3.

17. Ibid., p. ix.

18. Theodor W. Adorno, *Prisms,* trans. Samuel and Shierry Weber (Cambridge: MIT Press, 1981), p. 32.

19. Cf. Leo Strauss, "Social Science and Humanism," in *The State of the Social Sciences,* ed. Leonard D. White (Chicago: University of Chicago Press, 1956), pp. 424–25: "What claims to be the final triumph over provincialism reveals itself as the most amazing manifestation of provincialism."

Index